Convergences:
Inventories of the Present

Edward W. Said, General Editor

AMY KAPLAN

The Anarchy of Empire in the Making of U.S. Culture

HARVARD UNIVERSITY PRESS

Cambridge, Massachusetts, and London, England

First Harvard University Press paperback edition, 2005

Library of Congress Cataloging-in-Publication Data
Kaplan, Amy.
The anarchy of empire in the making of U.S. culture / Amy Kaplan.
p. cm. — (Convergences)
Includes bibliographical references (p.) and index.
ISBN 0-674-00913-4 (cloth)
ISBN 0-674-01759-5 (pbk.)
1. United States—Foreign relations—1865–1921.
2. United States—Foreign relations—1783–1865.
3. United States—Territorial expansion.
4. National characteristics, American.
5. Popular culture—United States—History—19th century.
6. Popular culture—United States—History—20th century.
7. Imperialism—Social aspects—United States—History.
8. Imperialism in literature.
9. Imperialism in motion pictures.
I. Title.
II. Convergences (Cambridge, Mass.)

E661.7 .K37 2002
327.73'009'034—dc21
2002027254

For Rose

Contents

The Anarchy of
Empire in the Making of
U.S. Culture

Introduction

The neatly ordered kitchen in Catharine Beecher's household manual seemed remote from the battlefields of Mexico in 1846—as far afield as Mark Twain's Mississippi was from the port of Honolulu in 1866; as far as the vaudeville houses showing the new moving pictures were from the shores of Cuba and the Philippines in 1898; and as far as the East St. Louis race riots were from the colonization of Africa in 1917. *The Anarchy of Empire in the Making of U.S. Culture* contends that these domestic and foreign spaces are closer than we think, and that the dynamics of imperial expansion cast them into jarring proximity. I intend my title, taken from a poem by W. E. B. Du Bois, to challenge the traditional understanding of imperialism as a one-way imposition of power in distant colonies, and to call attention instead to ambiguities and contradictions of imperial relations in the formation of a national culture. In this book I explore how international struggles for domination abroad profoundly shape representations of American national identity at home, and how, in turn, cultural phenomena we think of as domestic or particularly national are forged in a crucible of foreign relations. The idea of the nation as home, I argue, is inextricable from the political, economic, and cultural movements of empire, movements that both erect and unsettle the ever-shifting boundaries between the domestic and the foreign, between "at home" and "abroad."

The entanglement of the domestic and the foreign was articulated in particularly revealing ways in a Supreme Court case of 1901, *Downes v.*

Bidwell. This case contributed to the constitutional underpinning of U.S. imperialism at a pivotal juncture in its history, when the United States shifted from continental expansion to overseas empire, from absorbing new territories into the domestic space of the nation to acquiring foreign colonies and protectorates abroad. I argue that the language of this case demonstrates the slipperiness of these distinctions and expresses anxiety and ambivalence about the nature of the American Empire at the turn of the twentieth century. The court's decision played a key role in determining the political status of Puerto Rico, which, along with the Philippines and Guam, Spain ceded to the United States at the end of the Spanish-American War of 1898, the same war in which Cuba achieved nominal independence under U.S. occupation and subsequent domination.[1] While the United States waged a subsequent brutal war against the Philippine struggle for independence, Congress in 1900 installed a temporary civilian administration with limited powers to govern Puerto Rico, including the power to levy duties and taxes. In response to one of these laws, the business firm of Downes & Co. sued the collector of the Port of New York to recover the duties exacted on a shipment of oranges Downes had imported from the port of San Juan. Downes claimed that the tax was illegal because, as a territory, Puerto Rico was covered by the Constitution and therefore subject to its revenue clause mandating uniform taxation throughout the United States. Ruling against the plaintiff, the Court determined that Puerto Rico was a possession of the United States and therefore not immediately included within the jurisdiction of the Constitution without a specific act of Congress. Resolved by a narrow margin, the decision produced five different opinions, none of which was signed by a majority, but which together reveal the contested and complex issues that the case raised.

In his influential assenting opinion, signed by three other members, Justice Edward Douglas White concluded: "whilst in an international sense Porto [sic] Rico was not a foreign country, since it was subject to the sovereignty of and was owned by the United States, it was foreign to the United States in a domestic sense, because the island had not been incorporated into the United States, but was merely appurtenant thereto as a possession."[2] In the immediate case at hand, the Court ruled that Puerto Rico lay outside the province of the revenue clauses of the Constitution and was therefore taxable as "foreign," in contrast to the "domestic" status of the states and territories within the Constitution's domain. Although Puerto Rico could be taxed as an exporter of foreign goods, it had no claim to the sovereignty of an independent nation, a status that would make it foreign in the "international sense." The broader implications meant—paradoxically—that for international purposes the Court included Puerto Rico within the *domestic* sphere of the American nation. Yet in terms of the rights and privileges conferred by the Constitution, the court excluded Puerto Rico from that same sphere and thus deemed it *foreign* in a "domestic sense." To be domestic in the domestic sense would have made it a part of the nation, on parity with the states, and to be foreign in the foreign sense would have made Puerto Rico an autonomous nation. The court went to great rhetorical length to avoid both alternatives.

This Supreme Court decision had far-reaching consequences beyond the fine-tuning of tariff laws. Along with other related decisions that came to be known as the *Insular Cases,* it legislated the juridical and political terrain of Puerto Rico as a dependency of the United States. These cases constructed the foundation of an imperial regime and a social reality that still underlie the current status of Puerto Rico as a Commonwealth today.[3] This status hinged on White's discursive creation of a new legal category of the "unincorporated territory," a classification that meant that Puerto Rico could not become a part of the nation without a separate act of Congress to incorporate it. This new doctrine positioned Puerto Rico in a liminal space both inside and outside the boundaries of the Constitution, both "belonging to" but "not a part" of the United States. The *Insular Cases* thereby relegated the people of Puerto Rico to a state of limbo in space and time, where they were neither citizens at home nor aliens from another nation.[4]

My interest in this case lies in the cultural connotations of "foreign to the United States in a domestic sense," an ambiguous phrase that articulates an unstable paradox at the heart of U.S. imperial culture. What does it mean to be "foreign" in the "domestic sense"? "Domestic" and "foreign" are, of course, not neutral legal and spatial descriptions, but heavily weighted metaphors imbued with racialized and gendered associations of home and family, outsiders and insiders, subjects and citizens. When the Supreme Court employed metaphors of the nation as a household and a corporeal human form, it was drawing on and contributing to a vast reservoir of contradictory meanings that accrued over time and space, and it deployed them to create new discursive and social realities. My reading of this case introduces a major theme of this book, that domestic metaphors of national identity are intimately intertwined with renderings of the foreign and the alien, and that the notions of the domestic and the foreign mutually constitute one another in an imperial context. Locating Puerto Rico legally and spatially was not only the work of judges and cartographers, but also the work of culture in imbuing geography with meaning, in defining such common-sense notions as near and far, inside and outside, here and there. The Supreme Court justices in 1901 were participating in imperial culture's broader project of mapping the boundaries between the domestic and the foreign. I show this project at work in different cultural forms and historical periods, from domestic manuals and novels of the 1840s to *Citizen Kane* in 1941.

Reverberating throughout the Court's deliberations were urgent questions not only about the ambiguous status of Puerto Rico, but also—if not more so—about the ambiguous status of the United States as a nation, a republic, and an empire. While drawing the juridical boundaries of Puerto Rico, the justices seemed primarily concerned with securing the conceptual and political borders of the United States and the integrity of its national identity. If Puerto Rico was deemed foreign in the domestic sense, then where did that place the American nation? At stake for the justices was the fundamental meaning of "United States." Justice White raised the recurrent question of what "the words 'United States' signified at the time of the adoption of the Constitution."[5] Does this name include all territories as well as states? Does the Constitution automatically extend to all people and territories conquered or acquired by the United States? To answer these questions, the justices engaged in an enormous amount of interpretive and discursive work. They revisited the constitutional history of expansion from the Northwest Ordinance (1787) to the annexation of Florida (1819), from the Louisiana Purchase (1803) to the Treaty of Guadalupe Hidalgo (1848), from debates over the expansion of slavery in the territories leading to the Civil War, to the current status of New Mexico and Arizona. To map the ambiguous space of Puerto Rico in 1898, their discussions also ranged across the globe to other contemporary locations of the U.S. empire from Cuba to the Philippines, Guam and Samoa, Alaska and Hawaii.

Justices on both sides referred to Chief Justice Marshall's characterization of the United States in an 1820 case, *Loughborough v. Blake.* In this case about taxation in the District of Columbia, the Chief Justice asked, "Does this term designate the whole, or any particular portion of the American Empire? Certainly this question can admit but of one answer. It is the name given to our great republic, which is composed of States and territories."[6] For Marshall the "United States" were coextensive with the American Empire and both were constituted as a republic. Sixty years later, however, in *Downes,* Justice Henry Billings Brown found that this statement had "occasioned some embarrassment in other cases," and that it did not apply to the current context of new territorial acquisitions.[7] Instead, Brown contended that "in dealing with foreign sovereignties, the term 'United States' has a broader meaning than when used in the Constitution."[8] For him, "United States" had a double reference in which the terrain of the American Empire exceeded that of the American republic. In other words, in the international context, the meaning of the "United States" as a nation became broader and more inclusive, while within the domestic domain of the Constitution, the meaning narrowed in its reference and became more exclusive. Thus the protean definition of the United States shifted in different national and international contexts, when viewed from within and from without.

It is not hard to see that these questions of legal precedent were also ridden with anxiety about the grounding of American national identity. To the consternation of dissenting Chief Justice Melville Weston Fuller, "the occult meaning" of the "unincorporated territory" gave Congress the unrestricted power to keep any newly acquired territory "like a disembodied shade, in an intermediate state of ambiguous existence for an indefinite period."[9] Justice John Marshall Harlan expressed concern for the deathly consequences of the "unincorporated territory" that would leave Puerto Ricans floating in a spatial and temporal limbo. The other justices also repeatedly conjured an image of Puerto Rico as a "disembodied shade" that lurked around the edges of the embodied nation. The concept of "unincorporated territory" was supposed to lay this ghost to rest in a zone outside of statehood and thereby bury the contradictions between the American Empire and American republic, contradictions that the annexation of Puerto Rico kept bringing to life. As "occult," the "unincorporated territory" cast a dark shadow across the geographic and constitutional bonds of the incorporated nation. As "foreign" in "the domestic sense," "belonging to but not a part of," the ambiguous space of Puerto Rico both confounded and shored up the international boundaries of the United States. It unsettled the "domestic sense" of the American nation as home and threatened to turn it into a haunted house.

The great irony of this case is that from the perspective of Puerto Rico, the United States was the foreign object casting its shadow across every aspect of political, economic, and social life of the island; it was the foreign body that Puerto Rico had to incorporate.[10] Yet the language of the court inverted this relationship and rendered the annexation of Puerto Rico as a violation of the integrity of the United States. Menace infuses the legal discourse of *Downes v. Bidwell.* Justice Brown warned that "a false step at this time may be fatal to the development of what Chief Justice Marshall called the American Empire," and Justice White repeatedly used the phrase "fraught with danger."[11] The Court's conclusion presented three distinct positions that did not draw clear lines for or against imperialism, but all three shared the sense that the annexation of Puerto Rico could threaten the coherence of America as a nation.

What dangers might the justices have perceived in a case about the import of oranges, a product most likely to be "incorporated" only in the dining rooms of the middle classes? Of course the case was not primarily about keeping Puerto Rico at bay, but about bringing it closer by making it accessible to the circulation of American capital and trade. Obviously, it was not oranges that constituted the problem, but the people of Puerto Rico. Many of the threats articulated by the Court clustered around the perceived identity of the Puerto Ricans as an "alien and hostile people," in White's terms.[12] Even though "the annexation of distant possessions [may be] desirable," wrote Brown, the problem was that these possessions were "inhabited by alien races, differing from us in religion, customs, laws, methods of taxation, and modes of thought."[13] The pursuit of imperial desire risked absorbing aliens into the domestic sphere, and the resulting racial and cultural intermixing threatened ultimately to make the United States internally foreign to itself. To ward off this threat, Justice Brown advocated annexing Puerto Rico as a colony with qualitatively different legal status from the United States.

For the dissenting justices, however, this solution of annexation without incorporation posed an even greater danger: it would make the United States foreign to itself by turning the American republic into a European form of absolutism. "Action taken outside of the constitution," wrote Justice Harlan, may "engraft upon our republican institutions a colonial system such as exists under monarchical governments."[14] The dissenting justices thereby argued that for America to remain a republic, the Constitution must immediately follow the flag.[15] Both sides implicitly revived in an international scope the Enlightenment poles of anarchy and tyranny as twinned threats to democracy. The incorporation of alien races would introduce a kind of anarchy into the unity of the nation, according to the majority, while unincorporated annexation would turn the republic into a tyrannical empire, according to the minority. Each imagined scenario would turn the United States into a monstrous hybrid creature, either a mixture of alien races or a foreign form of government "engrafted" on the republic.

Justice White offered the category of "unincorporated territory" as a compromise of sorts, but rather than resolve contradictions, this solution proliferated them. The "unincorporated territory" turned the space of Puerto Rico into a buffer zone, a blurred borderland between the domestic and the foreign on to which White could project these threats of hybridity which the others envisioned within the nation. He claimed that without this buffer, the alternative of immediate incorporation would do irrevocable damage to the same republican institutions that the dissenting justices wished to uphold. By deeming Puerto Rico as "foreign to the United States in a domestic sense"—neither a European-style colony nor a fully fledged territory on the way to statehood—White rhetorically protected the American republic from becoming foreign to itself.

To make his case for the doctrine of incorporation, White's major rhetorical strategy was hyperbole; he dramatized catastrophic scenarios that could hypothetically annihilate the integrity of the United States if the opposing argument held sway. He rendered the "evils of immediate incorporation" as a hydra-headed peril to the state, the body politic, citizenship, and the family. "Millions of inhabitants of alien territory," warned White, "if acquired by treaty, can, without the desire or consent of the people of the United States speaking through Congress, be immediately and irrevocably incorporated in the United

States, and the whole structure of the government be overthrown."[16] Reversing the trajectory of imperial power outward, he depicted the acquisition of Puerto Rico as a phantasmic invasion of the United States. Who are those millions he feared, a number far exceeding the population of Puerto Rico? His examples included both Cuba and the Philippines, though one was nominally sovereign and the other was fighting the United States for its independence. At the same time, his rhetoric echoed nativist fears of immigrants at the turn of the century, which imagined foreigners as the bearers of revolution and anarchy with the power to overthrow "the whole structure of government." Indeed, contemporaneous debates about both imperialism and immigration revolved around the perceived incapacity of nonwhites for self-government. White rendered this innate lack as excessive power, as the desire to rule others and to destroy the government of the United States. The expansion of the Constitution would lead to the demise of the very nation-state it brought into being and paralyze all branches of government, for "although the House of Representatives might be unwilling to agree to the incorporation of alien races, it would be impotent to prevent its accomplishment."[17] Ultimately, argued White, Congress would be stripped of its capacity to guard the people of the United States from these "evil consequences," an impotence that extends hyperbolically in time as well as space "beyond all future control of or remedy of the American people."[18]

White imagined the "evil of immediate incorporation" not only as undermining the structure of the national government, but also, in even more intimate terms, as damaging the body politic, as the word "incorporation" connotes. He rendered the United States as a body (presumably male) made vulnerable and impotent by the assertion of its imperial power on others. Ironically, this same force was heralded at the time as the embodiment of masculine prowess (as I discuss in Chapter 3). White claimed, on the contrary, that "for the purpose of incorporating foreign territory into the United States domestic territory must be disincorporated. In other words, that the Union must be, at least in theory, dismembered for the purpose of maintaining the doctrine of immediate incorporation of alien territory."[19] The United States here appears as a distended body that could be hacked apart, that could implode internally from its ingestion of foreign bodies. The appeal to the dismembered body of the Union would have evoked images from the Civil War, as though the absorption of alien territory threatened to maim again the recently healed body sutured together in the aftermath of that conflict. As we shall see in Chapter 4, the 1898 war with Spain was popularly viewed as an external antidote to this internal divisiveness. Yet in White's evocation, the fruits of this war in the annexation of foreign territory could dismember the Union again. Thus in turning to historical precedents, the justices not only adapted new forms of imperial conquest to a narrative teleology of national expansion and unification, but they also evoked past threats that could unravel this narrative.

The basis of American citizenship itself would be undermined, claimed White, if Puerto Rico were incorporated as domestic territory. To include Puerto Ricans as citizens would imply "that all citizenship of the United States is precarious and fleeting, subject to be sold at any moment like any other property. That is to say, to protect a newly acquired people in their presumed rights, it is essential to degrade the whole body of American citizenship."[20] While disinterring the dismembered body of the Civil War, White also resurrected the memory of slavery. Yet rather than see the "possession" of Puerto Rico and its "newly acquired people" as reminiscent of chattel slavery, he implied that if the Constitution automatically granted citizenship to Puerto Ricans, then American citizenship might be dismantled and the people of the United States enslaved. If the expansion of the Constitution could turn aliens into citizens, then this expansion in turn threatened to alienate the inalienable right of the American citizen. Furthermore, the language of physical degradation suggests a moral and racial tainting, thereby rendering the body of the American citizen incapable of citizenship. Significantly, this case was decided only five years after *Plessy v. Ferguson,* which legalized segregation and endorsed Jim Crow laws that revoked African American rights achieved under Reconstruction. At the same moment that former slaves and their descendants were stripped of full citizenship at home, the inclusion of nonwhite citizens from abroad was rendered as the enslavement and darkening of white Americans, thereby placing them outside the domain of the proper citizen. Thus according to White's logic, the notion of "foreign" in "a domestic sense" maintains Puerto Rico as a "possession" and its people as quasi-slaves "acquired" to differentiate U.S. citizenship from the degradation of slavery.

In conjuring these images of slavery and immigration, the justices were engaging in a fundamental and oft repeated U.S. practice of viewing foreign people through the lenses of racial categories at home. This is another way in which Puerto Ricans became "foreign to the United States in a domestic sense"; they were rendered racially other through familiar and recognizable stereotypes of nonwhite noncitizens at home, who were seen as foreign within the domestic space of the nation. The justices insisted that, legally, the treatment of Indians in conquered territories did not provide a precedent for the status of Puerto Ricans, who were prior subjects of Spain. Yet the language of *Downes v. Bidwell* resonates with the landmark decision of *Cherokee Nation v. the State of Georgia* in 1831, which rendered Indians as members of "domestic dependent nations," foreign to the rights guaranteed by states and territories, but domestic for federal purposes. As "alien races," Puerto Ricans were rendered "foreign" in the "domestic sense" by their perceived resemblance to alien races deemed to be incapable of self-government at home. The threat of millions of aliens incorporated by the U.S. empire was thus both amplified and muted through the domestic analogies of Indian-white relations, slavery, and immigration. This interplay among racial discourses across international borders did not work like an iron grid that was simply moved from the United States to the outposts of empire. Rather, as I will argue, the racialized analogies that empire deployed at home and abroad created dissonance as well as resonance, as they mutually defined and destabilized one another.[21]

If Justice White represented the "evils of immediate incorporation" as a racial menace to the body politic, he also perceived such incorporation as dangerous to the United States in its aspects of family and home. He worried that incorporation would make "America hapless in the family of nations"[22] and linked this crippled capacity to act in the world to the internal lineaments of the family weakened by the pressure of newcomers. Leading up to his final opinion, he used familial language to restore the "domestic sense" of the nation. "Incorporation does not arise," he averred, "until in the wisdom of the Congress it is deemed that the acquired territory has reached the state where it is proper that it should enter into and form part of the American family."[23] He did not completely wall off the American family in an insular state, but left its boundaries somewhat permeable. The category of the "unincorporated territory" held out the possibility of absorbing new members into the family while deferring this possibility to the indefinite future. White thereby left the image of the American family floating somewhat tenuously between the domestic and the foreign, a key image I explore in Chapter 1. Yet he maintained these boundaries as both firm and flexible by reasserting a hierarchy in the authority of Congress, which, like a father, has the "wisdom" to guard the gates of the family home and to determine who can enter. The ambiguous category of the "unincorporated territory" kept Puerto Rico safely outside the American family, yet close enough to control in a dependent position, like a ward or pupil. President McKinley made a similar paternalist argument when he referred to the colonization of the Philippines as "benevolent assimilation."[24]

Justice White acknowledged that his opponents might find "all the confusions and dangers above indicated . . . more imaginary than real."[25] While he raised this objection to dismiss it, I claim that the work of imagining these "confusions and dangers" is central not only to constructing the legal jurisdiction of Puerto Rico, but also to legitimating the project of American imperialism. Inverting the role of colonizer and colonized, the Court imagined a nightmare scenario that turned the acquisition of Puerto Rico and other territories into the foreign colonization of the United States, an act that could undo its sovereign government, dismember its body, enslave its citizens, and dissolve its familial bonds. This image turns U.S. aggression abroad into a defensive protection of the home in view of the peril of America becoming foreign and unrecognizable to itself. If Puerto Rico were deemed domestic in "a domestic sense," that is, a part of the nation, it would have even greater power to harm the United States than if it were foreign in a foreign sense, that is, an independent sovereign nation. The ambiguous space of Puerto Rico as "unincorporated," as "foreign to the United States in a domestic sense," both embodies and allays these fears. It maps a desirable space where the border of the United States can expand and contract; where Americans can go out into the world without bearing the foreign into the home. Yet the discourse of the Court also heightens the very confusion it is meant to allay. Its attempt to disentangle the meaning of the domestic and foreign, to draw clear boundaries between them, only further entangles them by creating a hybrid liminal space that is neither fully outside the

United States nor comfortably a part of it. The foreign both remains lodged within the "domestic sense" of the American nation and casts a dark shadow across its unstable borders.

The production of these elaborate fears and anxieties and the need to control and manage their disruptive potential is a key cultural process that interests me in this book. The language of *Downes* demonstrates that underlying the dream of imperial expansion is the nightmare of its own success, a nightmare in which movement outward into the world threatens to incorporate the foreign and dismantle the domestic sphere of the nation. The justices represented a double vision of U.S. imperialism as both expansive and contracting, on the one hand, constitutionally capable of boundless expansion, and on the other, narrowly protective of its own borders. As this Supreme Court case makes evident, imperialism does not emanate from the solid center of a fully formed nation; rather, the meaning of the nation itself is both questioned and redefined through the outward reach of empire.

This confounding of the borders between the foreign and the domestic lies at the heart of what I mean by my title, *The Anarchy of Empire in the Making of U.S. Culture.* "The Anarchy of Empire" comes from a poem by W. E. B. Du Bois, "A Hymn to the People," on the last page of his book entitled *Darkwater: Voices from Within the Veil,* the subject of my final chapter.[26] On the occasion of the Universal Congress of the Races in 1911, Du Bois composed the poem as a recasting and commentary on Kipling's "Recessional" (1897), a hymn seeking moral sanction for the British Empire. For Du Bois "The Anarchy of Empire, the doleful Death of Life!" refers to the violent destruction and havoc wreaked on the peoples and lands subject to colonial conquest and domination. In his poem, "The Anarchy of Empire" breaks down national boundaries to connect peoples subject to racial exploitation all over the globe, "Foreshadowing the union of the World."

In rewriting Kipling, Du Bois contested a common imperial trope that posits anarchy abroad as the prime cause of imperial intervention. "Anarchy" has often been used by imperial powers as a euphemism for revolution or independence struggles in order to justify their suppression by military intervention and colonial subjugation. In "Recessional," anarchy is embodied in the "lesser breeds without the law," like the Puerto Ricans in *Downes,* whose perceived chaotic qualities generate the need for the iron law of empire. While Du Bois saw empire itself as the prime cause of anarchy throughout its dominion, Kipling and other imperialists believed that the anarchic qualities of nonwhite peoples called forth the need for imperial rule. Indeed, Kipling dedicated "The White Man's Burden" to Theodore Roosevelt, to urge the United States to annex the Philippines. In advocating that the United States annex the territories acquired from Spain in 1898, Theodore Roosevelt warned that "if we had driven out medieval tyranny only to make room for savage anarchy, we had better not have begun the task at all."[27] Roosevelt's discourse, like that of the justices in *Downes,* produced the threat of "savage anarchy" to justify U.S. dominance, a role he also differentiated from the tyranny of Old World empires. The exceptional quality of the American Empire, in this way of thinking, transcends the ancient polarity between anarchy and tyranny.

Both Roosevelt and Du Bois posit a direct cause-and-effect relation between anarchy and empire, albeit opposing ones. I am interested in "the anarchy of empire" as an oxymoron of sorts, a contradiction in terms. The Oxford English Dictionary defines "empire" as a "supreme and extensive political dominion," and "anarchy" as a "state of lawlessness due to the absence or inefficiency of the supreme power; political disorder." If empire is identified with "an extensive territory," the meaning of anarchy is rarely rooted in geographic locations; instead, it conveys a sense of spatial dispersion and dislocation. Anarchy is also defined as a state of "absolute liberty," as the "non-recognition of moral law" and as "unsettledness or conflict of opinion." The oxymoron "the anarchy of empire" thus suggests the breakdown or defiance of the monolithic system of order that empire aspires to impose on the world, an order reliant on clear divisions between metropolis and colony, colonizer and colonized, national and international spaces, the domestic and the foreign. I am interested in the way anarchy becomes an integral and constitutive part of empire, central to the representation of U.S. imperialism in dispersed locations and at different historical moments. Anarchy is conjured by imperial culture as a haunting specter that must be subdued and controlled, and at the same time, it is a figure of empire's undoing.

The "anarchy of empire" thus suggests ways of thinking about imperialism as a network of power relations that changes over space and time and is riddled with instability, ambiguity, and disorder, rather than as a monolithic system of domination that the very word "empire" implies. If "the anarchy of empire" refers to the destruction and exploitation inflicted on the colonized world, it also suggests the internal contradictions, ambiguities, and frayed edges that unravel at imperial borders, where binary divisions collapse and fractured spaces open. In this understanding of imperialism, I am indebted to the insights of anthropologists and historians of empire as well as to postcolonial theorists who have radically challenged the traditional notion of imperialism as a unilinear assertion of power in remote colonies. In highlighting what Frederick Cooper and Ann Stoler have called the "tensions of empire," scholars have remapped imperial spaces as contact zones and sites of encounter. They have shown how imperial relations entail not only violent force but also conflict, negotiation, discipline, and fantasy, which together reshape the colonized world and the imperial metropolis.[28] These engagements, they insist, occur within political and social structures of power and domination that both form and are transformed by these colonial encounters. In the arena of representation, critics have shown how stereotypes do not simply impose hierarchies between the civilized and the savage, the colonizer and colonized, but how stereotypes themselves become unstable sites of ambivalence that distort and challenge the bedrock divisions on which they are founded.[29]

My work has also built on theories of empire and culture elaborated by Edward Said and more recently by Michael Hardt and Antonio Negri. I depart from their approaches, however, where they implicitly contribute to a paradigm of American exceptionalism by rendering imperialism a distinctly European phenomenon. Said's *Culture and Imperialism* powerfully demonstrates how the treasures of European high culture bear the traces of their foundation in the remote geographies of colonial violence and exploitation.[30] His title comments directly on Matthew Arnold's *Culture and Anarchy*, to contest the English writer's notion of culture as an autonomous sphere that transcends and ameliorates the anarchy of class conflict. On the contrary, argues Said, this concept of culture became a lethal weapon in abetting the power of the nation-state both at home and in the colonies, where Arnold's cultural canon took shape through the educational institutions of the

British Empire. In Said's revision of Arnold, the anarchy inflicted on colonial subjects bestows coherence and aesthetic value upon the order of European culture, thus masking its imperial origins. Said's approach emphasizes the distance, both geographic and conceptual, between Europe and its colonies, a model that cannot take into account the history of U.S. imperialism, where colonialism and anticolonialism, nation-building and empire-building joined together in geographic dominion over Native Americans, and where slavery and immigration brought people subject to imperialism to settle inside national borders. Furthermore, overseas expansion, as I have shown, relied on the creation of ambiguous spaces that were not quite foreign nor domestic, and it also created vast deterritorialized arenas in which to exercise military, economic, and cultural power divorced from political annexation. While my method borrows much from Said's reading of imperial culture, I emphasize the collapse of boundaries between here and there, between inside and outside, and the incoherence as much as the coherence that the anarchy of empire brings to the making of U.S. culture.

My idea of the anarchy of empire has more in common with Hardt and Negri's description of Empire than with their description of imperialism, even though they use "Empire" for our contemporary world order of globalization, where "in contrast to imperialism Empire establishes no territorial center of power and does not rely on fixed boundaries or barriers. It is a decentered and deterritorializing apparatus of rule that progressively incorporates the entire global realm within its open, expanding frontiers."[31] According to the authors, this new system has its basis in the U.S. Constitution, a foundation radically different from that of European imperialism. They therefore regard Theodore Roosevelt as pursuing an old-style European imperialism, and Woodrow Wilson with his League of Nations as foreshadowing the emergence of today's postmodern regime, in which the sovereignty of the nation dissolves in the borderless world of Empire. I would argue that these two tendencies are not as distinct as Hardt and Negri contend, but that both are at work in varied configurations throughout the history of U.S. imperialism. The American Empire has long followed a double impetus to construct boundaries and patrol all movement across them and to break down those borders through the desire for unfettered expansion. To separate Empire from imperialism is to foreclose the history of American imperialism and breathe new life into the belief in American exceptionalism.[32]

A key paradox informs the ideology of American exceptionalism: it defines America's radical difference from other nations as something that goes beyond the separateness and uniqueness of its own particular heritage and culture. Rather, its exceptional nature lies in its exemplary status as the apotheosis of the nation-form itself and as a model for the rest of the world.[33] American exceptionalism is in part an argument for boundless expansion, where national particularism and international universalism converge. The cultural expressions I analyze reveal an anxiety about the anarchic potential of imperial distension underlying this exceptionalist ideal. If the fantasy of American imperialism aspires to a borderless world where it finds its own reflection everywhere, then the fruition of this dream shatters the coherence of national identity, as the boundaries that distinguish it from the outside world promise to collapse.

The Anarchy of Empire in the Making of U.S. Culture sets these varied approaches in dialogue with the field of American studies to contribute to the current effort to remap that field from broader international and transnational perspectives. My focus, however, is less on the contact zones themselves than on what Lora Romero has called the "home fronts" of imperial culture.[34] A "home front" implies a line that seals off domestic space from a foreign battlefield, but as a front, it also provides a formidable line of attack and engagement. I am interested in how dominant representations of national identity at home are informed and deformed by the anarchic encounters of empire, even as those same representations displace and disavow imperialism as something remote and foreign to U.S. nationhood. The chapters that follow are all guided by a central question. How can the framework of the "anarchy of empire" challenge and decenter the national focus of some of the key paradigms that have shaped the study of U.S. culture? How might the contours of these fields of inquiry change, when viewed not solely from within the confines of U.S. borders, but from an international context of imperial encounters?

Historically, the examples I have selected range over a hundred years, from Catharine Beecher's *Treatise on Domestic Economy* to Orson Welles's *Citizen Kane*, from John O'Sullivan's concept of "Manifest Destiny" to Henry Luce's designation of the "American Century." The paradigms central to American studies that I address include the "cult of domesticity," the national identity of authorship, the crisis of masculinity in the 1890s, the rise of Jim Crow segregation, the history of American film, and Du Bois's critique of American racism in the early twentieth century. Although my essays do not aspire to provide historical coverage, a new periodization, or a developmental narrative, they are linked by common concerns about the historiography of U.S. culture and imperialism. I challenge the way the history of U.S. imperialism has often revolved around a central geographic bifurcation between continental expansion and overseas empire, and the related, yet not identical, division between territorial annexation and deterritorialized forms of global domination. This spatial splitting often takes the temporal form of a developmental narrative that moves from continental national expansion in the nineteenth century to formal colonial annexation at the turn of the century to the neo-imperial exercise of military and economic might in the twentieth. This overarching narrative has defined the so-called Spanish-American War of 1898 as a watershed or turning point, as either a leap from the domestic continental frontier to sites overseas, or a radical shift to a new stage of the "Open Door" policy of economic expansion.[35] My own project started as a study of imperial culture in the 1890s in order to counter the denial of empire that structures the discourse of American exceptionalism. Yet I found that this focus implicitly upheld an older exceptionalist historiography, which viewed 1898 as an aberration, as the only time that the United States became—inadvertently—a proper imperial power, and the only time imperialism was a subject for public consumption and debate. Thus the 1890s now appear as an episode in the middle chapters of this book, situated in relation to multiple historical trajectories of the anarchy of empire that include the massive and violent continental conquests of the 1840s and the American colonization of Hawaii in the Pacific, long before it was formally annexed in 1898. Nor do I end my story in 1898, but instead examine its mixed and contradictory legacy in the twentieth century, in the development of the early film industry and in Du Bois's articulation of the global color line.

Whereas some scholars have emphasized the break between continental expansion and overseas empire, others have underlined the continuity between the two through the export of policies and symbols of Indian wars and the "metaphysics of Indian hating" to new frontiers.[36] Although this approach has generated powerful and influential studies, it risks reproducing the teleological narrative that imperialism tells about itself, the inexorable westward march of empire. Furthermore, by taking as foundational the confrontation between white settlers and Native Americans, this approach also overlooks how intimately the issues of slavery and emancipation and relations between blacks and whites were intertwined with each stage of U.S. imperial expansion. In each of my chapters I explore how the representations of U.S. imperialism were mapped not through a West/East axis of frontier symbols and politics, but instead through a North/South axis around the issues of slavery, Reconstruction, and Jim Crow segregation. The conquest of Indian and Mexican lands in the antebellum period cannot be understood separately from the expansion of slavery and the struggle for freedom. As historian Thomas Hietala has argued about Manifest Destiny in the 1840s, "expansionist policies took place under the shadow of the unwanted black."[37] My first chapter shows how domestic ideology in the same period represented home and nation in relation to both westward expansion and debates about slavery and African colonization. Similarly, in Chapter 2, I demonstrate how Mark Twain's depiction of the colonization of Hawaii was intertwined with his memories of slavery and his ambivalence about emancipation. When I turn to the wars in Cuba and the Philippines at the turn of the last century, it is not to explore the export of the Western frontier overseas, but to highlight the relation of imperialism abroad to the assault on Reconstruction at home, and the way some African Americans seized war abroad as an opportunity to claim citizenship in an imperial nation. Thus I am interested in tracing not only the ways in which imperial relations abroad were rendered through the lenses of black/white relations at home, but the way these two arenas were intermeshed. The racial politics of *The Birth of a Nation* were inextricable from the birth of an Empire.

Chapter 1, "Manifest Domesticity," introduces the double meaning of "domestic" as both the space of the nation and of the familial household and shows how these notions are inextricably intertwined with shifting notions of "foreign." The chapter opens with a paradigm that may seem remote from the arena of empire: the discourse of domesticity and the ideology of separate gendered spheres in the 1830s–1850s. I argue that the female realm of domesticity and the male arena of

Manifest Destiny were not separate spheres at all but were intimately linked. Their ideologists reimagined the nation as home during a period of massive and violent expansion into Mexico and Indian lands, which raised the volatile question of the expansion of slavery. In an analysis of household manuals, women's magazines, and popular domestic fiction, I demonstrate that the rhetoric of empire both suffused and unsettled the representation of the home to produce a domestic sphere of empire that ranges from the Rio Grande to Africa. The home is a mobile space that became in one way encompassed and in another expelled the foreign within, and the ideology of separate gendered spheres reinforced the effort to separate races by rendering freed black slaves as foreign to the nation. The chapter ends by remapping the terrain of women's novels in the 1850s to show how the representation of domesticity and female subjectivity simultaneously contributed to and were enabled by narratives of nation and empire building.

In Chapter 2, "The Imperial Routes of Mark Twain," I turn to an author whose name has long been synonymous with American culture. Once perceived as the quintessential American author, Mark Twain has most recently been the locus for debates about racism and black-white relations that pervade the American literary tradition. In this chapter I argue that his international travels in the routes of empire profoundly shaped both the iconic stature of Twain as an American writer and his complex representation of race. Specifically, I show how Twain's trip to Hawaii in 1866 as a young journalist was pivotal in launching his career as a national figure. His newspaper letters reveal conflicts between the colonial preconceptions he brought with him to Hawaii and the tumultuous social changes he found there that overflowed and unsettled the imperial framework of his writing. In Hawaii's transformation to a sugar-based economy in the immediate aftermath of the American Civil War, Twain found uncanny parallels to slavery at home, a connection that fueled his greatest fiction about race in America twenty years later. The memories of this formative imperial encounter, I argue, would haunt his writing throughout his career. Twain is well known for his outspoken condemnation of imperialism at the end of his life. I am interested not only in how Twain viewed American imperialism abroad, but also in how his earliest voyage through the anarchic routes of empire helped to create an American Mark Twain.

The next chapter begins with Twain's anti-imperialist writing against the annexation of the Philippines in 1901. When turning to the 1890s in Chapters 3–5, I do not posit a radical break between continental and overseas expansion, nor do I endorse a teleological narrative that empire tells about itself, the westward march of empire. Instead, I show how popular novelists and politicians were wrestling with these very questions about rupture and continuity in their representation of America as an empire or a republic, as were the Supreme Court justices in *Downes v. Bidwell*. I show how the Spanish-American War was portrayed not only as the export of Indian wars to new frontiers abroad but also as a resolution of the internal divisions of the Civil War.

Chapter 3, "Romancing the Empire," explores a double discourse of American imperialism in the 1890s, which redefined imperial power as disembodied—that is, divorced from contiguous territorial expansion—and relocated it as embodied in the figure of American manhood. I read popular historical romances of the period in conjunction with works about masculinity and political debates about imperialism, to show how these novels created cognitive and libidinal maps of the world on which they projected fantasies of unlimited expansion. More than neat political allegories that transpose international conflict into chivalric tales, these novels represented the empire as a site where American masculinity could be rescued from threatening social changes at home. I argue that the spectacle of manhood and the nostalgia for an imagined heroic past worked to enlist American women as spectators of the imperial project as they denied agency and visibility to Cubans and Filipinos struggling for independence against both the Spanish and American empires.

Chapter 4, "Black and Blue on San Juan Hill," turns from fictional fantasies about overseas adventures to journalistic accounts of the war in Cuba to find striking parallels between them. I argue that the construction of imperial masculinity was challenged by the presence of African American soldiers who troubled the clear racial divisions between colonizer and colonized and the assumed affiliations between race and nationhood. When writing about Cuba in *The Rough Riders,* Theodore Roosevelt anxiously differentiated his image of American masculinity not only from Cubans and Spaniards but also from African American troops who were fighting alongside him. In letters to the black press, African American soldiers criticized the export of Jim Crow segregation to imperial outposts abroad, while they saw these sites as opportunities to claim a form of imperial citizenship and militant manhood at home. The representation of empire at the turn of the century functioned both as an external catalyst and as a medium for the resolution of domestic racial conflict. This complex interaction underlies one of the most enduring cultural icons in U.S. memory of the Cuban-Spanish-American war.

While the "yellow press" has long been identified with jingoism at the turn of the century, less well known is the role of the new medium of film in mustering support for the first American war to be recorded in "moving pictures." In Chapter 5, "Birth of an Empire," I explore how closely the development of this new medium was tied to the spectacle of imperialism in 1898, and how echoes of that connection reverberated in American films well into the twentieth century. Early "moving pictures" made the world accessible to a diverse public at home while they celebrated American mobility abroad. I argue that these war films played a pivotal role in the development of film's capacity to tell stories in the first decade of the twentieth century. I then examine veiled allusions to this imperial heritage in later landmark American films, D. W. Griffith's *The Birth of a Nation* (1915), Oscar Micheaux's *Within Our Gates* (1920), and Orson Welles's *Citizen Kane* (1941). There I argue that traces of U.S. imperial history surface at key moments of cinematic innovation and threshold periods of international crisis, to reimagine the global role of America on the brink of entering the two World Wars.

The chapter on film concludes with a look at Henry Luce's essay, "The American Century," which, in urging the United States to enter World War II, coined a phrase that would rename the twentieth century. The next chapter turns to W. E. B. Du Bois's vastly different description of that same century: "The problem of the twentieth century is the problem of the color line,—the relation of the darker to the lighter races of men in Asia and Africa, in America and the islands of the sea."[38] In "The Imperial Cartography of W. E. B. Du Bois," I show how Du Bois represents the complex interconnections among domestic and foreign spaces that implicitly inform the paradigms I explore in the other chapters. This chapter poses the question of the relation between Du Bois's Pan-African internationalism and his views of American imperialism. Du Bois not only condemned the United States as an imperial force in the world, but used the framework of empire to decenter America as a product of broader global forces, and at times to recenter his own international authority. The analysis focuses on *Darkwater: Voices from Within the Veil* (1920), one of Du Bois's most ambitious and formally innovative efforts to remap racial conflicts within the United States through transnational networks of imperial power. The imperial cartography of *Darkwater*, I argue, renarrates the histories inscribed in and erased from conventional maps of the world, maps that were ripped up and redrawn during the cataclysm of World War I. Through seismic shifts of perspective, *Darkwater* expands the geographical terrain of "world war" to encompass the colonization of Africa and Asia, post-Reconstruction America, and the U.S. empire abroad. In *Darkwater*, Du Bois redefines the meaning of "war" to include conflicts over representations of space and time. From vantage points along the global color line, he reconceives the meaning of "peace" to project alternative futures beyond the anarchy of empire.

Mapping the overlapping terrain of the foreign and the domestic involves contests over the writing of history. I am interested not only in how we write the history of imperialism, but also in how the participants and critics of the imperial projects historicized empire in their own time. As the opening example suggests, legislating the status of the newly acquired territory of Puerto Rico involved the justices in renarrating the history of the United States as empire and republic. They were not the only ones to have questions about the disjuncture or continuity of current imperial ventures with received histories of the American past. Each cultural response, I will show, involved a complex process of both remembering and forgetting the inextricable connections between national identity and imperial expansion.

CHAPTER 1

Manifest Domesticity

The April 1847 issue of *Godey's Lady's Book* opened with an article entitled "Life on the Rio Grande" that starts: "There they are pic-nic-ing in real gipsy style, enjoying the life of freedom [which] dwellers in the pent-up city would find so delightful—for a few days."[1] This picnic refers to the accompanying illustration of a white pioneer family in a small clearing surrounded by a dense, towering forest. The mother stands at the center of the picture, with her husband at her side holding his rifle, and her children at her feet, staring at a freshly killed deer. An open cooking fire, a crude log cabin, and a few stalks of corn complete the scene. This family tableau evokes a larger domestic sphere to show that Texas, once a "Mexican province," is now "a member of the great family of free states that form the American Union." In *Godey's* vision of Manifest Destiny in this new state, "cities are appearing as by the rubbing of the Aladdin's lamp, dwellings and villages dotting the wide prairies, and the school house and church rising side by side, as on our New England hills they stand."

This idyllic sketch was published in the midst of a year-long war between the United States and Mexico, only a month after General Taylor's heralded victories not far from the Rio Grande. *Godey's* strikingly made no mention of the war, which was provoked in part by the annexation of Texas in 1845, or of the fact that the Rio Grande was a disputed boundary between the two nations. Neither did it acknowledge that Texas entered the "great family of free states" as a slave state. The absence of this violent political context is mirrored in the illustration by the lack of any defining characteristics that would identify the landscape or settlers as specific to the region. Instead, this generic picture of pioneer domesticity could appear anywhere from Kentucky to Oregon in that amorphous shifting terrain known as "the frontier."

"Life on the Rio Grande" represents U.S. imperialism not through war and conquest, but through a narrative of progress measured by how "highly the influence of the sex is valued in this new state of Texas." As evidence, the article quotes at length a speech delivered by General H. Mcleod at the occasion of the opening of the public school system in Galveston. "The civilization of every age has been the reflection of female influence," he proclaimed, and then proceeded to narrate world history as woman's progress from the position of man's slave and hireling to that of the lady worshipped by the medieval chivalrous knight. Both roles, however, were "as far from woman's true sphere as were the purchased beauties that filled the harem of his Moslem enemy." Only in the homes of America today has woman found her "true sphere" in her role as mother. Women have an especially important mission on the frontier, where "liberty is ever degenerating into license and man is prone to abandon his sentiments and follow his passions. It is woman's high mission, her prerogative and duty to counsel, to sustain, ay, to control him." *Godey's* happily concluded that if these "sentiments of a Texan" are "acted upon . . . that state (or states) will soon be among the brightest in our galaxy." Adherence to woman's sphere guarantees adhesion to the larger family of the Union.

The general's speech epitomized the well-known nineteenth-century "cult of domesticity" or ideology of "separate spheres," which held that woman's hallowed place is in the home, the site from which she wields the sentimental power of moral influence. Scholars have explored in depth the multiple political uses and contexts of domesticity; they have amply deconstructed the permeable boundary between putatively separate spheres; and they have shown how the extension of female sympathy across social classes worked to uphold the very racial and class hierarchies that sentimentality claimed to dissolve.[2] Yet few have noted what "Life on the Rio Grande" clearly demonstrates: that the discourse of domesticity was intimately intertwined with the discourse of Manifest Destiny in antebellum U.S. culture. The "empire of the mother" developed as a central tenet of middle-class culture between the 1830s and 1850s, at a time when the United States was violently and massively expanding its national domain across the continent. The spatial representations of domesticity and Manifest Destiny seem to exemplify the divisions between female and male spheres: the home as a bounded and rigidly ordered interior space as opposed to the boundless and undifferentiated space of an infinitely expanding frontier. The ideology of separate spheres configures the home as a stable haven or feminine counterbalance to the male activity of territorial conquest. *Godey's* article suggests, however, that these gendered spaces were more complexly intermeshed; that "woman's true sphere" was in fact a mobile and mobilizing outpost that transformed conquered foreign lands into the domestic sphere of the family and nation. At the same time, the focus on domesticity could work to efface all traces of violent conflict, as the foreign qualities of the Rio Grande magically disappeared into the familiar landscape of New England.

To understand this spatial and political interdependence of home and empire, it is necessary to consider rhetorically how the meaning of the domestic relies structurally on its intimate opposition to the notion of the foreign. *Domestic* has a double meaning that links the space of the familial household to that of the nation, by imagining both in opposition to everything outside the geographic and conceptual border of the home. The earliest meaning of *foreign,* according to the *Oxford English Dictionary,* refers to the physical space "out of doors" or to concerns "at a distance from home." Contemporary English speakers refer to national concerns as domestic in explicit or implicit contrast with the foreign. The notion of domestic policy makes sense only when distinguished from foreign policy, and, uncoupled from the foreign, national issues are never labeled domestic. The concept of foreign policy depends on the idea of the nation as a domestic space imbued with a sense of at-homeness, in contrast to an external world perceived as alien and threatening. Reciprocally, a sense of the foreign is necessary to erect the boundaries that enclose the nation as home. Domesticity, furthermore, refers not to a static condition, but to a process of domestication, which entails conquering and taming the wild, the natural, and the alien. "Domestic" in this sense is related to the imperial project of civilizing, and the conditions of domesticity often become markers that distinguish civilization from savagery. Domestication implies that the home contains within itself those wild or foreign elements that must be tamed; domesticity monitors the borders between the civilized and the savage as it regulates the traces of savagery within its purview.[3]

This chapter poses the question of how the ideology of separate spheres contributed to creating an American empire; how the concept of domesticity made the nation into home at a time when its geopolitical borders were expanding rapidly through violent confrontations with Mexicans and Native Americans. I argue that domesticity is a mobile and often unstable discourse that can expand or contract the boundaries of home and nation, and that their interdependency relies on racialized conceptions of the foreign. I explore this idea of traveling domesticity in the writings of Catharine Beecher and Sarah Josepha Hale, whose work, despite their ideological differences as public figures, reveals how the internal logic of domesticity relies on, abets, and reproduces the contradictions of nationalist expansion in the 1840s and 1850s. My reading of Beecher's *Treatise on Domestic Economy* demonstrates that the language of empire suffused the rhetoric of domesticity, while my analysis of Hale's work uncovers the shared racial underpinnings of domestic and imperialist discourse through which the separateness of gendered spheres reinforced the effort to separate the races by turning blacks into foreigners. The chapter concludes by remapping the terrain of women's fiction of the 1850s to suggest how narratives of female subjectivity are scripted through the imperial reach of domesticity. Together, these examples demonstrate how domesticity worked as both a bulwark against and embodiment of the anarchy of empire, and how images of the nation as home were haunted by "disembodied shades" who blurred the boundaries between the domestic and the foreign.

Empire of the Home

Domesticity dominated middle-class women's writing and culture from the 1830s through the 1850s, at a time when national boundaries were in violent flux. During this period the United States increased its national domain by seventy percent, engaged in a bloody campaign of Indian removal, fought its first prolonged foreign war, wrested the Spanish borderlands from Mexico, and annexed Texas, Oregon, California, and New Mexico. As Thomas Hietala has shown, this convulsive expansion was less a confident celebration of Manifest Destiny than a response to crises of confidence about national unity, the expansion of slavery, and the racial identity of citizenship—crises that territorial expansion exacerbated.[4] Furthermore, these movements evoked serious questions about the conceptual border between the domestic and the foreign. In the 1831 Supreme Court decision on *Cherokee Nation v. the State of Georgia*, for example, Indians were declared members of "domestic dependent nations," neither foreign nationals nor U.S. citizens.[5] This designation made the domestic an ambiguous liminal realm between the national and the foreign, as it placed the foreign inside the geographic boundaries of the nation. The uneasy relation between the domestic and the foreign can also be seen in the debates over the annexation of new territory. In the middle of the Mexican-American War, President Polk insisted that slavery was "purely a domestic question" and not a "foreign question" at all, but the expansion he advocated undermined that distinction and threatened domestic unity by raising the question of slavery's extension into previously foreign lands.[6]

The language of domesticity permeated representations of national expansion. John L. O'Sullivan's *Democratic Review*, for example, claimed in 1847 that the war "unfortunately exists through the anarchy of Mexico," for "when a nation keeps a 'disorderly house', it is the duty of neighbors to intervene."[7] Military invasion is represented here as a form of good housekeeping. In debates about the annexation of Texas and later Mexico, both sides represented the new territories as women to be married to the United States; Sam Houston wrote of Texas presenting itself "to the United States as a bride adorned for her espousals"; and President Taylor accused annexationists after the Mexican-American War of trying to "drag California into the Union before her wedding garment has yet been cast about her person."[8] These visions of imperial expansion as marital union carried within them the prospect of marriage as racial amalgamation. While popular fiction about the Mexican-American War portrayed brave American men rescuing and marrying Mexican women of Spanish descent, political debate over the annexation of Mexico hinged on what was agreed to be the impossibility of incorporating a foreign, racially mixed people into a domestic nation imagined as Anglo-Saxon.[9] The "virtues of the Anglo-Saxon Race make their political union with the degraded Mexican-

Spanish impossible," wrote the *Democratic Review* to explain the annexation of Texas. Southerners, such as Senator Calhoun, used the same reasoning to argue against annexing all of Mexico.[10] In both cases, the language of political union and marital union merged in the common fear of racial intermixing.

One of the major contradictions of imperialist expansion is that while the United States strove to nationalize and domesticate foreign territories and peoples, annexation threatened to incorporate non-white foreign subjects into the republic in a way that was perceived to undermine the nation as a domestic space. The discourse of domesticity was deployed to negotiate the borders of an expanding empire and divided nation. Rather than stabilize the representation of the nation as home, this rhetoric heightened the fraught and contingent nature of the boundary between the domestic and the foreign, a boundary that broke down around questions of the racial identity of the nation as home. Domestic discourse, I argue, both redressed and reenacted the anarchic qualities of empire through its own double movement: to expand female influence beyond the home and the nation, and simultaneously to contract woman's sphere to that of policing domestic boundaries against the threat of foreignness.

At this time of heightened imperial expansion, proponents of "woman's sphere" applied the language of empire to the home and even to women's emotional lives. "Hers is the empire of the affections," wrote Sarah Josepha Hale, influential editor of *Godey's Lady's Book,* who opposed the women's rights movement as "the attempt to take woman away from her empire of home."[11] To educational reformer Horace Mann, "the empire of the Home" was "the most important of all empires, the pivot of all empires and emperors."[12] Writers who counseled women to renounce politics and economics, "to leave the rude commerce of camps and the soul hardening struggling of political power to the harsher spirit of men," urged them in highly political rhetoric to take up a more spiritual calling, "the domain of the moral affections and the empire of the heart."[13] Catharine Beecher gave this calling a nationalist cast in *A Treatise on Domestic Economy,* when, for example, she used Queen Victoria as a foil to elevate the American "mother and housekeeper in a large family" who is "the sovereign of an empire demanding as varied cares, and involving more difficult duties, than are exacted of her, who wears the crown and professedly regulates the interests of the greatest nation on earth, [yet] finds abundant leisure for theaters, balls, horse races, and every gay leisure."[14] This imperial trope might be interpreted as a compensatory and defensive effort to glorify the shrunken realm of female agency, in a paradox of what Mary Ryan calls "imperial isolation," whereby the mother gains her symbolic sovereignty at the cost of withdrawal from the outside world.[15] For these writers, however, metaphor has a material efficacy in the world. The representation of the home as an empire exists in tension with the notion of woman's sphere as a contracted space, because it is in the nature of empires to extend their rule over new domains while fortifying their borders against external invasion and internal insurrection. If, on the one hand, domesticity drew strict boundaries between the private home and the public world of men, on the other, it became the engine of national expansion, the site from which the nation reaches beyond itself through the emanation of woman's moral influence.

The paradox of what might be called "imperial domesticity" is that, by withdrawing from direct agency in the male arena of commerce and politics, woman's sphere can be represented by both women and men as a more potent agent for national expansion. The outward reach of domesticity in turn enables the interior functioning of the home. In her introduction to *A Treatise on Domestic Economy,* Beecher inextricably links women's work to the unfolding of America's global mission of "exhibiting to the world the beneficent influences of Christianity, when carried into every social, civil, and political institution" (12). Women's maternal responsibility of molding the character of men and children has global repercussions: "to American women, more than to any others on earth, is committed the exalted privilege of extending over the world those blessed influences, that are to renovate degraded man, and 'clothe all climes with beauty'" (14). Beecher ends her introduction with an extended architectural metaphor in which women's agency at home is predicated on the global expansion of the nation:

> The builders of a temple are of equal importance, whether they labor on the foundations, or toil upon the dome. Thus also with those labors that are to be made effectual in the regeneration of the Earth. The woman who is rearing a family of children; the woman who labors in the schoolroom, the woman who, in her retired chamber, earns with

her needle the mite to contribute for the intellectual and moral eleva-
tion of her country; even the humble domestic, whose example and influence may be molding and forming young minds, while her faithful
services sustain a prosperous domestic state;—each and all may be
cheered by the consciousness that they are agents in accomplishing the
greatest work that ever was committed to human responsibility. It is the
building of a glorious temple, whose base shall be coextensive with the
bounds of the earth, whose summit shall pierce the skies, whose splen-
dor shall beam on all lands, and those who hew the lowliest stone, as
much as those who carve the highest capital, will be equally honored
when its top-stone shall be laid, with new rejoicing of the morning
stars, and shoutings of the sons of God. (14)

The political charge of this metaphor is contradictory: it unifies
women of different social classes in a shared project of construction
while sustaining class hierarchy among women.[16] This image of social
unity depends upon and underwrites a vision of national expansion, as
women's varied labors come together to embrace the entire world. As
the author moves down the social scale, from mother to teacher to
spinster, her geographic reach extends outward from home to schoolroom to country, until the "humble domestic" returns back to the
"prosperous domestic state," an ambiguous phrase whose double
meaning refers at once outward to the nation and inward to the home.
Woman's work here performs two interdependent forms of national
labor; it forges the bonds of internal unity and pushes the nation outward to encompass the globe. This outward expansion in turn enables the internal cohesiveness of woman's separate sphere by making
women agents in erecting an infinitely expanding edifice.

Beecher thus introduces her detailed manual on the regulation of
the home as a highly ordered space by fusing the boundedness of
the home with the boundlessness of the nation. Her 1841 introduction bears a remarkable resemblance to the rhetoric of Manifest Destiny, particularly to this passage by one of its foremost proponents,
O'Sullivan, in his "The Great Nation of Futurity" of 1839:

The far-reaching, the boundless future will be the era of American
greatness. In its magnificent domain of space and time, the nation of
many nations is destined to manifest to mankind the excellence of di-
vine principles; to establish on earth the noblest temple ever dedicated

to the worship of the most high—the Sacred and the True. Its floor shall be a hemisphere—its roof the firmament of the star-studded heavens, and its congregation an Union of many Republics, comprising hundreds of happy millions, calling, owning no man master, but governed by God's natural and moral law of equality.[17]

While these passages exemplify the stereotype of separate spheres (one describes work in the home and the other the work of nation building), both use a common architectural metaphor, a biblical temple coextensive with the globe. O'Sullivan's grammatical subject is the American nation, which, while it remains unnamed in Beecher's passage, is the medium for channeling women's work at home to a Christianized world. The construction of an edifice ordinarily entails walling off the inside from the outside, but in these two cases there is a paradoxical effect whereby the distinction between inside and outside is obliterated by the expansion of the home/nation/temple to encompass the globe. The rhetoric of Manifest Destiny and that of domesticity share a vocabulary that turns imperial conquest into spiritual regeneration in order to efface internal conflict or external resistance in visions of geopolitical domination as global harmony.

Although in the reaches of imperial domesticity a home is ultimately coextensive with the entire world, the concept also continually projects a map of unregenerate outlying foreign terrain that gives coherence to its boundaries and justifies its domesticating mission. When in 1869 Catharine Beecher revised her *Treatise* with her sister, Harriet Beecher Stowe, as *The American Women's Home,* they downplayed the earlier role of domesticity in harmonizing class differences and enhanced domesticity's outward reach. The book ends by advocating the establishment of Christian neighborhoods settled primarily by women as a way of putting into practice domesticity's expansive potential to Christianize and Americanize immigrants in Northeastern cities and "all over the West and South, while along the Pacific coast, China and Japan are sending their pagan millions to share our favored soil, climate, and government." No longer a leveling factor among classes within America, domesticity could be extended to those perceived as foreign within and beyond American national borders: "Ere long colonies from these prosperous and Christian communities would go forth to shine as 'lights of the world' in all the now darkened nations. Thus the Christian family and Christian neighborhood would become the grand ministry as they were designed to be, in training our whole race for heaven."[18] Though Beecher and Stowe emphasize domesticity's service to "darkened nations," the existence of "pagans" as potential converts performs a reciprocal service in the extension of domesticity to single American women. Such Christian neighborhoods would allow unmarried women without children to leave their work in "factories, offices and shops," or reject their idleness in "refined leisure," to live domestic lives on their own, in some cases adopting native children. Domesticity's imperial reach allows the woman's sphere to include not only the heathen but also the unmarried Euro-American woman, who can be freed from biological reproduction to rule her own maternal empire.

If writers about domesticity encouraged the extension of female influence outward to civilize the foreign, their writings also evoked anxiety about the opposing trajectory that brings foreignness into the home. Analyzing the widespread colonial trope that compares colonized people to children, Ann Stoler and Karen Sánchez-Eppler have each shown how this metaphor can work not only to infantilize the colonized but also to portray white children as young savages in need of civilizing.[19] This metaphor at once extends domesticity outward to the tutelage of heathens and inward to regulate the threat of foreignness within the boundaries of the home. For Beecher, this internal savagery appeared to endanger the physical health of the mother. Throughout her *Treatise,* the vision of the sovereign mother with imperial power is countered by the description of the ailing invalid mother. This contrast can be seen in the titles of the first two chapters, "Peculiar Responsibilities of American Women" and "Difficulties Peculiar to American Women." The latter focuses on the pervasive invalidism that makes American women physically and emotionally unequal to their global responsibilities. In contrast to the ebullient temple building of the first chapter, Beecher ends the second with a quotation from Tocqueville describing a fragile frontier home centered on a lethargic and vulnerable mother, whose

> children cluster about her, full of health, turbulence and energy; they
> are true children of the wilderness; their mother watches them from
> time to time, with mingled melancholy and joy. To look at their

strength, and her languor one might imagine that the life she had given them exhausted her own; and still she regrets not what they cost her. The house, inhabited by these emigrants, has no internal partition or loft. In the one chamber of which it consists, the whole family is gathered for the night. The dwelling itself is a little world; an ark of civilization amid an ocean of foliage. A hundred steps beyond it, the primeval forest spreads its shade and solitude resumes its sway. (24)

The mother's health appears drained less by the external hardships inflicted by the environment than by her own "children of the wilderness," who violate the border between home and primeval forest. This boundary is partially reinforced by the image of the home as an "ark of civilization" whose internal order should protect its inhabitants from the "ocean of foliage" that surrounds them. Yet the undifferentiated inner space, which lacks "internal partition," replicates rather than defends against the boundlessness of the wilderness around it. The rest of Beecher's *Treatise,* with its detailed attention to the systematic organization of the household, works to "partition" the home in a way that distinguishes it from an external wilderness.[20]

Although the infirmity of American mothers is a pervasive concern throughout *Treatise,* its physical cause is difficult to locate. Poor health afflicts middle-class women in Northeastern cities as much as women on the frontier, according to Beecher, and she sees the cause in geographic and social mobility: "everything is moving and changing" (16). This movement affects women's health most directly, claims Beecher, by depriving them of reliable domestic servants. With "trained" servants constantly moving up and out, middle-class women must resort to hiring "ignorant" and "poverty-stricken foreigners," with whom they are said in *American Woman's Home* to have a "missionary" relationship (332). Though Beecher does not label these foreigners as the direct cause of illness, their presence disrupts the orderly "system and regularity" of housekeeping, leading American women to be "disheartened, discouraged, and ruined in health" (18). Throughout her *Treatise* Beecher turns the lack of good servants—at first a cause of infirmity—into a remedy; their absence gives middle-class women the opportunity to perform regular domestic labor that will revive their health. By implication, their self-regulated work at home will also keep "poverty-stricken foreigners" out of their homes. Curiously, then, the mother's ill health stems from the unruly subjects of her domestic empire—children and servants—who bring uncivilized wilderness and undomesticated foreignness into the home. The fear of disease and of invalidism that characterizes the American woman also serves as a metaphor for anxiety about foreignness within. The mother's domestic empire is at risk of contagion from the very subjects she must domesticate and civilize, who ultimately infest both the home and the maternal body.[21]

Beecher's concept of the domestic thus generates and is constituted by images of the foreign. On the one hand, domesticity's "habits of system and order" appear to anchor the home as an enclosed stable center against a fluctuating alien world of expanding national borders; on the other, domesticity must be spatially and conceptually mobile to travel to the nation's far-flung frontiers. Beecher's use of Tocqueville's ark metaphor suggests the rootlessness and the self-enclosed mobility necessary for the efficacy of middle-class domesticity to redefine the meaning of habitation, to make Euro-Americans feel at home in a place where *they* are initially the foreign ones. Domesticity inverts this relationship to create a home by rendering prior inhabitants alien and undomesticated and by implicitly nativizing newcomers. The empire of the mother thus embodies the anarchy at the heart of the American empire; the two empires follow a double compulsion to conquer and domesticate—to control and incorporate—the foreign within the borders of the home and the nation.

Domesticating the Empire

The imperial scope of domesticity was central to the work of Sarah Josepha Hale, throughout her half-century editorship of the influential *Godey's Lady's Book* and in her fiction and history writing. Hale has been viewed by some scholars as advocating a woman's sphere more thoroughly separate from male political concerns than the one Beecher promoted.[22] This withdrawal seems confirmed by the refusal of *Godey's* even to mention the Civil War throughout its duration, much less take sides. Yet when Hale conflates the progress of women with the nation's Manifest Destiny in her history writing, other scholars have judged her as inconsistently moving out of the woman's sphere into a conventional male political realm.[23] Hale's conception of separate spheres, I argue, is predicated on the imperial expansion of the nation. Although her writing as editor, essayist, and novelist focused on the interior spaces of the home, with ample advice on housekeeping, clothing, manners, and emotions, she gave equal and related attention to the expansion of female influence through her advocacy of female medical missionaries abroad and the colonization of Africa by former black slaves. Even though Hale seemed to avoid the issue of slavery and race relations in her silence about the Civil War, in the 1850s her conception of domesticity took on a decidedly racial cast, exposing the intimate link between the separateness of gendered spheres and the effort to keep the races apart in separate national spheres.

In 1847, in the middle of the Mexican-American War, Hale launched a campaign on the pages of *Godey's Lady's Book* to declare Thanksgiving Day a national holiday, a campaign she avidly pursued until Lincoln made the holiday official in 1863.[24] This effort typified the way in which Hale's map of woman's sphere overlaid national and domestic spaces; *Godey's* published detailed instructions and recipes for preparing the Thanksgiving feast, while it encouraged women readers to agitate for a nationwide holiday as a ritual of national expansion and unification. The power of Thanksgiving Day stemmed from its center in the domestic sphere; Hale imagined millions of families seated around the table on the same day, thereby unifying the vast and shifting space of the national domain through simultaneity. This domestic ritual would "unite our great nation, by its states and families" from "St. John's to the Rio Grande, from the Atlantic to the Pacific border," and it should therefore become an official holiday "as long as the Union endures."[25] If the celebration of Thanksgiving unites individual families across regions and brings them together in an imagined collective space, Thanksgiving's continental scope endows each individual family gathering with national meaning. Furthermore, the Thanksgiving story commemorating the founding of New England—which in Hale's version makes no mention of Indians— could create a common history by nationalizing a regional myth of origins and transposing it to the territories most recently wrested away from Indians and Mexicans. Hale's campaign to transform Thanksgiving from a regional to a national holiday grew even fiercer with the approach of the Civil War. In 1859 she wrote, "If every state would join in Union Thanksgiving on the 24th of this month, would it not be a renewed pledge of love and loyalty to the Constitution of the United States?"[26] Thanksgiving Day, she hoped, could avert the coming civil war. As a national holiday celebrated primarily in the home, the cross-country Thanksgiving celebration serves to write a national history of origins, to colonize newly acquired Western territories, and to unite North and South.

The domestic ritual of Thanksgiving could expand and unify the nation, provided its borders were fortified against foreignness; for Hale, the nation's boundaries not only defined its geographical limits but also set apart nonwhites within the national domain. In Hale's fiction of the 1850s, Thanksgiving polices the domestic sphere by making black people, whether free or enslaved, foreign to the domestic nation and homeless within America's expanding borders. In 1852 Hale reissued *Northwood*, the novel which had launched her career in 1827 with a highly publicized chapter about a New Hampshire Thanksgiving dinner, showcasing the values of the American republic to a skeptical British visitor. For the 1852 version Hale changed the subtitle from "A Tale of New England" to "Life North and South," to highlight the new material she added on slavery.[27] Pro-union yet against abolition, Hale advocated sending all black people to settle in Africa and Christianize its inhabitants. Colonization in the 1850s had a two-pronged ideology: to expel blacks to a separate national sphere, and to expand U.S. power through the civilizing process; black Christian settlers would become both outcasts from and agents for the American empire.[28]

Hale's 1852 *Northwood* ends with an appeal to use Thanksgiving Day as an occasion to collect money at all American churches "for the purpose of educating and colonizing free people of color and emancipated slaves" (408). This annual collection would contribute to "peaceful emancipation" as "every obstacle to the real freedom of America would be melted before the gushing streams of sympathy and charity" (408). While "sympathy," a sentiment associated with woman's sphere, seems to extend to black slaves, the goal of sympathy in this passage is not to free them but to emancipate white America from their presence. Thanksgiving for Hale thus celebrates national cohesiveness around the domestic sphere by simultaneously rendering blacks within America foreign to the nation.

For Hale, colonization would also transform American slavery into a civilizing and domesticating mission. One of her Northern characters explains to the British visitor that "the destiny of America is to instruct the world, which we shall do, with the aid of our Anglo-Saxon brothers over the water. . . . Great Britain has enough to do at home and in the East Indies to last her another century. We have this country and Africa to settle and civilize" (167). When his listener is puzzled by the reference to Africa, the American explains "that is the greatest mission of our Republic, to train here the black man for his duties as a Christian, then free him and send him to Africa, there to plant Free States and organize Christian civilization" (168). The colonization of Africa becomes the goal of slavery by making it part of the civilizing mission of global imperialism. Colonization thus not only banishes blacks from the domestic union, but, as the final sentence of *Northwood* proclaims, it proves that "the mission of American slavery is to Christianize Africa" (408).

In 1853 Hale published the novel *Liberia*, which begins where *Northwood* ends, with the settlement of Liberia by freed black slaves.[29] Seen by scholars as a retort to *Uncle Tom's Cabin*, it can also be read as the untold story of Stowe's novel, starting where she concludes, with former black slaves migrating to Africa.[30] Although the subtitle, "Mr. Peyton's Experiment," places colonization under the aegis of a white man, the narrative turns colonization into a project emanating from woman's sphere in at least two directions. In its outward trajectory, the settlement of Liberia appears as an expansion of feminized domestic values. Yet domesticity is not only exported to civilize native Africans; the framing of the novel also makes African colonization necessary to the establishment of domesticity within the United States as exclusively white. While Hale writes that the purpose of the novel is to "show the advantages Liberia offers to the African," in so doing it construes all black people as foreign to American nationality by asserting that they must remain homeless within the United States. At the same time, Hale paints a picture of American imperialism as the embodiment of the feminine values of domesticity: "What other nation can point to a colony planted from such pure motives of charity; nurtured by the counsels and exertions of its most noble and self-denying statesmen and philanthropists; and sustained, from its feeble commencement up to a period of self-reliance and independence, from pure love of justice and humanity?" (iv). In this passage America is figured as a mother raising her baby, Africa, to maturity; the vocabulary of "purity," "charity," "self-denial" represents colonization as an extension of the values of woman's separate sphere.

The narrative opens with a scene fraught with danger to American domesticity. The last male of a distinguished Virginia family is on his deathbed, helpless to defend his plantation from a rumored slave insurrection. The women of the family, led by his wife, Virginia, rally with the loyal slaves to defend their home from the insurrection that never occurs. Thus the novel's separate spheres have gone awry, with the man of the family abed at home, while white women and black slaves act as protectors and soldiers. The ensuing plot to settle Liberia overtly rewards those slaves for their loyalty by giving them freedom and a homeland; it also serves to reinstate separate spheres and reestablish American domesticity as white.

When the narrative shifts to Africa, the black colonizers, now deprived of American nationhood, have the task of Americanizing that continent through domesticity. A key figure in the settlement is the slave Keziah, who has nursed the white plantation owners. She is the one most responsive to Peyton's proposal for colonization, because of her desire to be free and to Christianize the natives. Her future husband, Polydore, more recently arrived in the United States as a slave and thus less "civilized," is afraid to return to Africa because of his memory of native brutality and superstition. This couple represents two faces of enslaved Africans central to the white imagination of colonization: the degenerate heathen represented by the man, and the redeemed Christian represented by the woman. Keziah, however, can only become a fully domesticated woman at a geographic remove from American domesticity. When Keziah protects the plantation in Virginia, her maternal impulse is described as that of a wild animal—a "fierce lioness." Only in Africa can she become the domestic center of the new settlement, where she establishes a home that resembles Beecher's Christian neighborhood. Keziah builds a private home with fence and garden, and civilizes her husband while she expands her domestic sphere to adopt native children and open a Christian school.

Keziah's domestication of herself and her surroundings in Africa can be seen as part of the movement in the novel (noted by Susan Ryan) in which the freed black characters are represented as recognizably American only at the safe distance of Africa.[31] Once banished from the domestic sphere of U.S. nationality, they can be resurrected as American in a foreign terrain. The novel narrates the founding of Liberia as a story of colonization, but Hale's storytelling also colonizes Liberia as an imitation of America, replete with images of the frontier, the *Mayflower,* and the planting of the American flag. A double narrative movement at once contracts U.S. borders to exclude blacks from domestic space and simultaneously expands those borders by re-creating that domestic space in Africa. Thus the novel ends with a passage that compares the Liberian settlers to the Pilgrims and represents them as part of a global expansion of the American nation:

> I do not doubt but that the whole continent of Africa will be regenerated, and I believe the Republic of Liberia will be the great instrument, in the hands of God, in working out this regeneration. The colony of Liberia has succeeded better than the colony of Plymouth did for the same period of time. And yet, in that little company which was wafted across the mighty ocean in the *May Flower,* we see the germs of this already colossal nation, whose feet are in the tropics, while her head reposes upon the snows of Canada. Her right hand she stretches over the Atlantic, feeding the millions of the Old World, and beckoning them to her shores, as a refuge from famine and oppression; and, at the same time, she stretches forth her left hand to the islands of the Pacific, and to the old empires of the East. (303)

In Hale's view, both slavery and domesticity are necessary to the imperial mission; African slaves are brought to America to become Christianized and domesticated, but they cannot complete this potential transformation until they "return" to Africa.

Hale's writing makes race central to woman's sphere. Nonwhites are excluded from domestic nationalism; moreover, the capacity for domesticity becomes an innate defining characteristic of the Anglo-Saxon race. Reginald Horsman has shown how in political thought by the 1840s the meaning of Anglo-Saxonism had shifted from a historical understanding of the development of republican institutions to an essentialist definition of a single race that possesses an innate and unique capacity for self-government.[32] His analysis, however, limits this racial formation to the traditionally male sphere of politics. Hale's *Woman's Record* (1853), a massive compendium of the history of women from Eve to the present, establishes woman's sphere as central to the racial discourse of Anglo-Saxonism. To Hale the empire of the mother spawns the Anglo-Saxon nation and propels its natural inclination toward global power. In her introduction to the fourth part of her volume on the present era, Hale represents America as manifesting the universal progress of women that culminates in the Anglo-Saxon race. To explain the Anglo-Saxon "mastery of the mind over Europe and Asia," she argues that

> if we trace out the causes of this superiority, they would center in the moral influence, which true religion confers on the female sex. . . . There is still a more wonderful example of this uplifting power of the educated female mind. It is only seventy-five years since the Anglo-Saxons in the New World became a nation, then numbering about three million souls. Now this people form the great American republic, with a population of twenty-three millions; and the destiny of the world will soon be in their keeping! Religion is free; and the soul which woman always influences where God is worshipped in spirit and truth, is untrammeled by code, or creed, or caste. . . . The result before the world—a miracle of advancement, American mothers train their sons to be men.[33]

Hale here articulates the imperial logic of what has been called "republican motherhood," which ultimately posits the outward expansion of maternal influence beyond the home and the nation's borders.[34] The Manifest Destiny of the nation unfolds logically from the imperial reach of woman's influence emanating from her separate domestic sphere. Domesticity makes manifest the destiny of the Anglo-Saxon race, while Manifest Destiny becomes in turn the condition for Anglo-Saxon domesticity. For Hale domesticity influences national expansion in a double manner: it casts the image of the nation as a home delimited by race, and the image of the nation as propelled outward through imperial female agency.

Advocating domesticity's expansive mode, *Woman's Record* includes only those nonwhite women who contributed to the spread of Christianity to colonized peoples. In the third volume, Hale designates Ann Judson, a white American missionary to Burma, as the most distinguished woman to 1830 (152). The fourth volume of *Woman's Record* focuses predominantly on American women as the apex of historical development. In contrast to the aristocratic accomplishment of English women, "in all that contributes to popular education and pure religious sentiment among the masses, the women of America are in advance of all others on the globe. To prove this we need only examine the list of American female missionaries, teachers, editors and authors of works instructive and educational, contained in this 'Record'" (564). While Anglo-Saxon men marched to conquer new lands, female influence had a complementary outward reach from within the domestic sphere.

The argument for African colonization can be seen as part of the broader global expansion of woman's sphere. In 1853 Hale printed in *Godey's Lady's Book* "An Appeal to the American Christians on Behalf of the Ladies' Medical Missionary Society," in which she argued for the special need for women physicians abroad because they would have unique access to foreign women's bodies and souls.[35] Her argument for training female medical missionaries both enlarged the field of white women's agency and feminized the force of imperial power. She saw female medical missionaries as not only curing disease but also raising the status of women abroad: "All heathen people have a high reverence for medical knowledge. Should they find Christian ladies accomplished in this science, would it not greatly raise the sex in the estimation of those nations, where one of the most serious impediments to moral improvement is the degradation and ignorance to which their females have been for centuries consigned?" (185). Though superior to heathen women in status, American women would accomplish their goal by taking gender as a common ground, which would give them special access to women abroad. As women they could be more effective imperialists, penetrating those interior colonial spaces, symbolized by the harem, that remain inaccessible to male missionaries:

> Vaccination is difficult of introduction among the people of the east, though suffering dreadfully from the ravages of small-pox. The American mission at Siam writes that thousands of children were, last year, swept away by this disease in the country around him. Female physicians could win their way among these poor children much easier than doctors of the other sex. Surely the ability of American women to learn

and practice vaccination will not be questioned, when the more difficult art of inoculation was discovered by the women of Turkey, and introduced into Europe by an English woman! Inoculation is one of the greatest triumphs of remedial skill over a sure loathsome and deadly disease which the annals of Medical Art record. Its discovery belongs to women. I name it here to show that they are gifted with genius for the profession, and only need to be educated to excel in the preventive department.

Let pious, intelligent women be fitly prepared, and what a mission-field for doing good would be opened! In India, China, Turkey, and all over the heathen world, they would, in their character of physicians, find access to the homes and harems where women dwell, and where the good seed sown would bear an hundredfold, because it would take root in the bosom of the sufferer, and in the heart of childhood. (185)

In this passage the connections among women branch out in many directions, but Hale charts a kind of evolutionary narrative that places American women at the apex of development. Though inoculation was discovered by Turkish women, it can only return to Turkey to save Turkish children through the agency of English women transporting knowledge to Americans, who can then go to Turkey as missionaries and save women who could not save themselves or their children. The needs of heathen women allow American female missionaries to conquer their own domestic empire without reproducing biologically. Instead, American women are metaphorically cast as men in a cross-racial union, as they sow seeds in the bodies of heathen women who will bear Christian children. Through female influence, women physicians will transform heathen harems into Christian homes.

Thus the concept of female influence in Hale's writing, so central to domestic discourse and at the heart of the sentimental ethos, was underwritten by and abetted the imperial expansion of the nation. While the empire of the mother advocated retreat from the world-conquering enterprises of men, this renunciation promised a more thorough kind of world conquest. Both the empire of the mother and the American Empire sought to encompass the entire world outside their borders, yet this same outward movement contributed to and relied on the contraction of the domestic sphere to exclude persons conceived of as racially foreign within those expanding national boundaries.

Imperial Subjectivity

The imperial reach of domesticity extended not only to racially foreign subjects inside and outside the home, but also to the interiority of female subjectivity, the major focus of popular women's fiction in the 1850s. While critics such as Gillian Brown, Richard Brodhead, and Nancy Armstrong have taught us how domestic novels represent women as model bourgeois subjects, these novels also produced a racialized national subjectivity in contested international spaces.[36] Understanding the imperial scope of domesticity and its relation to the foreign should help us map the broader international and national contexts in which unfold narratives of female development that at first glance seem anchored in local domestic spaces. These narratives construct domestic locations in complex negotiation with the foreign. To take a few well-known examples from the 1850s, Susan Warner's *The Wide Wide World* sends its heroine to Scotland, while the world of Maria Cummins's *The Lamplighter* encompasses India, Cuba, the American West, and Brazil. The geographic coordinates of *Uncle Tom's Cabin* extend to Haiti, Canada, and, most notably, Africa; in E.D.E.N. Southworth's *The Hidden Hand,* the resolution of multiple domestic plots in Virginia relies on the participation of the male characters in the Mexican-American War.[37] This remapping involves more than seeing the external settings anew; it means turning inward to the privileged space of the domestic novel—the interiority of the female subject—to find traces of foreignness that must be domesticated or expunged. The imperial struggle to control foreignness within "woman's sphere" shapes the representation of female subjectivity, the empire of the affections and the heart.

Many domestic novels open at physical thresholds—such as windows or doorways—to problematize the relation between interiors and exteriors. As we have seen in Hale's *Liberia,* they introduce the sphere of domesticity as fragile and under siege. *The Wide Wide World* opens at a window, with the heroine's "thoughts traveling dreamily . . . perfectly regardless of all but the moving world without" (9). *The Lamplighter* starts at the stoop of an unwholesome tenement, while *The Hidden Hand* opens with a view of the ancestral mansion battered by tempestuous winds. *Uncle Tom's Cabin* politicizes this boundary between inside and outside, where the slave trader violates the domestic stability of the slave and the master. The plots of these novels are propelled in part by the effort to reconstitute the domestic sphere, both by enlarging its domain beyond the narrow definition of familial bloodlines and by purging it of the foreign bodies this expansion incorporates.

These novels explore the breakdown of the boundaries between internal and external spaces, between the domestic and the foreign, as they struggle to renegotiate them. This struggle takes place not only within the home but also within the "empire of the heart," within the interior subjectivity of the heroine. Where the domestic novel turns inward into the private sphere of female subjectivity, we often find that subjectivity scripted by narratives of nation and empire. In contrast to its title, *The Wide Wide World,* for example, presents a heroine who appears narrowly closeted in domestic interiors. Jane Tompkins has viewed Ellen Montgomery's paradoxical achievement of a female self through Christian self-abnegation as the paradigm of sentimental power, while Richard Brodhead has shown how the activity of reading functions as a method of disciplining the bourgeois self.[38] He does not note, however, that Ellen's favorite book is Parson Weems's *Life of Washington.* In rereading and memorizing this story, "whatever she had found in the leaves of the book, she had certainly lost herself" (329). If reading creates individual subjectivity, at the core of the female self we find a national narrative about the fathering of the nation. Weems's popular biography contributed to a shift in the representation of Washington: from a public statesman to a private man embodying domestic virtues, the father of his nation whom Weems portrayed as a loving son to his mother.[39] Thus Ellen's turn inward not only breaks down the boundary between separate spheres, but also incorporates the father of the nation into the empire of the mother.

Critics have debated whether the sentimental heroine submits or indirectly rebels against patriarchal dictates of woman's sphere. I am arguing that Ellen's submissive and rebellious acts are both underwritten by imperial narratives. She escapes from confining domestic labor, "seated on a little bench in the chimney corner, when the fire blazed up well, before the candles were lighted. To forget the kitchen and the supper and her bustling aunt and sail around the world with Captain Cook" (336). Reading about imperial adventures also sanctions the kind of self-indulgence that defies the dictates of domesticity, allowing her to read "like an epicure . . . she would be lost in her book, perhaps hunting the elephant in India or fighting Nelson's battles over again." The more inward she turns and self-abnegating she becomes, the more expansive and adventurous her reading sphere.

In the final test of self-discipline, Ellen brings her reading into the world, where she reenacts the American struggle for independence against the British Empire. She is forced to leave America to live with her newly discovered Scottish relatives, who first tease her for being an American "rebel," "one of those who makes a saint of George Washington." Her uncle then more seriously demands that she renounce her national identity and exchange her national patrimony for her bloodline: "Forget that you were American, Ellen—you belong to me; your name is not Montgomery any more—it is Lindsay;—and I will not have you call me 'uncle'—I am your father, you are my own little daughter, and must do precisely as I tell you" (510). Ellen vows to obey, to submit to authority. Like the heroine of a captivity narrative in reverse, where Scotland is the site of the removal from home, she maintains her memories and affectionate ties to home while she submits to the foreign power around her. In this dialectic between submission and rebellion, Ellen's achievement of a Christianized feminized self is scripted as an enactment of national independence through the female virtues of self-sacrifice and submission rather than revolution. By submitting to a foreign yet familial authority, she finally achieves a home in America.

It is well known that domestic novels end with marriage and the promise of a future state of domestic bliss. In many domestic novels written in antebellum America, that marriage has an incestuous quality as it often unifies the heroine with her adopted "brother," usually a childhood playmate or mentor figure. In *Wide Wide World*, for example, when Ellen comes of age, she chooses fraternity—her allegiance to her American "brother" John, over paternity—the authority of her Scottish "father." This symbolic incest plot might be understood as a disavowal of adult female sexuality by representing marriage as a return to childhood. In addition, this near incest has racial connotations—it answers the question of how to break with parental bloodlines of the Old World, to create a new family and nation, while keeping that new family untainted by racial intermixing in the New World. This union between adopted brother and sister may enact the desire for a domestic space in which the family members are as alike as possible without violating the taboo of incest. Yet if the bloodlines of European aristocracy are rejected in the figure of the cruel despotic father, then the capaciousness of the new adopted fraternal families can potentially include anyone—the orphan, the half-breed, the savage. Marriage with a symbolic brother counterbalances this promiscuous mobility and keeps foreign bodies out of the domestic union.[40]

The wider and more foreign the world is in the novel, the more excessive these near incestuous marriages. *The Lamplighter,* a popular rewriting of *Wide Wide World,* flirts with multiple incestuous relationships. When the heroine, Gerty, meets her unknown father, everyone treats their relationship as a courtship. The older sister figure, Emily, who adopts Gerty, is already the adopted sister of her father and is reunited with him at the end. Gerty, of course, marries her childhood playmate and "brother," William. The novel avoids father/daughter incest by ending with a double marriage between adopted brother and sister in two generations. *The Lamplighter* references a much wider global geography than does Warner's *Wide Wide World* to map the separateness of male and female spheres in international dimensions, as the most important male characters spend most of their lives traveling the globe. Gerty's father, in despair at his violent separation from his adopted sister/lover, travels to Brazil, the American West, and Asia, where he runs across William in Calcutta, working for a New England firm. These male travel narratives are told indirectly and are subordinated to the focus on women characters trying to maintain fragile domestic spaces at home. Indeed, Gerty's major stand against her despotic adopted father takes the form of choosing to stay home to care for William's ailing parents, rather than take her much anticipated opportunity to travel to Havana with her wealthy adopted family.

Although Cummins seems to reject and displace the male adventure narrative with female domesticity, a closer look shows more profoundly how they are intertwined. William's imperial enterprise in India is economically necessary to support his mother and to sustain the domestic sphere in America.[41] Furthermore, domesticity has the role of protecting men abroad from the allure and the threat of foreign domains. When Gerty turns down the trip to Cuba, her guardian taunts her with the claim that William has been seduced: "I dare say he's married to an Indian." Although no Indian, Cuban, or Brazilian men or women enter the novel, the threat of these colonized spaces and foreign women merges with that of a decadent European aristocracy. Thus William is tempted not by the women of India, where he spends eleven years, but by the glitter of Parisian high society, where he spends a few weeks, and from which only the memory of his mother saves him. The "empire of the mother" thus reaches beyond the grave to rescue men from the foreign influence that may break their "ties which bound the exile to his native home." Home here refers both to family and nation.

Women in *The Lamplighter* do not wait passively at home. If men must prove their masculinity and national allegiance by remaining immune to foreign influence, women have the work of purging both themselves and their homes of foreignness. In fact, the narrative of disciplining the female subject, so central to the domestic novel, can be viewed as a kind of civilizing process in which women play the roles of both missionary and heathen. Gerty first appears in the novel as a godless uncivilized street urchin, filled with rage and vengeance. Female anger is often figured as darkness and savagery, an assault on domesticity and the civilized self. Gerty literally breaks a window—the border between the home and the outside—with her rage. Emily vows to cure Gerty of her "dark infirmity," which positions her as a little heathen whose "unruly nature" must be tamed (63). In a scene that recalls Sunday schoolbooks depicting pagan children, Gerty looks at a picture of the young Samuel praying and asks, "why is he kneeling?" "what's praying?" "who is god?" We later find out that Gerty herself was born in a foreign climate to the daughter of a ship captain in Brazil, surrounded by disease, by the "inhospitable southern disease, which takes the stranger for its victim" (321). The fragile domestic bond between her parents could not withstand such a hostile foreign environment. Thus Gerty's conversion into an exemplary Christian woman enacts a civilizing narrative wherein she must purge herself of her origins in a dark, diseased, uncivilized terrain, and of the savage female anger associated with those foreign realms. This internalized split between the colonizer and colonized within a single heroine appears racially externalized in *Uncle Tom's Cabin* onto Eva and Topsy.[42]

Feminist approaches to *Uncle Tom's Cabin* have shown how, for Stowe, the empire of the mother extended beyond the home into the national arena of antislavery politics. This expansive movement of female influence, I have been arguing, has an international dimension that helps the separate gendered spheres coalesce in the imperial expansion of the nation by redrawing domestic borders against the foreign. Read in relation to Hale's *Liberia,* Stowe's delineation of domestic space, as both familial and national, can be seen as relying upon and forwarding the colonization of Africa by the novel's free black characters. Rather than just an afterthought at the end of the novel, there is what Toni Morrison calls an "Africanist presence" throughout the text.[43] Africa appears as both an imperial outpost and a natural embodiment of woman's sphere, a kind of feminized utopia that is strategically posed as an alternative to Haiti, which hovers as a menacing image of black revolutionary agency. The idea of African colonization does not simply emerge at the end as a racist failure of Stowe's political imagination; rather, colonization underwrites the racial politics of the domestic imagination. The "Africanist presence" throughout *Uncle Tom's Cabin* is intimately bound to the expansionist logic of domesticity itself.

The extension of woman's sphere to Africa through debates about slavery within the United States can be understood as part of the imperial reach of the ideology of separate spheres, what I have been calling Manifest Domesticity. As noted in the beginning of the chapter, debates about westward expansion into the lands of Native Americans and Mexicans were inseparable from conflicts about the spread of slavery and the future of slaves and free blacks. These interconnections between outward national expansion and inward divisiveness both informed and menaced the images of the nation as home. These overlapping spheres of Manifest Domesticity converge in Southworth's *The Hidden Hand.* Published on the verge of the Civil War, the novel tells a tale about reconstituting domesticity on a Virginia plantation during the Mexican-American War.

The high-spirited and rebellious heroine of the novel, Capitola Black, is constantly in need of the domestication she defies. Her guardian rescues her from the foreigner-ridden streets of New York City, where she is disguised as a boy and raised by a mulatto woman. When she returns to Virginia, she continues to test his authority and the boundaries of woman's sphere through her adventurous escapades and lack of female sensibility: she "abhorred sentiment" (108). Toward the end of the novel, the Mexican-American War irrupts as a seeming reinforcement of the separate male/female spheres, as all the men go off to war and the women remain at home. Transgressing those boundaries, Capitola rescues the traditional feminine heroine of the novel from a coerced marriage by disguising herself as the bride; she thereby substitutes female rebellion for acquiescence. At the moment she triumphantly reveals her identity and thwarts the wedding, Capitola's real fiancé enters to tell her about the outbreak of war with Mexico. He immediately announces his plan to enlist, as though he were determined to repossess the narrative of rescue for the sphere of manhood. But the war at first has the effect of feminizing men, for Southworth does not represent the major conflict during the war as a military engagement with the enemy; instead, it is a form of class warfare between American men. The aristocratic villain, Le Noir, abetted by his working-class sergeant, gangs up on the aspiring middle-class private, Traverse, the most feminized hero in the novel—and most connected to his mother. Southworth restages the war as a triumph of domestic values over Le Noir, himself a composite figure of the corrupt Old World aristocracy and degenerate Mexicans (and as his name obviously implies, a figure of blackness). Thus she turns a foreign war of imperial conquest into a triumph of feminine domestic values. Even though Southworth includes comments critical of the U.S. military engagement with Mexico, the war intercedes as a *deus ex machina* that reconstitutes the imperial dimensions of domesticity.

Meanwhile, on the home front, the mock-heroic voice of the narrator keeps drawing our attention away from the battlefield to "our little domestic heroine," "a Napoleon in petticoats." While the men are away fighting on foreign territory, Capitola protects the integrity of the home from threats of the foreign that come from within the interior of the domestic sphere and the empire of the heart. All along Capitola has been attracted to the bandit, Black Donald, the henchman for the villain, Le Noir. In one of the final climactic scenes, Black Donald sneaks into her bedroom to rape her. Capitola tries to dissuade him with an uncharacteristically lofty and sentimental homily about the baseness of his attempted seduction as opposed to the manly courage she admires in him. When he does not yield to her moral suasion, she reluctantly pulls a lever that opens a trapdoor onto a deep pit dug under the house. She thereby protects the sanctity of her own body and her private domestic space and also expels that part of her rebellious self identified with him (though she does help him escape from prison at the end).

The trapdoor at the foundation of the home collapses the distinction between gendered spheres, as the heroine reenacts the founding story of the original plantation in the conquest of Indian lands. The colonial owner had tried to buy land from Indians, but they refused to sell. He then built the pit and invited the obdurate Indian chiefs to the house under the guise of a feast, at which he promptly dropped them into the pit and stole their land (67). While other Indians burned down the original house in revenge, the property remained in the hands of the white owner, who built a new house over the pit that remained. It is striking that Capitola repeats that founding gesture of imperial violence to protect the borders of her domestic empire and the inviolability of the female body. While the men are promoting Manifest Destiny in Mexico in an ongoing narrative of the conquest, the woman reproduces that narrative in the empire of the home. On the threshold of the Civil War, Southworth turned to the Mexican-American War to expose and to expel the threat of Indians and blacks as foreigners within the intimate recesses of woman's sphere.

The pit expands metaphorically beyond the literal foundation of the domestic estate in Southworth's Virginia plantation; it represents the hidden foundation, the gaping hole upon which the ideology of middle-class domesticity was constructed and reinforced. Under the self-contained orderly home lies the anarchy of imperial conquest. Not a retreat from the masculine sphere of empire building, domesticity both reenacts and conceals its origin in the violent appropriation of foreign land. Buried in the pit closely accessible to the domestic space, ghosts from prior imperial encounters haunt the self-enclosed household of the family and the nation. "Manifest Domesticity" turns an imperial nation into a home by producing and colonizing specters of the foreign that lurk inside and outside its ever-shifting borders.

CHAPTER 2

The Imperial Routes of Mark Twain

One of the best-known moments of American literature occurs at the end of *The Adventures of Huckleberry Finn,* when Huck declares his intention to "light out for the Territory ahead of the rest" to escape from Aunt Sally and her plan to "adopt me and sivilize me." In the context of "Manifest Domesticity," Huck appears as the savage child who revolts against the colonizing impulse of woman's sphere rather than internalize its discipline, and in eschewing domesticity, he joins the masculine arena of territorial conquest. This flight from domesticity has been viewed in literary history as a hallmark of Mark Twain's writing; his rugged vernacular realism was seen to emerge from his rejection of the sentimental and genteel writing of the domestic tradition. His rejection of the domestic sphere, moreover, has characterized Twain as "domestic" in another sense of the word, that is, as a representative national author, an "American" writer by virtue of embracing the flight from civilization to the freedom of the unfettered wilderness.

Though this particular paradigm of the American author has been amply debunked, Mark Twain has long been considered the quintessential American author, from William Dean Howells's nomination of him as "the Lincoln of our Literature" to Jonathan Arac's critical assessment of *The Adventures of Huckleberry Finn* as a "hypercanonized" novel.[1] Twain's iconic stature has often relied on a paradigm of doubleness: homespun Southwestern vernacular versus the Eastern literary establishment; a pre-Civil War slave-holding culture versus postwar Northern commercial society; a white author drawing on African American sources of oral culture.[2] In these critical paradigms, division itself characterizes Twain's resonance as the author who embodies the splits that constitute the nation. What this internal bifurcation omits, however, is that Twain's career, writing, and reception as a national author were shaped by a third realm beyond national boundaries: the routes of transnational travel, enabling and enabled by the changing borders of imperial expansion. Twain wrote about an internally divided America in his most famous fiction of the 1880s and 1890s only after writing about Hawaii, Europe, and the Near East; he wrote about travel on the Mississippi only after crossing the Pacific and Atlantic oceans. His famous "homespun" qualities were thus woven from the tangled threads of imperial travel.

I propose that the national identity of Mark Twain, his "Americanness," was forged in an international context of imperial expansion. Twain is well known for his vocal opposition to U.S. annexation of the Philippines in the last decade of his life, when he turned his keen sense of injustice at home to the violent oppression of imperial conquest abroad.[3] Yet his passage between the domestic and the foreign was neither linear nor unidirectional, for he first engaged with the reality of imperialism early in his career as a journalist traveling across the continent and abroad. I contend that his first overseas trip to Hawaii in 1866 had a formative and lasting effect on Twain's career as a public lecturer and writer; that Hawaii in fact Americanized Mark Twain. In his imperial encounter with Hawaii, Twain honed the lenses—and blind spots—that he later turned on the legacy of slavery and race relations within the United States. While Mark Twain's status as a "national treasure" has been recently complicated by reevaluations of his ambivalence toward race in America, it is equally important to understand how this national treasure was derived from international plunder. Rather than focus on Twain's views of U.S. imperialist actions abroad, the question here is how the anarchy of empire created an American Mark Twain.

Imperialist Melancholia

At the beginning of his last travel book, *Following the Equator* (1897), Mark Twain tells a story about a young American family he met in Hawaii in 1866. "They had among their belongings," he writes, "an attractive little son of the age of seven—attractive but not practically companionable to me, because he knew no English. He had played from his birth with the little Kanakas on his father's plantation, and had preferred their language and would learn no other."[4] The family soon left Hawaii for upstate New York, where the boy learned English: "by the time he was twelve he hadn't a word of Kanaka left; the language had wholly departed from his tongue and his comprehension." With the swimming skills he learned as a child in Hawaii, the boy grew up to become a professional diver. When Twain visited the family some years later, he found the twenty-one-year-old son bedridden from a recent underwater accident. He had been investigating a sunken passenger boat that had just gone down in a storm, when

> something touched him on the shoulder, and he turned and found a dead man swaying and bobbing about him and seemingly inspecting him inquiringly. He was paralyzed with fright. His entry had disturbed the water, and now he discerned a number of corpses making for him and wagging their heads and swaying their bodies like sleepy people trying to dance. His sense forsook him, and in that condition he was drawn to the surface. He was put to bed at home and was soon very ill. During some days he had seasons of delirium which lasted several hours at a time; and while they lasted he talked Kanaka incessantly and glibly; and Kanaka only. (48–49)

As in their first encounter in Hawaii, Twain did not understand a word the diver was saying to him, although he was intrigued by the return of the forgotten Hawaiian tongue. Twain concludes his story by recommending that doctors study cases like the diver's "and find out how to multiply them. Many languages and things get mislaid in a person's head, and stay mislaid for lack of this remedy" (49). The diver's breakdown becomes at once an emblem of and cure for forgetting.

Although Twain and the young diver never interact in a common language, the story communicates an image of the treacherous routes of memory. The diver's job presumably was to retrieve the corpses for proper burial so that they could be mourned and laid to rest. Instead, his entry into the water rouses the corpses to cross the line between the living and the dead, as they beckon him to dance. This paralyzing encounter with the unburied dead rouses internalized corpses from his own past, buried memories of his original home and his mother tongue. For the diver these unassimilated traces of traumatic loss break the surface of the present, and his past returns to him as a foreign language that divides him from himself and others.

Twain recounts this haunting story of dancing corpses and mislaid languages just as he was about to revisit a formative location from his own past: his six-month trip to Hawaii in 1866. Almost thirty years later, Honolulu was his first scheduled stop on the worldwide lecture tour he described in *Following the Equator.* On a ship anchored a mile offshore, he eagerly anticipated a triumphant and nostalgic return to the islands he had toured as a journalist at the start of his career. He was shattered to find the port quarantined because of an outbreak of cholera, and "thus suddenly did my dream of twenty-nine years go to ruin" (46). In lieu of his physical return to Hawaii, he dedicated a chapter of *Following the Equator* to revisiting memories of his earlier encounter.

Twain's depiction of his own memories contrasts markedly with the diver's traumatic descent underwater. Lounging on deck, Twain gazes longingly at the inaccessible shore and lets his thoughts float dreamily on the sea's luminous surface. In contrast to the diver, gazed at and touched by dancing corpses, Twain must maintain his distance in time and space as a spectator; his memories appear as "an enchanting procession" of the "pictures—pictures—pictures" that pass before his eyes. These pictures highlight scenes of unchanging natural beauty, visions of "Paradise" that merge the present and the past by transcending historical time. Twain briefly acknowledges that in thirty years "change has come" to the islands, but those changes are "political and not visible from the ship." His nostalgic pictures contribute to the invisibility of political change over time and keep him afloat on the surface of his memories.

Yet the irresistible pressure of change inevitably disrupts the calm surface as Twain implicitly links his aborted return to Hawaii in 1895 to deeper historical movements that undercut his dreams of paradise. While Twain was anchored offshore during the cholera epidemic, Hawaiian Queen Liliuokalani was imprisoned in a Honolulu jail for leading the struggle to maintain the last traces of Hawaiian sovereignty. American residents would achieve their goal of annexation three years later, in 1898. The epidemic that prevented Twain's entry into Honolulu was only the latest outbreak of devastating diseases inflicted on

Hawaiians by successive waves of colonial incursions. Reviewing the history of Hawaii in his chapter, Twain ends with statistics from censuses that starkly record the decimation of the native population from the arrival of Captain Cook in 1788 to the present. He specifically notes that in the time between his two visits the population was reduced by half. Disease and death thus implicate Twain's return to the islands as inseparable from this violent lineage of colonial encounters.

Immediately after numerating the Hawaiian dead, Twain recounts the tale of the diver, which evokes a deeper and more unsettling narrative of his first visit to Hawaii than do his enchanted pictures of a timeless paradise. Sugar brought both Twain and the young boy to Hawaii. The boy grew up on a sugar plantation at a time when the burgeoning industry, dominated by Americans, was radically transforming the economy and the social and political landscape of the Hawaiian Kingdom. The boy's childhood took place during the American Civil War, which opened vast new markets for Hawaiian sugar in the North and West when these regions were cut off from Southern producers. *The Sacramento Union,* a powerful California newspaper, hired Twain immediately after the war to report on the sugar industry for investors and consumers in California. He wrote twenty-six letters to the newspaper that faithfully promoted the sugar trade and U.S. economic and political interests in Hawaii. The letters also catered to readers' taste for the exotic in descriptions of the landscape, people, and culture he saw in his travels across three of the islands. The swaying corpses of the diver's tale recall Twain's fascination in those letters with the hula, which he saw performed at a royal funeral for a Hawaiian princess and which intrigued him with the merging of dancing and death.

Twain's six-month trip provided him with his first sustained writing assignment and with the material for his first highly successful lecture tour. Yet just as the boy could not sustain both languages simultaneously, Twain had trouble writing about his memories of Hawaii to which he so often referred. He planned to collect his *Sacramento Union* letters as a travel book but could not find a publisher. Instead, he tacked on selections from the letters to the end of *Roughing It* (1872), a section which is less well realized than the rest of the book and never fully incorporated into the Western frontier narrative that precedes it.[5] In 1884, between writing *The Adventures of Huckleberry Finn* and *A Connecticut Yankee in King Arthur's Court,* Twain worked on what he called his "Sandwich Islands Novel" but never completed it. Although he referred to Hawaii with increasing nostalgia in his later writing, this repeated return to a subject that so eluded him points to the unsettling presence, or telling absence, of Hawaii in his corpus, as a text that cannot be written or a forgotten language that might possess him only at the risk of breakdown.

In the story of the diver Twain offers a compressed and poignant analogue for his own career as a writer. As a young man, Twain was cut off from his original language in the slave-holding South by the Civil War, and soon after from his Southwestern vernacular by his move East and marriage into a genteel New York family. As the diver's encounter with dancing corpses reawakened his childhood language and led to his breakdown, Twain's encounter with Hawaii in 1866 disinterred memories of his own childhood in prewar Missouri. In his best-known fiction of the 1880s and 1890s, Twain endured treacherous self-divisions to dive into the pre-Civil War past and to stir up the shallow-buried and mislaid corpses of slavery and the war. Furthermore, the story of the diver would have resonated with Twain's deep personal grief for the traumatic losses in his own family. In 1858, his brother Henry was killed in a steamboat explosion, an accident for which Twain blamed himself, and which dramatically altered his relation to his memories of Mississippi as profoundly as the Civil War would do. Almost forty years later, when he sat down to write *Following the Equator,* his daughter Susy had just died of meningitis while he was on the last leg of his worldwide lecture tour that started at the port of Honolulu. Twain wrote the story about the diver from Hawaii under the shadow of enormous loss and unresolved grief, and these losses became linked in his imagination to the imperial site of Hawaii.

Twain's recollections of Hawaii might be understood as an expression of what Renato Rosaldo has called "imperialist nostalgia," the longing to salvage an imagined pristine pre-colonial culture by the same agents of empire—missionaries, anthropologists, travel writers—who have had a hand in destroying it.[6] Imperialist nostalgia disavows the history of violence that yokes the past to the present, as in Hank Morgan's longing for the "Lost Land" of Camelot, which he destroys at the end of *Connecticut Yankee.* Yet in Twain's efforts to write about Hawaii, memories of colonial violence erupted through his nostalgia, like dancing corpses tapping him on the shoulder. Twain expressed what we might call "imperialist melancholia," a form of blocked mourning for both the victims of imperial violence and the lost privileges of imperial power, which for him were intertwined with the loss of slavery. As melancholia feeds on unresolved ambivalence toward the lost object, Twain kept revisiting memories of Hawaii he could never fully embrace and realize in his writing or relinquish and lay to rest in the historical past. Like the diver, Twain was seized by the lost language of colonial origins he could neither consciously remember nor forget.[7]

Twain's encounter with Hawaii represents a "mislaid" language that links imperialism abroad with slavery at home, a memory Twain buried and never fully assimilated when he came to write about America as a nation. As he delved into his own past in his writing of the post-Reconstruction era, the forgotten discourses of empire and emancipation threatened to shatter the coherence of his national idiom, just as the boy needed to forget Hawaiian when he learned English. At the same time, however, those forgotten languages also enabled that national idiom. Hawaii, for Mark Twain, became a site of what Ernest Renan called the necessary forgetting, which is a "crucial factor in the creation of a nation."[8] For Twain and his nation, it was necessary to forget the interconnections between slavery and imperialism—that is, to remember to forget—in the re-creation of American national identity in the aftermath of the Civil War.

The Sandwich Islands and the Americanization of Mark Twain

Most scholars agree with Twain's own assessment of his six-month trip to Hawaii in 1866 as a major turning point in his career.[9] After several years as a journalist and humorist in Nevada and California under his recently minted pen name, he returned to San Francisco from Honolulu to launch a new phase of his career as public lecturer, and he spoke exclusively about his trip to the islands. Catapulting him into the national limelight, his "Sandwich Islands Lecture" appealed to full houses in California and Nevada, and Twain repeated it to break into the Eastern lyceum circuit in New York.[10] Success there gave him access to the highly publicized *Quaker* tour to Europe and the Holy Land, which became the basis for his first best-selling book, *The Innocents Abroad* (1869). Upon returning from that trip with new lecture material, Twain continued to give his "Sandwich Islands Lecture," which he also revived for his immensely popular tour to England in 1873. On both sides of the Atlantic, the press called upon him as an authority on the current crisis of political accession to the throne in Hawaii and the possibility of U.S. annexation. Thus Mark Twain made his well-known transition from the Western frontier to America's Eastern literary center and on to Europe by pursuing the less well-known course of empire in the Pacific. Twain refashioned himself from a regional journalist to a national figure of international renown by lecturing about the islands he called "so far away from any place and in an out of the way locality."[11] Yet Twain's journey there belied its remoteness, as Hawaii put his name on the map at a time when the United States, turning outward after the Civil War, was increasingly drawing Hawaii into its economic and political orbit.

When Twain began lecturing in San Francisco, he found that "public lectures were almost an unknown commodity in the Pacific market."[12] He marketed this new commodity by turning the material culled from the Sandwich Islands into a form of cultural capital that could also sell his new public persona. By assuming authority about a "primitive" people abroad, he contradicted his early reputation as another kind of "primitive" at home. He had gained that after the publication of his first story in New York, the year before traveling to Honolulu. At that time the New York press hailed him as a budding celebrity, identifying him with his provincial subject matter as a local exotic, a rough-hewn journalist, "the wild humorist of the Pacific Slopes."[13] Twain complained about this characterization in a letter to his mother and sister: "To think that after writing many an article a man might be excused for thinking tolerably good, those New York people should single out a villainous backwoods sketch to compliment me on!—'Jim Smiley & his Jumping Frog'—a squib which would never have been written but to please Artemus Ward."[14] His postscript to that letter also expressed disappointment that he could not afford to accept an invitation to travel to Honolulu on the inaugural trip of the ocean steamer *Ajax,* along with "the cream of the town—gentlemen & ladies both" (329).

Travel abroad appeared to him as an opportunity to raise his class status and gain literary cachet. He pursued those goals a year later, finally making the trip to Honolulu on the *Ajax.* His strategy worked; on his return, newspapers consistently applauded his lecture debut in

San Francisco as superior even to the popular lectures of Artemus Ward. They praised Twain's delivery as more natural and unpolished with less straining for effect. They also commended him for combining humor with edification and information, for conveying first-hand knowledge of the Sandwich Islands unavailable in books, calling him the "future historian" of the islands. Given his reputation as a humorist, reviewers were surprised and delighted by his "eloquent description of the volcano of Kilauea, a really magnificent piece of word painting."[15] A paper in his home state of Missouri applauded him for trumping the recent visit of Emerson and other "literary magnates" by the way "he interested and amused a large and promiscuous audience."[16] Although Twain's American voice has long been identified with Southwestern vernacular, it is striking that he did not achieve this public speaking voice by telling tall tales in the tradition of Ward. Rather, he displayed his homespun vernacular by merging the colonial discourse of the educated traveler with the "western character of ludicrous exaggeration and audacious statement."[17] Mark Twain became audible as an "authentic" American voice while speaking as an authority about those whom he called "Our Fellow Savages."

Critics have long stressed the importance of Twain's lecture style in developing his writing and his public persona, but none has linked this development to the Hawaiian subject matter of his lectures. Randall Knoper has recently analyzed his deadpan style as a mode of negotiating the increasing divisions of gender, class, and race in the formation of middle-class taste. His lectures could appeal to newly established conventions of the respectable theater, often associated with a bourgeois domesticity, while playfully evoking the specter of male subcultures from the "tavern and the minstrel hall."[18] These negotiations take place, I contend, through the routes of imperial travel. By lecturing about "savage" Hawaiians on stage, Twain could playfully cross the line between the civilized and uncivilized, performing both sides of that divide. He merged the persona of the rough-hewn frontiersman with that of the educated traveler through their shared difference from his nonwhite subjects. Twain's lecture rendered native Hawaiians as both exotic and familiar in their unspoken resemblance to stereotypes of black slaves at home: "rich, dark brown, a kind of black and tan. The tropical sun and easy going ways inherited from their ancestors have made them rather idle."[19] He called the Hawaiians liars of "monstrous incredible" proportion, thereby curiously mirroring his own tall tales while distinguishing his own lies as self-conscious performance and ultimately as purveyors of truth (278). Twain's lectures thus positioned him in an implicitly racialized discourse of national identity where he could perform as a civilized white American by virtue of his travels among primitive peoples.

In his celebrated "word painting" of the volcano of Kilauea, Twain describes the eruption as a "carnival of destruction," a phrase that might be applied to his own treatment of his subject matter (281). He turns the anarchy wreaked by colonialism into the carnivalesque, a world turned upside down where Hawaiians "do everything differently from other people" (281). The humor in Twain's lectures erupts from the incongruous juxtapositions of colonial encounters, in which he takes local history, customs, and culture out of context and recasts them in an American idiom. Twain's double-edged humor also destabilizes the familiar ground of those "other people" by which the exotic Hawaiians are measured. The strange Hawaiian custom of eating dogs becomes funny, for example, when compared to "our cherished American sausage" (279). On a darker note, Twain summarizes the enormous number of Hawaiian lives lost to diseases brought by white men, using the incongruous language of economics: "To speak figuratively, they are retiring from business pretty fast" (277). Twain's humor also works to mock his own civilized stance and to tease his audience with their colonial fantasies. He parodies his listeners' expectations of finding cannibals in the South Seas by claiming that he only found one foreign cannibal with an office in Honolulu, and by offering to demonstrate cannibalism with an infant volunteered from the audience (280). Using humor, Twain titillated his audience with his backwoods bawdiness, yet reassured them with his worldly knowledge.

In 1867 a young Welsh immigrant, Henry Morton Stanley, enthusiastically covered Mark Twain's St. Louis lecture on the Sandwich Islands as a reporter for the *Daily Missouri Democrat*. Twain was less enthusiastic about the fact that Stanley printed the lecture nearly verbatim and thus deprived the lecturer of the value of repeating it. The two, however, would become good friends and meet five years later in London, where each arrived to great fanfare, Twain for his exotic American humor and Stanley for his dauntless expedition to Africa for the *New York Herald*. Years later Twain introduced Stanley on a lecture tour in

Boston, with praise for his "intrepid Americanism," as a "product of institutions that exist in no other country on earth." The name Henry Stanley may be as synonymous with European imperialism in Africa as is Mark Twain's with America. But the two first crossed paths neither in England nor the Congo, but right near the Mississippi, where Twain lectured about his trip to Hawaii.[20] In different ways, they each built their national and international reputations by traveling in multiple directions on the transnational routes of empire. Both climbed the social scale to become famous white men and national heroes by lecturing and writing about their exploits among nonwhite peoples. If his trip to Hawaii helped Americanize Mark Twain, it also introduced him into an international circle of other travelers and writers, who were serving and selling the rapidly expanding empires to their audiences at home.[21]

Dancing Corpses

If Twain could confidently package the Sandwich Islands for the lecture platform, writing about the islands during his travels proved less manageable and more unsettling. *The Sacramento Union* hired him with clearly defined goals to promote California's economic interest in the growing sugar industry and to market the islands as accessible to American travel and business and equally available to popular knowledge and fantasy. On the one hand, Twain enthusiastically pursued this task to offer representations of Hawaii as palatable as the sugar that was shipped to mainland ports. On the other, the letters expressed ambivalence and irony toward his own participation in the imperial project. His representations of the colonial violence of the past and the present overflow and destabilize the framework that underwrote his travels. His letters from Hawaii reveal how his position as traveler and journalist became inextricably enmeshed in the "carnival of destruction," which his lectures may have safely contained in the frame of a "word painting."

In both public and private venues, Twain used imperial metaphors to refer to his writing about Hawaii. On the eve of his departure, he wrote to his mother and sister that he was headed to "ransack the islands, the great cataracts & the volcanoes completely, & write twenty or thirty letters to the Sacramento *Union*—for which they pay me as much money as I would get if I staid at home."[22] He here equates travel writing with looting—of questionable economic profit—a theme he would develop in the image of the "American Vandal," the title of a lecture based on his travels for *The Innocents Abroad.*[23] Right before leaving Honolulu he wrote to a friend there to apologize for stealing a copy of James Jarves's *History of the Hawaiian or Sandwich Islands:* "I 'cabbage' it by the strong arm, for fear you might refuse to part with it if I asked you . . . The honesty of the transaction may be doubtful, but the policy of it is sound—sound as the foundation upon which the imperial greatness of America rests."[24] Twain ironically renders American imperialism as the theft of both land and history and positions his own writing within that display of power. In his published letters he quotes extensively from Jarves, a writer from Boston, and uses his book as an authoritative guide to Hawaiian history, which Jarves renders as a narrative of redemption from ancient savagery and feudal cruelty to an enlightened Christian civilization. While Twain both parodies and praises missionary work throughout his letters, upon his return to San Francisco he referred to himself irreverently as "St. Mark, Missionary to the Sandwich Islands" in publicity for his lecture tour.[25] If these public references playfully identified him with the major imperial agents in Hawaiian colonial history, in his journal on the way there he made a more ominous connection between his trip and prior histories. When he fell sick on his voyage, he wrote: "I suppose I am to take a new disease to the Islands & depopulate them, as all white men have done heretofore."[26] The metaphors of pillage, strong-arming, and depopulation powerfully script Twain's journey through prior narratives of violent colonial encounters.

Twain's ambivalence about his role in this script surfaces in his letters, which show him trying to dissociate his position as a traveler and writer from these overt assertions of imperial force. In one of his first encounters in Honolulu with a resident not identified as either native or foreign, he goes to great length to explain that he is not a missionary, a whaler, a government official, or a navy officer but instead "only a private personage—an unassuming stranger—lately arrived from America."[27] Distinguishing himself from these entrenched roles of colonial governance, Twain is welcomed lavishly by one resident as noble and unthreatening. Twain then characteristically debunks his own assumption of American innocence by concluding, "I then took what small change he had and 'shoved'" (43).

To understand the representation of cross-cultural encounters, it is important to analyze the process of travel itself—the point of departure and the experience of transit—as material and symbolic practices that mediate the contact between cultures.[28] Twain's perception of Hawaii was framed by his voyage out, which had the purpose of reporting on the new steamship service between Honolulu and San Francisco. Like his more celebrated trip to Europe and the Holy Land on one of the first organized middle-class tours, his writing from Hawaii did not only report on a foreign land, but also advertised a new form of travel. His first letters from the ship described in laudatory details the speed, efficiency, power, and comfort of the steamship *Ajax*. Twain also advocated government subsidies for an extensive steamship line that would make Hawaii more immediately accessible to American business and link it to wider trading networks across the Pacific to China. Steamship technology, he argued, would make it possible to "populate the islands with Americans and loosen French and English grip" (12).

By rendering Americanization as liberation from the stranglehold of Old World empires, Twain represented Hawaii as a passive arena and lucrative reward for the contest between American and European powers in the Pacific. On board ship, for example, he undermines the expectations made by a young man reared on European discovery narratives by criticizing Balboa, "that infatuated old ass," for misnaming the ocean "Pacific" and "christening this sleeping boy-baby by a girl's name" (11). Against this effeminate misnaming, Twain proposes the more virile names "Wild" and "Untamed," in the image of the American frontier. Masculine renaming reflects Twain's effort to clear a space for himself as an American writer against prior European narratives. If he represents European colonialism as a form of maternalism that feminizes its conquests, American paternalism, by contrast, promises to awaken the "sleeping boy-baby," and bestow masculinity on the inhabitants of the Pacific. At the time of Twain's trip, Hawaiian leaders had long been playing off the interests of imperial nations against one another in order to preserve a measure of autonomy. Throughout his letters, however, Twain characterizes Hawaiian opposition to increasing American control as the result only of British or French manipulation. Thus in advocating America's masculine liberation of Hawaii from Europe, Twain contributes metaphorically to depopulating Hawaii and clearing space for repopulating the islands with Americans. His representation of a dyadic contest between a masculine America and feminized Europe has the effect of voiding Hawaiian actors as agents in their own history.

As much as Twain distances his American journey from European narratives, he structures his scene of arrival through a well-known myth of origins: the first colonial contact between Captain Cook and the Hawaiians. When Twain's ship enters the port of Honolulu on a Sunday, he hears the peal of church bells over lands "which were peopled by naked, savage, thundering barbarians only fifty years ago! Six Christian Churches within five miles of the ruins of a pagan temple, where human sacrifices were daily offered up to hideous idols in the last century! We were within pistol shot of one of a group of islands whose ferocious inhabitants closed in upon the doomed and helpless Captain Cook and murdered him, eighty-seven years ago; and lo! their descendants were at church! Behold what the missionaries have wrought!" (27). Twain frames his first glimpse of Hawaii through a well-worn grid that divides ancient savagery from Christian civilization, but his hyperbolic language describing the profusion of churches points to the unstable ground on which this hierarchy is built.

When Twain disembarks from the ship, he feels disoriented walking on "solid ground": "it was unpleasant to lean unconsciously to an anticipated lurch of the world and find that the world did not lurch, as it should have done" (29). In this comic reversal, being at sea feels more comfortable than walking on land, because the foreign terrain of Hawaii does not "lurch" in ways that fulfill his unconscious expectations. Instead, its continually shifting ground unsettles the framework he brings with him. More than just a description of sea legs, Twain's walk through the city dislodges the conceptual solid ground he could maintain at sea. The binary grids of colonial discourse he brought with him immediately break down as he makes his way, with a profound sense of dislocation, through a "mixed crowd" (26). Instead of viewing clear demarcations between savage and civilized, American and European, feminine and masculine, he finds himself jostled by men and women of mixed races and multiple nationalities in different sorts of dress, styles of comportment, and deference, representing a complex class system illegible to Twain's preconceptions of racial and gendered categories.

This theme of physical discomfort and mental disorientation recurs throughout his travels whenever he comes into closer proximity with the people and the land, whether riding horses or sleeping on small boats packed with native travelers. When he first leases a horse to see more of the island, for example, he returns with blistering saddle boil and blames his uncomfortable ride on the "shrewd Kanakas" who sell crippled and unusable horses to white tourists (48). This stereotype of the conniving native inadvertently acknowledges the traveler's foreignness and vulnerability, and his dependence on native knowledge and resources to gain access to the landscape. Even Twain's innocent haggling over hiring a horse takes place within the colonial struggle over the possession and dispossession of the land.

The sense of dislocation Twain conveys in his letters may stem not from his perception of the uncivilized and exotic qualities of Hawaii, but from his unexpected recognition of its modern and cosmopolitan qualities that seemed uncomfortably close to home. Rather than savage heathens in a tropical paradise, Twain found a struggling independent nation in the midst of profound political turbulence and social change. The development of capitalist plantations, which replaced a formerly lucrative whaling trade with a new sugar-based economy, was in the process of transforming the social landscape of Hawaii. Its demography was also changing dramatically through devastating diseases, immigration of white settlers, and the importation of contract labor from China to work on the plantations. Only twenty years before Twain's visit, the Hawaiian land, which had been held for generations by the King and chiefs, was legally transformed into private property. The "Great Mahele"—the division of land, allowed foreigners to own land for the first time. American missionaries as well as businessmen encouraged this "land reform" on the grounds that it would teach the common people the values of work and private property and alter traditional kinship relations and sexual practices under a new regime of domesticity. While the Great Mahele only led to greater dispossession of the Hawaiian people, it had a more successful effect on the missionary families, whose children amassed huge plots of land and led the way in establishing the plantation system.

Politically, the Kingdom of Hawaii in the 1860s was also in upheaval.

In a constitutional monarchy that included foreign residents and native Hawaiians in its legislature, American settlers were fighting for universal suffrage in a stronger constitution, which would give them even greater control over the government and enable closer ties to the United States. The Hawaiian monarchy was struggling to center power in its own sovereignty rather than the constitution. The monarchy at that time sought closer alliances with a British religious and political presence on the island to distance Hawaii from American missionary control and fend off the threat of annexation.[29] The same year Twain arrived in Honolulu on the *Ajax,* Hawaiians protested the presence of an American man-of-war assigned to the harbor of Honolulu "for an indefinite period of time" and commanded by a well-known advocate of annexation.[30]

Thus as Twain traveled through Hawaii, he crossed an unsettling terrain that refused to "lurch" to his preconceived rhythms. His letters jockey back and forth between registering jolts of dislocation and seeking strategies to relocate him on solid ground. Searching for spaces outside the turbulence of the political present, Twain repeatedly turns his gaze on Hawaiian women and on funeral rites and burial sites, as if sex and death could anchor him in a reality untouched by the very social transformations that brought him to Hawaii. Throughout his letters, Twain curiously associates native women with death and represents their sexuality as embodying remnants of a dying ancient culture that occasionally comes alive again. I will argue that he turns both the bodies of native women and the remains of the dead into exotic sites for the projection of colonial desire, sites apparently frozen in time and divorced from the historical struggles over colonization in which his journey is enmeshed. Twain's eroticization of Hawaii renders colonial desire as a kind of necrophilia. In constructing these timeless exotic spaces, however, Twain's letters also expose them as tense arenas for political conflict and struggles over the production of meaning.

In a commonplace colonial trope, Twain voyeuristically focuses on the eroticized female body in various degrees of nudity: native women bathing "promiscuously with the opposite sex," dancing the "lascivious hula," riding bareback through the streets both underdressed and over-perfumed with oils and flowers. Twain reproduces two related stereotypes, drawn from colonial discourse of missionaries and travelers in the Pacific, that linked Hawaiian women with a pre-Christian uncivilized past. Women become the yardsticks for measuring the barbarism of traditional Hawaiian society and the ancient system of "tabu." In his lecture Twain claimed that "away down at the bottom of this pile of tyranny and superstition, came the women, and they were abject slaves of all; they were degraded to the level of beasts, and thought to be no better" (238). Related to this social degradation was the stereotype of Hawaiian women as excessively sexual, demonstrated by their actively taking multiple sexual partners and their apparent disregard of marriage and domesticity. Missionaries blamed unrestrained female sexuality for spreading the venereal disease brought by sailors and traders, and they held women responsible for the decline of the population, claiming that in their native licentiousness women abjured their maternal duties to bear and raise children.[31] In this discourse, women's uncivilized sexuality becomes the source of disease and death, and the spread of disease by civilizing forces is projected onto the native female body.

One of Twain's letters suggests how the control of female sexuality is central to the colonial regime. The writer contrasts the current market days in Honolulu with a grand gala day of the past, when "white folks had to stay indoors" as Hawaiians from all over the countryside thronged into the city. The day's festivities culminated with "the lascivious hula-hula," performed by a "circle of girls with no raiment upon them to speak of" (70). He notes that "this weekly stampede of the natives interfered too much with labor and the interests of the white folks, and by sticking in a law here, and preaching a sermon there . . . they gradually broke it up." The demoralizing hula-hula "was forbidden to be performed, save at night, with closed doors, in presence of few spectators, and only by permission duly procured from the authorities and the payment of ten dollars for the same" (71). The hula changes venue from a public practice of Hawaiian culture to a confined spectacle regulated by business, religion, and law. In his characterization of the hula as lascivious and demoralizing, Twain adopts the missionary narrative of the civilizing process, but also reveals the way that narrative is intertwined with the needs of business and colonialism to regulate the movement of bodies and labor.

In the figure of Hawaiian women Twain may have expected to find a comforting exoticism, but instead was disturbed by discomfiting excess. He could not simply position women at bottom of the social hierarchy, because he learned that they wielded formidable political power in the monarchy, chiefdom, and Protestant church, and that they were active agents in breaking the system of tabus.[32] Yet he continually tries to relegate them to the sphere of the erotic and the dying past. In his lectures we can hear echoes of this past, when he jokes about a plantation where a worker claimed to have a plethora of mothers and therefore did not come to work regularly because he had to attend all their funerals.[33] The excess of mothers, even in their graves, works against incorporating Hawaiian men into the plantation system. Yet who has the last laugh? In Twain's joke, dead mothers—real or otherwise— have an authority that contests that of the plantation overseer.

Throughout his travels Twain was obsessed with death and its traces, as though death were a signature of Hawaiian culture. He attributed to Hawaiians a special intimacy with death, repeating often that they would just decide to die and do so, as though the people as a whole had willed their own demise. As a tourist, Twain collected bones scattered through the landscape, explored ancient burial sites where he imagined human sacrifices, and searched for the exact location where Captain Cook was eaten. This obsession both exposes and disavows the colonial violence that linked the history of conquest to the present of his own journey.

In a trip in the countryside with other American tourists, Twain parodies their activity of collecting bones:

> Presently we came to a place where no grass grew—a wide expanse of deep sand. They said it was an old battleground. All around everywhere, not three feet apart, the bleached bones of men gleamed white in the moonlight. We picked up a lot of them for mementos. I got quite a number of arm bones and leg bones—of great chiefs, maybe, who had fought savagely in that fearful battle in the old days, when blood flowed like wine where we now stood. . . . All sorts of bones could be found except skulls; but a citizen said, irreverently, that there had been an unusual number of "skull hunters" there lately. . . . A gentleman said: "Give me some of your bones, Miss Blank; I'll carry them for you." . . . "Mr. Brown, will you please hold some of my bones for me a minute?" And, "Mr. Smith, you have got some of my bones; and you have got one too, Mr. Jones; and you have got my spine, Mr. Twain. Now

don't any of you gentleman get my bones all mixed up with yours so that you can't tell them apart." (59–60)

This has a macabre and promiscuous quality: promiscuous in the obvious sense of sexual innuendo, where bones of native chiefs serve as the meeting ground for the bodies of white men and women. But also promiscuous in the sense of dissolving boundaries that collecting is meant to maintain, turning the American tourists into cannibals and headhunters.

Twain concludes that "nothing whatever is known about this place —its story is a secret that will never be revealed" (60). Yet he still tries to excavate that history and finds multiple interpretations from different sources: the legends of the "oldest natives" who have seen the bones there since their childhood; his historian guide Jarves, who writes about native warfare; a source that suggests the bones may be a mass burial from a terrible epidemic of 1804. Twain leaves the site without an explanation, overwhelmed by the sheer amount of unburied bones, as he rode "considerable distance over ground so thickly strewn with human bones that the horses' feet crushed them, not occasionally, but at every step" (62). Collecting the bones as souvenirs may be a way of making the traveler comfortable on these violent grounds, by divorcing these remains from their historical context and making them instead evidence of the traveler's presence when he returns home. The collection of bones, specimens, talismans, or souvenirs does not simply commemorate or refer to a known place or historical event; rather, collections manufacture their own reference as a way of making tourists at home by both representing and disavowing the colonial violence that links the history of conquest to the present journey. Twain's obsession with relics turns the complexity of the historical present into a mere overlay of a deeper dead past by rendering what appears as authentic native culture as necessarily dead or dying.

A highlight of Twain's trip to Hawaii was the royal funeral for Princess Victoria Kamamalu, which fascinated him and which he represented as an event where loss and sexuality merged. Although Twain was in Honolulu only toward the end of the four-week mourning period during which her body lay in state, he filled three letters with accounts of the ceremonies (the only other subjects to which he gave so much attention were sugar and the shipwreck of an American vessel). Sister of the current King Kamehameha V, and the last female descendent of King Kamehameha I, Princess Victoria would have been heir apparent to the throne when she died at the young age of 27. Her death represented the end of an era of a royal lineage that had founded the Hawaiian Kingdom, and her youth evoked the hundreds of thousands of premature deaths to disease among all classes. Following the early death of her brother King Kamehameha IV three years before, Princess Victoria's funeral would have been an overdetermined occasion for mourning in Hawaii, for her as a popular leader, for the link she represented between the past and the continuity of a Hawaiian future, and for countless other deaths. Twain, in contrast, saw the funeral as an opportunity to escape from the present into a "Glimpse of the Heathen Ages" (164). His letters repeatedly referred to the funeral rites as a "funeral orgy," a "wild scene" where "unbounded license prevailed." His writing transformed unbounded expressions of grief into enticing spectacles of sexual excess, as he looked forward to seeing the "forbidden hula," one part of the Hawaiian mourning ritual, which in his eyes served as a metonymy for native sexuality.[34]

Twain was disappointed at first, however, to find that access to the site and sight of mourning had become the grounds for political tension. The King restricted foreigners from entering the palace gates until the last night, at the same time that he gave unrestricted entry to crowds of native Hawaiians traveling from all over the islands. Twain complained that all "this time we strangers have been consumed with curiosity to look within those walls and see the pagan deviltry that was going on there. But the thing was tabu (forbidden—we get our word "taboo" from the Hawaiian languages) to foreigners—haoles" (161). Only when barred from access to Hawaiian space was Twain compelled to translate the word "haoles," thereby designating himself as "foreign" through the Hawaiian language and its influence on English. The political contest over access to cultural space and to the position of insiders was tied to the control of representation. When Kamehameha IV died three years earlier, the new King did invite foreign spectators onto the palace grounds. They used the occasion both to satisfy their scopic desire and then to deride the immorality of Hawaiian religious customs in the press and from the pulpit. As Twain notes, "the performances at the palace at the time the corpse of the late King lay there in state were criticized and commented upon too freely" by "scribblers like myself" (127).

This struggle over seeing and representing mourning continues throughout the letters. Locked out of the palace grounds, Twain goes to look at the coffin being built and raves about its wood and elegant craftsmanship: "It produces a sort of ecstasy in me to look at it, and it holds me like a mesmeric fascination" (128). Only while gazing at the unfinished walls of the coffin does Twain unabashedly expresses his own desire to look at the dead and the bereaved. He expresses a rapturous sense of his own unboundedness, as though the bounded empty space of the coffin could safely contain him. When he witnesses, in contrast, Hawaiian people mourning through chants, dances, vigils, cries, and prayers, his feelings shift between the poles of attraction and repulsion. When Twain is allowed to see the last night of funeral rites along with a few privileged haoles, his vision is both confined and protected by his assignment to a space from a verandah overlooking the palace grounds. On the one hand, this placement positions them as outsiders, as an audience in a theater balcony. On the other, they can imagine the rituals performed for their own pleasure, as they safely survey the crowd below.

For Twain the anticipated highlight of the ceremony is the "famous hula-hula we had heard so much about and so longed to see—the lascivious dance that was wont to set the passions of men ablaze in the old heathen days, a century ago." His expectation of an erotic display seems close to fulfillment when

> about thirty buxom young Kanaka women, gaily attired . . . formed themselves into half a dozen rows of five or six in a row, shook the reefs out of their skirts, tightened their girdles and began the most unearthly caterwauling that was ever heard, perhaps; the noise had a marked and regular time to it however, and they kept strict time to it with writhing bodies; with heads and hands thrust out to the left; then to the right; then a step forward, and the right hands all projected simultaneously forward, and the right hands placed on the hips; then the same repeated with a change of hands; then a mingling together of the performers—quicker time, faster and more violently excited motions more and more complicated gestures—(the words of their fierce

chants meantime treating in broadest terms, and in detail, of things which may be vaguely hinted at in respectable newspaper, but not distinctly mentioned)—then a convulsive writhing of the person, continued for a few moments and ending in a sudden stop and a grand caterwaul in chorus. (168)

Twain tries to contain the hula in the frame of an erotic spectacle while the sights and sounds overflow and unsettle that framework. What he hears as noise becomes an unexpected rhythm, and he watches movements that are not meant to rouse "passions" of the foreign male spectator. The women instead are attuned to one another, "mingling together" in unison as a collective body. Instead of a line of buxom showgirls, passive objects of display, the women move violently and chant fiercely, and their hula actively creates meanings that Twain cannot understand. When he cannot comprehend their "complicated gestures" from within his vantage on the verandah, he tries to control their meaning by translating it into the sexual innuendo of the "respectable newspaper." The hula seems to arouse and then thwart his erotic anticipation by producing a bodily excess of sight and sounds that seem more sinister than enticing.

Twain immediately distances himself from the scene he "so longs to see"—but watches with such discomfort—by launching into a diatribe against the Anglican Lord Bishop Staley for resurrecting these "heathen orgies." Since Twain represents his own desire as a regressive glimpse into ancient rites, he seems unsettled by the active agency of the mourners and their production of meanings in the immediate present. He displaces his own ambivalent feelings of desire and fear onto excoriation of the white man whom he blames for sponsoring these rituals as "a sort of master of ceremonies":

It is reported that the King has said: "The foreigners like their religion—let them enjoy it, and freely. But the religion of my fathers is good enough for me." Now that is right. At least I think so. And I have no fault to find with the natives for the lingering love they feel for their ancient custom. But I do find fault with Bishop Staley for reviving those customs of a barbarous age at a time when they had long been abandoned and were being forgotten—when one more generation of faithful adherence to the teaching of the American missionaries would have buried them forever and made them memories of the past—things to be talked of and wondered at, like the old laws that made it death for a plebeian to stand erect in the presence of his King, or for a man to speak to his wife on tabu day—but never imitated. (169)

By positioning the Bishop as the master puppeteer, Twain disavows the purpose of those Hawaiians in the present; they solicited the support of the British church with its more lenient view of Hawaiian tradition, as a part of a complex struggle against American missionary dominance of religious and cultural life. Twain also cannot acknowledge the hybrid nature of these rituals, which would have combined elements of traditional Hawaiian religion with American Calvinism and practices of the British high church. By excoriating Bishop Staley for reviving ancient rites, Twain thereby tries to reinscribe the Hawaiian present as a mere echo of a dying past. He represents the Hawaiian interest in traditional religion as a harmless and natural recidivism, a lingering affection for quaint outdated customs. To the bishop, in contrast, he attributes active political agency working to undermine the progress of the American missionaries. By using the frame of the nationalist struggle of the United States against Europe, pre-colonial Hawaii disappears into a mirror of tyrannical European monarchies. Hawaiians in the present are rendered only capable of imitating their own past.

As in the scene of the hula, the overwhelming impression Twain conveys of the funeral is of the powerful sounds of mourning permeating the streets of Honolulu. He expresses irritation at the "nightly wailing" performed by "a multitude of common natives [who] howl and wail and weep and chant the dreary funeral songs of ancient Hawaii" (160). These sounds of grief overflow and dissolve the boundaries of the visual spectacle he expects to enjoy. Just as he tries to reduce the physical expressions of mourning to excessive sexuality, he renders the music of mourning as sublingual noise-making, referring to the sounds as "caterwauls," as "harrowing," "extravagant lamentations," "dismal howls," and "distressing noises." Throughout his trip Twain was puzzled by the Hawaiian expression of emotion: "they wept and chanted their distressing songs and wailed their agonizing wails; for joy at the return of a loved one and sorrow at his death are expressed in precisely the same way with this curious people" (126). This ambiguity for Twain deconstructs the binary oppositions that construct meaning in his cultural grammar. Twain could only interpret these sounds as the meaninglessness or incomprehensibility of Hawaiian culture. Yet the unassimilated sounds of mourning resonate through his letters to suggest meanings that exceed his own understanding or capacity for translation.

During the final funeral procession, Twain seems to regain solid ground as a spectator who can parody the ornate pageant of social rankings. Yet there too the wails of mourning disrupt his parody: "The slow and measured tread of the marching squadrons; the mournful music of the bands; the chanting of the virtues of the dead and the warrior deeds of her ancestors, by a gray and venerable woman here and there; the wild wail that rang out at times from some bereaved one to whom the occasion brought back the spirit of the buried past— these completed the effect" (179). The "wild wail" disrupts Twain's desire to gaze at the procession for its visual effects. The sounds disinter "the spirit of the buried past" while mourning in the present opens a conduit to innumerable past losses of colonization. At the arrival of the procession to the mausoleum, Twain complains that the "multitude set up such a dismal heartbroken wailing as I hope never to hear again." Unable to let go at the conclusion of the ceremonies, Twain then quotes five pages from Jarves's *History* about the death of Kamehameha I. He both keeps alive and tries to bury the present scene of mourning in the colonial narrative of an ancient past, as though the "dismal heartbreaking wailing" of the multitude could be translated and silenced by the superabundance of an English text.

Throughout Twain's writing about Hawaii, however, these sounds of grief return to haunt him, breaking through the semantic frame of his nostalgic pictures. Though he approaches the funeral with voyeuristic curiosity about "ancient deviltry," the sounds that he wishes never to hear again revive the spirit of the unburied past that rises in the present. Like the diver, Twain returns from Hawaii with resurfaced corpses of forgotten languages, corpses that keep turning their gaze upon him and inviting him to dance.

Hawaii and the Reconstruction of the Old South

At the end of *Roughing It,* Twain framed his trip to Hawaii as an extension of his frontier narrative. The last leg of his journey west, the Sandwich Islands, appealed to his "vagabond spirit" as an escape from the routine of his work as a daily correspondent in San Francisco. Yet this journey further westward across the Pacific also led in another direction that confounded this fantasy of escape; it took Twain homeward into the American South to explore the meaning of slavery and freedom. In the culture of the sugar plantation Twain found striking parallels between the colonization of Hawaii and the changes convulsing the slave-holding South. The remnants of imperial violence that would not stay buried in the Hawaiian landscape evoked uncanny echoes of the ongoing violence of slavery, which was not laid to rest by emancipation. Traveling in the immediate aftermath of the Civil War, Twain brought to Hawaii unspoken questions and assumptions about slavery, emancipation, and race relations at home, and in the islands he found them refracted back to him from the apparently remote colonial context. It is well known that the outbreak of the Civil War severed Twain from his own past, the loss of which became a rich repository of memories that would fuel his greatest fiction. Yet critics remain puzzled that Twain did not write about slavery and race relations until twenty years after the war's end. I am arguing that his trip to Hawaii in the immediate aftermath of the war led him to the memories of the prewar past, both the nostalgia for and the nightmare of slavery. It therefore allowed him to defer these memories and offered a form for their displaced expression.

References to the Civil War fill Twain's depiction of his voyage from San Francisco to Honolulu. One of his first letters proudly notes that the *Ajax* was built as a powerful warship and was in its present service piloted by veterans of both the Civil War and the Mexican-American War (19). The refurbishing of this warship suggests that the military force deployed in an internecine conflict could be turned outward toward building a commercial empire, one that extends farther west of the lands conquered from Mexico in 1848. Twain's depiction of this same voyage in *Roughing It* focuses on a boisterous retired captain of a whaling ship. Dubbed by Hawaiians with the honorific "Admiral," he was revered by the "simple natives," who "regarded him as children regard a father. It was a dangerous thing to oppress them when the roaring Admiral was around" (*Roughing It*, 332). The same fierce attachment to the underdog turned the "frantic and bloodthirsty Union man" into a "rampant and inexorable secessionist" when he saw the

South losing the war (33). The Admiral also has a passion for political argument that he bases on what Twain calls "manufactured history." He argues that the war was started in retaliation against two Northern clergymen who tarred, feathered, and burned alive two visiting Southern ladies. Another passenger outwits him by taking his "manufactured history" for real and reminding him that these atrocities avenged even worse atrocities against women and children committed by two Southern clergymen. Most directly, this anecdote parodies Southern narratives of chivalry that Twain would target throughout his writing. Furthermore, by ridiculing these narratives of historical causation, Twain implicitly calls attention to the omissions out of which such stories are "manufactured": the history of slavery and the struggle for emancipation. The passengers on the *Ajax* may be sailing far away in space and time from the battlefields of the Civil War, but the unspoken issue of slavery resurfaces in the Admiral's paternalistic protection of the Hawaiians. The depiction of childlike loyal natives echoes the pro-slavery position of the prewar South and the racist arguments against the capacity of nonwhite people to govern themselves. Thus while Twain may have retrospectively structured his voyage to Hawaii in *Roughing It* as a flight west to freedom, what he found instead was that the colonial hierarchies of the islands conjured memories of the prewar South and its racial hierarchies of slavery.

When Twain arrived in Honolulu, he heard echoes of the American Civil War all around him. Complaining in a letter about the "popular-song nuisance that follows us," he exclaims:

> at the very outpost and fag-end of the world, of a little rock in the middle of a limitless ocean, a pack of dark skinned savages are tramping down the street singing it with a vim and vigor that makes my hair rise!—singing it in their own barbarous tongue! They have got the tune to perfection—otherwise I never would have suspected that "Waikiki lantani oe Kaa hooly hooly wahoo" means "While we were marching through Georgia." If it would have been all the same to General Sherman, I wish he had gone around by the way of the Gulf of Mexico, instead of marching through Georgia. (65)

The joke here erupts from the incongruous transposition of both language and geography that ricochets from the boundaries between the foreign and the domestic. The familiarity of the tune stems not only from the music, but also from the sight of "dark-skinned savages." Like the funeral dirges that defy Twain's comprehension, he translates the "barbarous tongue" into the once familiar language of race at home. While Twain represents Hawaii geographically as the epitome of remoteness, a rock devoid of human history, his mapping of Hawaii through the grid of the American North and South produces emptiness, but ironically brings Hawaii closer to home. By turning the Hawaiian language he does not understand into a translation of an American song, Twain remains deaf to the history that preceded him. Yet his imposition of a North/South grid does not remain stable on this shifting ground. His multilayered parody also places the Hawaiian singers in the position of the translator and parodist that Twain cannot hear, and suggests uncanny echoes of marching for conquest and marching for freedom at home and abroad. In wishing that Sherman had taken a more indirect route, it is Twain himself who has taken a circuitous path to the American South.

On his voyage out, Twain meditates on the meaning of labor and emancipation. The ocean voyage in his first letter gives him a "strange new sense of entire and perfect emancipation from labor and responsibility coming strong upon me," which he parodies as the "tranquil delight in that kind of labor which is such a luxury to the enlightened Christian—to wit, the labor of other people" (5). After he returns home in *Roughing It,* he refers to his trip as "half a year's luxurious vagrancy in the islands" (414). If emancipation in the United States had recently abolished the luxury of other people's labor in the South, Twain represented the sugar plantation in Hawaii as a replacement for the loss of slave labor at home. He claimed that sugar in Hawaii was much more lucrative than in Louisiana. Not only was the land more fertile, but the "free" labor of "Kanaka men and women" was much cheaper: "The hire of each laborer is $100 a year—just about what it used to cost to board and clothe and doctor a Negro—but there is no original outlay of $500 to $1,000 for the purchase of the laborer" (260). Thus the cultivation of sugar in plantations in Hawaii promised to recover the economic value of slave labor at home by replacing black slaves with native Hawaiian workers.

For Twain, the social relations of colonialism in Hawaii may have in addition recovered the racialized cultural value of slavery. Throughout his journey, he continually compared his impressions of native Hawaiians to memories of black slaves at home. When he took a schooner between the islands, for example, he described Hawaiians lying on the deck as "thick as Negroes in a slave pen" (195). When he read about a Hawaiian custom of praying an enemy to death, he compared it in his journal to "similar superstitions in the south."[35] On the long sail home from Honolulu, he jotted notes for what would turn into his later fiction about his boyhood. The Pacific evoked for him memories of the Mississippi, and his cursory knowledge of Hawaiian customs brought up fragmented memories of slave culture from the summers he spent as a child on his uncle's farm. In his journal he made a list of "superstitions" he recalled from his childhood and included the following: "niggers tie wool up with thread to keep the witches from riding them" (160). This thread of memory would become the story that introduces Jim in *Huckleberry Finn*, when Jim expresses his desire for freedom in a story about witches riding him "all over the world."

If, on the one hand, Hawaii seemed a throwback to his childhood memories of slavery, on the other hand, its growing sugar industry made its social landscape more similar to the South in 1866, in the immediate aftermath of the war. Despite Hawaii's physical distance, the Civil War had a major impact on the Hawaiian economy. The demand for new sources of sugar to replace those from the South gave a major boost to sugar production in Hawaii and drew it into even closer economic and political ties to the United States by the war's end. And sugar in Hawaii was indeed a big business, concentrated in the hands of a few landowners—for the most part sons of American missionaries—who also controlled banking, marketing, and the export business. This boom required disciplined workers, who would submit to the conditions of sugar production that was a unique "synthesis of field and factory."[36] The relatively new class of planters in Hawaii faced a problem familiar to Southern planters after the war: how to create and control a "free" labor force of nonwhite workers in an evolving capitalist economy. Whereas Southern U.S. planters, like those in the postemancipation Caribbean, were concerned with turning former slaves into free labor, Hawaiian planters were contending with new laborers freed not from slavery—but "freed" from the land that sustained them through subsistence farming, and cut off from kinship networks and relations to chiefs and priests. While most planters in Hawaii were displaced New Englanders who supported the Union during the war, some also longed for what they imagined to be the more productive conditions of slavery; they compared their own plantations "unfavorably with those in the Caribbean—not, they hastened to add, because they wanted slavery in the Hawaiian kingdom, but because they wanted to show what might be done with a disciplined work force."[37] Hawaiian planters, along with their U.S. counterparts, were involved in a broader international struggle to coerce "free" workers in a slave-like system of labor under the conditions of capitalist agricultural production.[38]

Hawaiian workers actively resisted the slave-like conditions of the plantation system through a variety of strategies of recalcitrance, subversion, and outright refusals to work. In response, the government aided the planters with harsh vagrant laws and anti-emigration laws designed to control Hawaiian mobility.[39] As Twain notes, "the contract with the laborer is in writing and the law rigidly compels compliance with it; if a man shirks a day's work and absents himself, he has to work for two days for it when his time is out. If he gets unmanageable and disobedient, he is condemned to work on a reef for a season" (270). At the time Twain wrote this from Hawaii, Southern states right after the war were legislating the "Black Codes" regulating vagrancy, labor contracts, and apprenticeship to keep freed people as close to the status of slaves as possible.[40] Though Radical Reconstruction voided these laws, the paradoxical effort to impose a coercive system of free labor continued. Twain found Hawaii and America closer than he imagined geographically, on a map of an international struggle that linked emancipation and imperialism in creating a coercive system of nonwhite free labor.

Along with the legal system, changing representations of the Hawaiians were mobilized to discipline labor as well. The dominant stereotype that early missionaries held of Hawaiians as heathens and savages shifted to focus primarily on native idleness and laziness.[41] In 1869, for example, *The Pacific Commercial Advertiser* wrote: "if only we could compel our idlers, loafers or vagrants . . . to work for their own good and for the good of the kingdom, we would have at once a supply of perhaps 5,000 able-bodied men and women."[42] Active resistance to the time-work discipline of the plantation was rendered as the deficiency of the civilized qualities of individual ambition, hard work, and collective responsibility. Similar to the language characterizing blacks in the

South and the North, "idleness" was increasingly viewed as an innate racial characteristic. A Democratic Party circular against Reconstruction in Pennsylvania, for example, offered a picture of a stereotyped Negro happily resting on his back while a white man chops wood in the background. The caption reads: "The Freedman's Bureau: an agency to keep the Negroes in idleness at the expense of the white man."[43] In Hawaii, Twain at times presents an ironic view of this definition of civilization as paid labor. He parodies the missionary narrative of braving a "thousand privations" to teach the Hawaiians "what rapture it is to work all day long for fifty cents to buy food for the next day, as compared with fishing for pastime and lolling in the shade through eternal summer, and eating of the bounty that nobody labored to provide but nature" (53). Though he mocks the Protestant work ethic, he also contributes to the discourse of Hawaiian idleness. Twain could not imagine a way of life before colonialism as involving productive labor, but only as a prelapsarian form of harmony with nature.

This sheds interesting light on the hackneyed but dominant image of Hawaii as paradise, one that Twain promoted throughout his writing and which has continued in the tourist trade today. As Hawaiians were forced into a postlapsarian capitalist system of commodified labor, the image of Hawaiian paradise as a place without labor or history became increasingly available as a commodity to attract foreign settlers and tourists. Racial discourse splits the same qualities of a labor-free Eden into opposing values. The reputed indolence of Hawaiians derided as a form of racial degradation becomes lauded as a natural luxury, as leisure or vacation, for white residents and travelers. Although Twain arrived in Hawaii to work as a journalist, he contrasted Honolulu to the "place of the hurry and bustle and noisy confusion of San Francisco," as "I moved in the midst of a summer clime as tranquil as dawn in the Garden of Eden."[44] When Twain returned to his nostalgic memories of Hawaii, he increasingly recalled it as a paradise, a place without labor, where he enjoyed his "luxurious vagrancy" without being subject to the legal system against vagrancy. His letters suggest how this image of Hawaii as a natural paradise outside of history was historically produced by capitalist development that dispossessed Hawaiians of land to turn them into "free labor." In 1866, at an early stage of the "Sugar Kingdom" in Hawaii, Twain glimpsed the ironic meaning of "paradise" that Stannard Baker Ray would spell out in 1911: "Hawaii

has been called . . . the Paradise of the Pacific. But it is also a paradise
not only of natural beauties and wonders; it is also a paradise of modern industrial combination."[45]

The flip side of that paradise, the myth of Hawaiian laziness, was
strangely held responsible in colonial discourse for their dwindling
numbers. Twain noted that no matter how draconian the discipline of
Hawaiian labor, the "sugar product is rapidly augmenting every year,
and day by day, the Kanaka race is passing away" (270). The representation of Hawaiians as incorrigibly idle also contributed to what was becoming the economic mainstay of the sugar industry in Hawaii: the import of contract labor, from China during the time of Twain's visit, and
extending over the century to Japan, Portugal, Norway, Korea, Puerto
Rico, and the Philippines. Twain heartily endorsed the import of in-
dentured labor from China, and he advocated the employment of
"coolie labor" in the California businesses of mining, mills, and rail-
roads. He viewed Chinese labor at this time not as a threat to American workers, but instead as a means to emancipate them from the
"drudgery which all white men abhor and are glad to escape from"
(272). Chinese labor, argued Twain, would create an elite white working class: "all the best class of the working population who might be
emancipated from the pick and shovel would find easier and more
profitable employment in superintending and overseeing the coolies"
(272). Chinese laborers allowed Twain to imagine restoring the role of
plantation overseer, lost with the abolition of slavery. Thus in Hawaii
Twain found not only an opportunity for American investors and
planters, but also a model for the formation of a white working class.
Just as he escaped from the drudgery of San Francisco to the Garden
of Eden in Hawaii, he imagined men working in his old job of mining to be liberated by the import of Chinese labor and thereby free
to become white men. Twain ends this letter on sugar in Hawaii with
a paean to the rise of an American empire in the Pacific, an empire that relies not only on the extension of American enterprise and
power abroad, but also on the importation of foreign labor at home to
whiten the American working class. In what he saw as the remote isolated locale of Hawaii, Twain learned a lesson in the transnational dimensions of whiteness that emerged from the movement of labor, capital, and racial discourses across the globe.

The international image of nonwhites as naturally indolent and incapable of self-discipline supported a related image of the same people as childlike and incapable of self-government. If Twain's depiction of the problem of free labor in Hawaii echoed that of post-emancipation America, so did his representation of the Hawaiian government. At a time of intense struggle over the possibilities and extent of black citizenship at the beginning of Reconstruction, Twain reported on Hawaii's interracial legislature with fascination and repulsion. The first thing he noticed when he walked into the legislature was its racial composition: "half a dozen white men and some thirty or forty natives. It was a dark assembly" (107). His comic picture of the legislature's activities derives from the incongruity he highlights between the foreign, uncivilized nature of the Hawaiians and their enacting a familiar role of citizens at home. He goes to great length to maintain this distinction, even as he blurs the boundary between the civilized and savage. Thus when he describes the 80-year-old president as noble and well dressed, he thinks to himself: "This man, naked as the day he was born, and war club and spear in hand, has charged at the head of a horde of savages . . . worshipped wooden images . . . seen hundreds of his race offered up in heathen temple as sacrifices to hideous idols . . . and now look at him; an educated Christian . . . a man practiced in holding the reins of an enlightened government. . . . Look at him sitting there presiding over the deliberations of a legislative body, among whom are white men" (108–9). Though Twain's ostensible purpose is to emphasize how far the president has risen up the ladder of civilization, the focus on the contrast between past and present has the effect of making the present look like window-dressing on an unyielding savage past, which can burst out at any moment. Twain spends a lot of time describing the president's clothing, which serves to emphasize his nakedness underneath. Twain intrigues his readers with a back and forth movement here, describing how the savage has become remarkably civilized yet emphasizing his savage past.

Twain's double-edged parody often uses his mockery of the Hawaiian legislature to ridicule legislatures at home as well. Under the heading "Familiar Characteristics," he describes a Kanaka member "who paddled over here from some barren rock or other out yonder in the ocean—some scalawag who wears nothing but a pair of socks and a plug hat when he is at home, or possibly is even more scantily arrayed in the popular mall—got up and gravely gave notice of a bill to authorize the construction of a suspension bridge from Oahu to Hawaii, a matter of a hundred and fifty miles! . . . Up came Honorable Ku and Luluiaui and Kowkow and Kiwawhoo and a lot of other clacking geese" (112). While Twain renders the procedures as play-acting, as the trappings of decision-making overlaying nakedness and ignorance, he cautions his readers: "do not do an unjust thing now and imagine Kanaka legislators do stupider things than other similar bodies." He then tells a story about a Wisconsin legislature, in the midst of affixing a penalty to the crime of arson, when "a member got up and seriously suggested that when a man committed the damning crime of arson they ought to make him marry the girl" (112). While describing here the universal stupidity of legislatures, Twain makes the Wisconsin legislature look all the more absurd because its ignorance outstrips that of naked savages. His description of the Hawaiian government has the overall effect of portraying children at play mimicking adults: "we see in this little land of fifty thousand inhabitants the complete machinery in its minute details of a vast and imposing empire done in miniature" (180). Entranced by the costumes of governance, Hawaiians, implies Twain, are incapable of true democracy.

Twain's mockery of Hawaiian citizens governing themselves would resonate at home with the postwar debates about the capacity of black people for participating in government. What may have looked comic abroad appeared more threatening at home to many white people in the North and South. Twain was in Hawaii the same year that Congress passed the landmark Civil Rights bill, which President Andrew Johnson vetoed and which would later become the Fourteenth Amendment. In his third annual message to Congress, Johnson stated that "in the progress of nations negroes have shown less capacity for self-government than any other race of people. No independent government of any form has ever been successful in their hands. On the contrary whenever they have been left to their own devices they have shown an instant tendency to lapse into barbarism."[46] I am not arguing that Twain's depiction of the Hawaiian nation would have been read as directly endorsing or negating this stereotype of blacks in the United States, but rather that his comic rendering of Hawaiian self-government would have had resonance and dissonance for those debates at home. While Twain brought stereotypes of blacks to frame his representation of Hawaiians, his depiction of Hawaiians also refracted back on racial politics at home when both were in upheaval. How would American readers of Twain in 1866 have perceived the image of dark-skinned Hawaiians presiding over white men? Racial discourses do not move in a unidirectional way with the outward course of empire, but they circulate among different imperial sites to build, reinforce, and contest meanings in relation to one another.

Not only white Americans transported their experiences and discourses of race back and forth across the Pacific. As members of the Hawaiian royalty traveled to the United States and Europe, their sense of American racism in their home was reinforced by their experience of racism abroad. When the current King, then Prince Lot, and his brother Prince Liholiho Alexander visited the United States as young men in 1850, a conductor threw them off a train bound for Baltimore because they were not white. On a Hudson River boat in New York they were refused entry to a dining salon for the same reason. In his journal on the way home, Twain referred to this trip as the reason for the current King's purported irrational disdain for Americans: "It riles me to hear an American . . . stand up and pay titular adulation to this heathen blackamoor—to this man who remembers to this day, & grieves over a trifling unintentional offense offered in the U.S. years ago to his private individuality, not to his official rank—& who hates America and Americans for it yet."[47] Twain could not see the King as a credible observer of American racism, which the monarch contrasted with his favorable reception in Europe. Instead, Twain portrayed the Hawaiian leader as a puppet manipulated and misled by the British and French, from whom he lapped up "gew-gaws of cheap adulation." Twain cast Hawaiian opposition to America as a childish grudge against "the strong and steadfast <American> hands that have lifted her up . . . Dam! Royalty!—I don't think much of Hawaiian royalty!"[48] Twain claimed not to blame the princes for feeling insulted at the time, but accused them of *not forgetting*, of refusing "to wipe out of their minds the memory of the affront . . . the king has never forgotten that trifling stab at his little vanity" (149–50). While Twain blamed the King for still grieving and not forgetting an incident that occurred twenty-six years before, the writer was the one who could not let go. He repeated the story twice in two pages with such vitriolic denunciation and rhetorical overkill that his own responses appear raw and present. In his retelling, Twain combined the two incidents and misplaced them in a location he would well remember: a Southern steamship. In trying to bury the Hawaiian response to American racism as a "trifling" from the past, Twain himself brought to life the unburied corpses of racism and imperialism dancing across the routes of his Pacific travel.

Anxieties about the self-government of nonwhites at home and abroad—the legacy of slavery and imperialism—come together in Twain's account of a visit to the government prison on his first tour of Honolulu. There he is introduced to another traveler who has taken a strange, circuitous course from the United States to Hawaii,

> General George Washington, or, at least, to an aged, limping Negro man, who called himself by that honored name. He was supposed to be seventy years old, and he looked it. He was as crazy as a loon, and sometimes, they say, he grows very violent. He was a Samson in a small way; his arms were corded with muscle, and his legs felt as hard as if they were made of wood. He was in a peaceable mood at present, and strongly manacled. They have a hard time with him occasionally, and some time or other he will get in a lively way and eat up the garrison of that prison, no doubt. The native soldiers who guard the place are afraid of him, and he knows it. (75)

The history of this man, concludes Twain, is a "sealed book." He is said to have set off on a ship of black sailors from a New England port twenty years ago, but he is fond of reminiscing in his "dreamy, incoherent way, about the Blue Ridge in Virginia, and seems familiar with Richmond and Lynchburg. I do not think he is the old original General W.," concludes Twain.

Twain ends the letter by praising "a model prison for the western half of the world"—a model that centers on a chained black man. In a prison recently designed to impose colonial discipline among native Hawaiians, Twain locates a powerful and contradictory image of American nationhood in the aftermath of the Civil War. Though harmless and powerless, this black man appears dangerous and menacing, capable of tearing down the prison walls like Samson. His origins are mysterious, though they seem to include both the North and the South. On a ship of black sailors, he was once free to travel outside national borders before the war, while its end finds him immobilized and manacled on a Pacific island. His lunacy lies in his fantasy of sovereignty, imagining himself as General W. leading a war for independence. He seems to represent both the imprisonment of nonwhite people at home and abroad and their struggle for independence. Also symbolic of American imperial power, George Washington would devour the native guards if he were free. Like Melville's description of Queequeg as "George Washington cannibalistically developed," this description both acknowledges and ridicules the desire for independence by nonwhite peoples, and it renders U.S. force as cannibalistic.

Twain was visiting the prison in Honolulu at a time when prisons in the American South were being restructured to reproduce the conditions of slavery in the aftermath of emancipation. In the colonial prison of Hawaii, Twain may have discovered a comforting reconstruction of the American South, a model of a black nation reenslaved in an imperial setting. Or he may have seen a prophetic image of the postwar South, not as an imperial occupation by the North, as Southerners claimed, but as emancipation that would recolonize African Americans. Twain may have later rewritten this scene as the nightmare of Jim manacled in the cabin from which Tom Sawyer stages the freeing of a free man. As a photographic negative of the founding father, this enchained black George Washington suggests the enfeeblement and limits of American independence and freedom built upon the corrosive foundations of slavery and empire. Thus, behind the bars of a Honolulu prison, Twain discovered both the consoling reconstitution of slavery and the threatening figure of a black man about to break his chains and bring down the entire edifice with him.

Forgotten Languages

While General George Washington dropped out of Twain's later work, the writer repeatedly returned to another figure he met in Hawaii: Bill Ragsdale, the translator who mesmerized Twain with his voluble and skillful performance in the Hawaiian legislature. Twain describes him in a letter as "half white," adding parenthetically "(half white and half Kanaka)." His biracial character introduces his extraordinary bilingual fluency:

> Bill Ragsdale stands up in front of the Speaker's pulpit, with his back against it, and fastens his quick black eye upon any member who rises, lets him say half a dozen sentences and then interrupts him and re-

peats his speech in a loud, rapid voice, turning every Kanaka speech into English and every English speech into Kanaka, with a readiness and felicity of language that are remarkable.[49]

Twain applauds Ragsdale's facility at publicly performing his translations, at nimbly crossing back and forth between the two languages and cultures. And Ragsdale indeed played an important role in a tension-ridden legislature "filled with white members who refused to learn Hawaiian and native members who refused to speak English," which at a point in 1866 broke out into a fistfight between the two sides.[50] Ragsdale, however, attracted Twain not for his facilitation of smooth communication, but for the way his fluency seemed to yield him subversive power to channel the flow of that communication. Twain calls attention to the

> spice of deviltry in the fellow's nature, and it crops out every now and then when he is translating the speeches of slow Kanakas who do not understand English. Without departing from the spirit of the member's remarks, he will, with apparent unconsciousness, drop in a little voluntary contribution occasionally in the way of a word or two that will make the gravest speech utterly ridiculous. (113)

Portraying Ragsdale as trickster, a master of parody who subversively skews his translation with "apparent unconsciousness," Twain seems to find in his style a mirror of his own writing, of what would become his renowned deadpan style. We have seen throughout his letters and lectures how Twain translates elements of Hawaiian culture into an American idiom, which makes them look ridiculous. Yet what Twain could not hear, but what his description implies, was that Ragsdale was probably translating English speeches with the same parodic effect that made them look ridiculous as well. Translation can go both ways. Indeed, Twain's response to Ragsdale mirrors his own writing from Hawaii. He translates Hawaiian culture and society into a racialized American idiom that does not remain stable and unilinear, but unleashes echoes of counter-translations that Twain himself cannot understand.

Twain returned to Ragsdale in 1884 as the hero for his unfinished "Sandwich Islands Novel," a novel he worked on between completing *Huckleberry Finn* and beginning *A Connecticut Yankee in King Arthur's Court*. From the few fragments of the manuscript and his letters, it appears that Twain planned to write a historical novel that starts with Ragsdale's fictionalized birth during the period the first American missionaries arrived in the 1820s. It includes his romance with another "half-caste" young girl and a plot to kill the King by stealing his spittoon and praying him to death, and it ends with a fictional account of Ragsdale's actual death of leprosy in the 1870s.[51] Although Twain did not complete the novel, many of its elements were incorporated into *Connecticut Yankee,* where Hank Morgan violently translates the premodern English of Camelot into the language of nineteenth-century American capitalism, as Twain ridicules both. Hawaii returned to his mind at a time when he was confronting the legacy of slavery in post-Reconstruction America and the history of imperialism and capitalist development abroad. For his hero he sought a vibrant biracial and bilingual translator who moved with such facility between two languages and two races, just after Twain had translated African American oral culture into the idiom of a vernacular fiction in the voice of a young white boy. He turned to a half-caste figure in Hawaii who crossed racial boundaries at a time when segregation was drawing stricter boundaries among racial hierarchies in America. He chose to highlight Ragsdale's voluntary segregation in a leper colony just before he wrote about the threat and impossibility of crossing boundaries of race and language in *Pudd'nhead Wilson.* But it is *Connecticut Yankee* that came closest to his Sandwich Islands novel in its superimposition of Reconstruction in the American South with imperialism abroad. The word "Yankee" itself was shifting geographically at the time, referring not only to Northerners in relation to Southerners but also to the nation as a whole in international locations of imperial intervention.

On a page of notes for his Sandwich Islands novel, Twain twice mentions a figure who traveled between Hawaii and the American South to play an active role in Reconstruction: Samuel Armstrong.[52] The name is listed with no identifying context or connection to the rest of the novel. Although Twain would not have met Armstrong in Hawaii in 1866, he would have at least heard of, if not met, members of his powerful family there, and by 1884 he would have recognized his name as that of the founder of Hampton Institute, renowned for its program of industrial education for blacks.[53] Samuel was born in Hawaii, where his missionary father, Richard Armstrong, was the first minister of "public instruction"; in this capacity he developed schools for Hawaiian youth that relied heavily on a program of manual labor, a system that would prepare them for work on plantations and ranches. Samuel worked with his father until he went to Williams College in 1860 and soon after enlisted in the Union Army. He led a black regiment and then worked for the Freedmen's Bureau, before he founded Hampton Institute. I can only speculate on why Twain mentioned him in his notes for the novel. Twain wrote to Howells in 1884 that he had a large stack of books for his novel, which might have included Armstrong's *Lessons from the Hawaiian Islands,* published that same year. Twain certainly would have heard of Armstrong's work in Hampton, as he traveled extensively in the 1880s to publicize and raise money for the Institute.

Perhaps Armstrong embodied for Twain, however unconsciously, precisely the dynamic I have been charting in his work, whereby he found both dissonance and resonance between the representations of race in Hawaii and the United States. While Twain would learn how to write about black-white relations in America in part through the experience of writing about colonial relations in Hawaii, Armstrong is a figure for whom these connections were much more pronounced. We tend to think of U.S. imperialism as the exporter of racial ideologies abroad in a one-way linear direction, pursuing new Indians on new frontiers abroad, or exporting black stereotypes to the plantations of Cuba and Puerto Rico. And indeed I have been arguing that Twain represented Hawaiians through the lenses of race relations at home. But this route is not linear as it criss-crosses the globe. Armstrong is an example of a Hawaiian-born American who transposed his images of nonwhite people and institutions for educating them from the imperial site of Hawaii to the Reconstruction landscape of Virginia. Armstrong grouped Polynesians, Africans, and Indians as people lacking "true morality" and self-control. And he proposed the same methods of education for the "negro" and "Polynesian": "Of both it is true that not mere ignorance, but deficiency of character is the chief difficulty, and to build up character is the true objective of education . . . conditioned very largely on a routine of industrious habit. Morality and industry go together. Especially in weak tropical races, idleness like ignorance breeds vice."[54] My purpose is not to argue that Twain and Armstrong simply took fully formed images of Hawaiians and superimposed them on American blacks or vice versa, but that these images evolved, solidified, and fractured in relation to one another. Though Hawaii obviously had a much greater influence on Armstrong than on Twain, both men followed parallel routes to the postwar South, Armstrong in his building of institutions, and Twain in his travel and writing. When Twain turned to write fiction about race relations and the legacy of slavery in America, he had for many years been engaged in a global imperial conversation with men such as Samuel Armstrong, Anson Burlingame, Henry Stanley, and Rudyard Kipling about the incapacity of nonwhite people to govern themselves, and the power of international capitalism to transform them into a modern labor force. This is not to say, by any means, that all toed a common ideological line as a solid block of imperialists, but to argue that we need to rethink Mark Twain as an "American" writer through these transnational routes of empire.

Ragsdale, a local character who lived his life in ever narrowing circles and ended up confined to a leper colony, was a very different figure from Armstrong, who traveled from Hawaii to bring his ideas of colonial education to the American South. But it was Ragsdale, not Armstrong, whom Twain had planned to feature in his uncompleted novel. Moreover, Twain returned to Ragsdale once more in 1896 in the chapter of *Following the Equator* that includes the story of the diver. Twain concluded that chapter of his aborted return to Hawaii with an elegy for Ragsdale that recalls his brilliance as a translator and laments his untimely death of leprosy. Though Twain had known of his death years before, he mourns him as if hearing the tragic news for the first time, disinterring Ragsdale's memory to lay it to rest once again. In expressing such an immediate sense of loss, Twain may have been identifying with Ragsdale's exile and lamenting the prohibition against revisiting the island he first encountered thirty years before and could now only see from afar. Ragsdale makes a striking contrast with the bilingual diver, a figure who can neither translate nor mourn. English dominates his psyche through an imperial order in which his original Hawaiian language resurfaces as anarchy, as a delirious breakdown. Ragsdale, conversely, thrives on translation as parody, as a means of subverting the bifurcated hierarchy of imperial translation. In mourning Ragsdale, perhaps Twain was grieving over his own efforts to write a novel as a form of translation between languages, cultures, and geographies that seemed at once so remote and so uncannily close.

In his journey to Hawaii in 1866, Twain both displaced and discovered the origins of his own divided national identity at the intersecting global routes of slavery and empire. In the colonization of Hawaii he saw the irony of freeing free men that would fuel his best-known fiction and his powerful anti-imperial writing later in his life. Although Twain never completed his novel about Hawaii, the insistent memories of that imperial encounter continue to haunt the corpus of his writing about America, like corpses tapping him on the shoulder inviting him to dance.

CHAPTER 3

Romancing the Empire

In his well-known anti-imperialist tract of 1901, "To the Person Sitting in Darkness," Mark Twain claimed: "There must be two Americas: one that sets the captive free, and one that takes a once-captive's new freedom away from him and picks a quarrel with him with nothing to found it on; then kills him to get his land."[1] One America had rushed to the aid of Cuban independence in the war against Spain in 1898, when it was "playing the usual and regular *American* game." The other America annexed the Philippines at the end of that same war and was currently conducting a brutal war against its people's struggle for independence. Twain saw this America as not acting American at all, but as slavishly imitating the European game of colonial conquest. His powerful condemnation of imperialism works here in part by disavowing its centrality to U.S. identity, by representing imperialism as a foreign activity, an aberration from the national commitment to freeing the captive. Splitting America in two does not acknowledge how the narrative of liberation legitimated the exercise of imperial power. What Twain's anti-imperialism had in common with imperialist arguments was the representation of U.S. intervention as a narrative of rescue: of Cuba and the Philippines from the tyranny of an Old World empire on the one hand, and from the anarchy of revolution and self-rule on the other.

Proponents of imperialism merged Twain's two Americas through another narrative of liberation; they saw imperial warfare as an opportunity for the American man to rescue himself from the threatening forces of industrialization and feminization at home. In a 1900 speech urging the United States to annex the Philippines, for example, Senator Albert Jeremiah Beveridge asked: "What does all this mean for every one of us?" and then readily answered: "It means opportunity for all the glorious young manhood of the republic—the most virile, ambitious, impatient, militant manhood the world has ever seen."[2] Without specifying the opportunities for particular actions, Beveridge implied tautologically that the empire offered the arena for American men to become what they already were, to enact their essential manhood before the eyes of a global audience. In subduing the Philippines, asserted another imperialist, a man could escape the thrall of modern life and be rejuvenated as a "free, glorious man, the real sinews of the republic in the days when too many of us are city bred."[3] By fighting abroad, this logic held, an American man could return home to his republican origins.

A similar rescue mission was conducted on the pages of the popular historical romance, where heroes whose American identity was thinly veiled pursued chivalric adventures in bygone eras. In the opening scene from the 1898 bestseller, *When Knighthood Was in Flower,* the heroine, catching her first sight of the hero in the midst of fighting a duel, declares passionately: "For once I have found a real live man, full of manliness."[4] In these novels, mythical kingdoms in historical settings function as the fictional equivalent of the Philippines for Beveridge, as the site where a man can reassert his "militant manhood." In these romances, a woman serves both as the damsel in distress for the hero to rescue and as the eyes of the world for which masculinity is performed.

Many contemporary readers linked the jingoistic clamor for foreign wars to what William Dean Howells called the "horrid tumult of the swashbuckler swashing on his buckler" in "the new historical romances" in the 1890s.[5] Looking back at his youth, Henry Seidel Canby wrote in 1934, "Scott and the near-Scotts and the school-of-Scotts were such real determinants of inner life for readers brought up in the eighties and nineties that no one will ever understand the America of that day without reading and pondering upon not only *Ivanhoe* but also *To Have and To Hold* and *Richard Carvel* and *Monsieur Beaucaire* and *Under the Red Robe.*"[6] These novels, for Canby, linked the private psyche of the reader to the public enthusiasm for the Spanish-American War: "I cannot separate in my own memory the bands and cheering of '98,

Hobson, Dewey, and manifest destiny in an expectant world, from the extravagant romanticism of the shallow, unphilosophical, unpsychological novels we had all been reading. One carried over into the other, and the same color was infused through both" (205). Overlooked by later critics in their characterization of the period as the Age of Realism, historical romances, in fact, were the major bestsellers on the earliest published lists from 1895–1902.[7]

Popular journalism has long been accorded a major role in galvanizing public support for U.S. entry into war against Spain. The yellow press of Joseph Pulitzer and Randolph Hearst rapidly built its circulation by rallying support for *Cuba Libre,* underwriting filibustering expeditions, excoriating the treatment of Cuban civilians by the Spanish regime, and fanning the flame of patriotic outrage at the explosion of the *Maine.* Less well known is the contribution of popular fiction to creating this jingoistic atmosphere that Canby recalled. Yet many journalistic narratives followed the script of the historical romance, rendering America as a manly hero rescuing a foreign princess and her land from a tyrannical master. Critics, however, have long dismissed the popular romance as a nostalgic escape from modernity to the heartier life of the chivalric warrior; as a collective form of blowing off steam. Reproducing the terms of imperialist discourse itself, this approach ignores how nostalgia can abet modern imperial force, and how an outworn genre can be refurbished to represent a new political context.[8]

The nostalgia for a lost wholeness in the distant past expressed in the swashbuckling romances of the 1890s created fanciful realms on which to project contemporary desires for unlimited global expansion. These novels offer a cognitive and libidinal map of the geopolitical shift from continental expansion to overseas empire, marked by the heralded close of the frontier. Through the medium of the white male body, they work to close the gap between Twain's two Americas, to merge the narratives of liberation and domination, to narrate the new empire as consistent with the history of the republic, to map overseas colonies as contiguous to continental expansion. Like the Supreme Court justices in *Downes v. Bidwell,* the novelists were in search of historical continuity to suture the gaps between the present imperial movements abroad and an understanding of prior U.S. history as anticolonial. They figured the world outside the United States as both a new frontier and a return to the lost past of the American nation.

By transposing international conflict into tales of chivalric heroism, these novels combat imagined threats to masculinity on the home front as well as abroad, and they contribute to refiguring the relation between manhood and nationhood in a changing international context. The romance hero asserts his virility in more complex forms than the imagined simple violence of the self-reliant frontiersman. The chivalric rescue narrative makes him dependent on the liberation and subjugation of the willing heroine, who serves as a composite figure for the New Woman at home and the subjects of the new empire abroad. In contrast to the domestic novels of the 1850s, heroines of the 1890s romances escape from the home to participate in imperial adventures. Furthermore, in staging the spectacle of masculinity for the female gaze, the romances liberate women readers from the confines of domesticity to re-domesticate them as spectators enjoying the "pleasures of imperialism."[9] The heroine in these novels also represents the supposed desire of colonized peoples to be liberated from their backward traditions and to subject themselves to modern forms of power. The novels render resistance to empire as anarchy, as they dramatize, in Twain's terms, how America sets the captive free by subjecting him to imperial power.

The Double Discourse of American Imperialism

Nationhood and manhood have long been intimately related in the representation of the dynamic of territorial expansion. The frontier where Frederick Jackson Turner located the formation of American individualism became for later historians the site of conflict with Native Americans, which forged the ideology of white masculinity. What happened to the link between nationality and masculinity when U.S. expansion shifted course from the continent to an overseas empire in the 1890s? The traditional explanation finds both nationalism and masculinity physically revitalized by imperial conquest. Congruence between the body and the state underlies the characterization of the period by the title of Theodore Roosevelt's speech, "The Strenuous Life," and the commonplace phrase "national muscle-flexing," which deploys the body as a metaphor for international aggression. For revisionists, the contradictions that inhere in masculine regeneration on the frontier are exported and reproduced at the turn of the century in the confrontation with new "Indians" abroad. These explanations, however, demand reconsideration, because they assume both a continuous history of expansion and a natural connection between the identification of the nation with the land and with the male body.[10]

A more complex double discourse of American imperialism emerged in the 1890s: politicians, intellectuals, and businessmen on both sides of the debate were redefining national power as *disembodied*—that is, divorced from contiguous territorial expansion. In the same period, and often in the same breath, masculine identity was reconceived as *embodied*—that is, cultivated—in the muscular robust physique.

The disembodiment of American nationalism can be seen in the much-heralded close of the frontier, which was inseparable from the call for open doors abroad. With the end of continental expansion, national power was no longer measured by the settlement and incorporation of new territory consolidated into a united state, but rather by the extension of vaster yet less tangible networks of international markets and political influence. Even the annexation of Hawaii and the Philippines was valued primarily as providing way stations to the fabled China markets, just as Cuba became the gateway to the Caribbean, itself the key to the isthmus that would become a canal and open the door to worldwide shipping. We have seen how the ambiguous status of Puerto Rico as "unincorporated territory" expressed this tension between embodiment and disembodiment. These islands, despite their bounded nature, became projections of the desire for an ever-growing expansion that seemed directed at noncorporeal goals. Disembodiment might describe the cultural fantasy underlying what historians have called the economically determined "informal empire," the desire for total control disentangled from direct political annexation.[11]

In fact, America's "New Empire," as Brooks Adams dubbed it, defined itself ideologically against the territorially based colonialism of the old European empires. While the frontier environment may have characterized the exceptional nature of America's past for Turner and his followers, the spatially unbounded quality of the New Empire promised to reconstitute national uniqueness. Thus, as Myra Jehlen has shown, if Manifest Destiny "rests its case on the integrity of the continent," what she calls "incarnation," then the shift from continental to global expansion in the 1890s can be seen as a form of "disincarnation."[12]

In this light, the representation of U.S. nationhood might be seen to undergo a "reincarnation" in the image of the American man. The culture at large was in the process of redefining white middle-class masculinity from a republican quality of character based on self-control and social responsibility to a corporeal essence identified with the vigor and prowess of the individual male body.[13] Imperialist discourse drew on and reinforced this process, as novelist and critic Maurice Thompson testified: "The war has made startlingly clear how great a thing is physical health and strength. Probably no army and navy since the best days of the Roman Empire ever equaled ours man for man in the best results of athletic training."[14] Despite the evidence of war's physical ravages, caused by disease as much as combat, Thompson continued: "In looking at our soldiers and sailors I was filled with admiration of their lithe and muscular forms and their show of virile health." This view reduces the empire to one among other rugged settings— the playing field, the boxing ring, the newly discovered wilderness— and relegates the war to such vigorous activities as athletics, bicycling, weight lifting, hiking. Virility is less the means to the end of empire-building than is empire the occasion for body-building, an inversion which ideologically effaces the violent conflict with foreign bodies on alien terrain. The discourse of U.S. imperialism is therefore double, because it delineates national power that is simultaneously disembodied from territorial boundaries and embodied in the American man.

The question remains, however, what links geographic disembodiment and masculine embodiment in this double discourse? Elaine Scarry's analysis of war suggests that an ideological spotlight on the individual body might concretize an otherwise abstract political struggle.[15] If the political and territorial ends of John Hay's "splendid little war" seemed murky, the male body could thus provide an anchor of meaning in a sea of distended world power. The problem of conceptualizing American imperialism, however, lay less in its abstract political nature in the present than in its rupture with a vision of the past. Anti-imperialists opposed the forced annexation of noncontiguous islands as a radical departure from what they considered the organic growth of the nation, an unnatural act that Justice Harlan warned would "engraft upon our republican institutions a colonial system such as exists under monarchical governments."[16] Furthermore, anti-imperialists like Twain protested such conquest as antithetical to America's republican anticolonial tradition.

"Engrafting" the image of the American male body on to the disembodied empire implicitly addressed the question of whether imperialism was continuous with U.S. history, the problem facing the Supreme Court in *Downes v. Bidwell* in 1901. In the introduction to his book *Democracy and Empire,* sociologist Franklin Giddings explicitly posed and resolved this contradiction: "The world has been accustomed to think of democracy and empire as antagonistic phenomena. It has assumed that democracy could be established only on the ruins of empire, and that the establishment of empire necessarily meant the overthrow of liberty by a triumphant reign of absolutism. Yet in our day we are witnessing the simultaneous development of both democracy and empire."[17] What Giddings saw as a distinctly modern development, others envisioned through the lens of nostalgia, which located the empire as the site for recuperating a primitive corporeal virility. Writers such as Frank Norris represented a historically changing construction of masculinity as simply the return to a mythical origin: "somewhere deep down in the heart of every Anglo-Saxon lies the predatory instinct of his Viking ancestors—an instinct that a thousand years of respectability and tax-paying have not quite succeeded in eliminating."[18] This instinctual self could only be recovered, paradoxically, on an externalized frontier remote from the United States, whose internal national identity appeared threatened by the influx of non-Anglo-Saxon immigrants.

If the idea of an international empire seemed discordant with U.S. democracy, the representation of that empire in the primitive male body figured reassuringly as a return to a fundamental Anglo-Saxon heritage. In a period of the New Woman, the New Negro, the New South, and the New Empire, the New White American Man was invented as a tradition, to use Hobsbawm's term (and unlike the others, as a tradition it remains tellingly unlabeled), as nothing new at all, but rather a figure from an enduring recoverable past.[19] Thus in the revitalized male body, geographic distension and overseas conquest figure as a temporal return to origins, literally as nostalgia, *nostos,* the return home.

As we have seen through Mark Twain's memories of Hawaii, "imperialist nostalgia" for the indigenous forms of life destroyed by empire also entails nostalgia for an imagined past of the imperial nation, a longing not only for the "way they were," but the "way we were."[20] Whereas Twain's nostalgia was disrupted by the melancholic return of colonial violence, in this discourse the empire is where you can be all that you can no longer be at home—a "real live man"—where you can recover the autonomy denied by social forces of modernization, often aligned in this way of thinking with feminization. In the 1890s the lament for the close of the frontier loudly voiced such nostalgia for the formative crucible of American manhood; imperial expansion overseas offered a new frontier, where the essential American man could be reconstituted in his escape from modernity and domesticity.[21]

Yet if the empire appeals to an antimodern desire to retrieve primitive origins, there is a counter-dynamic at work as well. Rather than an untouched wilderness, the empire is represented as the setting where the primal man is staged as a highly theatrical spectacle by deploying the technologies of mass destruction and mass media he fled from at home. He proves his virility not in a bloody contest with a native other, but by acting before the eyes of a domestic audience. This double dynamic of recovering the primitive and staging it as a high-tech spectacle, of what Elliott Gorn in another context has called "controlled atavism," was epitomized by Theodore Roosevelt, whose foray into the West to recover his health—literally to restore his body—and whose later adventures fighting in Cuba and hunting in Africa were manifestly theatrical. He highlighted his bodily vigor by purchasing custommade "authentic" costumes from the tailors of New York, and he relied on the modern technology of photography to publicize his primitive virile image back home.[22] As his case suggests, the primitive male body proves to be as disembodied as the empire it represents; it becomes a carefully constructed simulation. Rather than a bedrock reality underlying the veneer of corporate civilization, the primal male body becomes another layering of veneers.

One well-known biological metaphor justifying territorial expansion in the nineteenth century compared national growth to an organic body, which must continue to grow or die.[23] But the stable part of this metaphor—the body—was being destabilized in this period as an artificially composed spectacle. Thus the analogy between nationhood and manhood in the 1890s ultimately relies on their spectacular nature rather than on their rooted physical organicism. Furthermore, the tension between the disembodied empire and the embodied American man is reproduced within the figure of masculinity itself, between nostalgia for the body and the spectacle of its display.

Reviving the Romance

"The return to romance," argued Thompson, "is simply a young, strong, virile generation pushing aside a flabby one. The little war we had with Spain did not do so much for us: the thing was already done by our schools, churches, gymnasiums, out-door sport; the war acted simply as a faucet through which our vigor began to act."[24] To the athletic field and battlefield, Thompson added the revival of the historical novel, with its "distinction of large masculine power." Whereas Howells and Canby treated this revival as a collective regression into "the feverish exuberance of an unhealthy child," a view seconded by later critics, Thompson welcomed the historical romances, with their "virile ancestry," not as antimodern regression but as part of a progression suitable to America's new global role, "signs in the air of great world changes." To him, the return to the romance represented a step into the future: "If the map of the world and the atmosphere of civilization are changing radically, a corresponding change in art should not be surprising." The revival of the romance turns a potential rupture with tradition into cultural and political continuity, a return to a healthier, more authentic American past.

The formulaic plot of the romance uncannily parallels the popular narrative of the Spanish-American War as a chivalric rescue mission that in turn rejuvenates the liberator. The historical romance opens with its own lament for the closed frontier, as the hero mopes, discontented with the dwarfed opportunities of his contemporary society. He then seeks adventure on a primitive frontier abroad, where he falls in love with a beautiful aristocratic woman, often the ruler of a kingdom and sometimes a genteel American. The hero, usually a disinherited or "natural" aristocrat, saves the kingdom from falling to its barbaric enemies and thereby modernizes it, and liberates the heroine from outdated class constraints by marrying her. The heroine of the novel, an athletically daring New Woman (often a Gibson girl in the illustrations), actively abets her own liberation by rescuing the hero and then embracing him in marriage. At the end, the hero returns home with his bride, after relinquishing political control of the realm he has freed.

This formula is strikingly pliable to radically different settings and eras, from Richard Harding Davis's *Soldiers of Fortune* (1897),[25] in which an American mercenary saves a fictional Latin American dictatorship from revolution and marries an upper-class American girl whose father owns mines there; to Charles Major's *When Knighthood Was in Flower* (1898), in which Brandon wins the heart of Mary Tudor and wrests her away from the power of the monarchy; to George Barr McCutcheon's *Graustark* (1901),[26] set in a mythical kingdom which a footloose American rescues from hostile neighbors to marry its princess; to Mary Johnston's *To Have and To Hold* (1900),[27] in which a colonist of Jamestown, Virginia, saves a female ward of the King from the evil designs of Lord Carnal, while simultaneously defeating the last Indian attack on the colony. These four bestsellers, from which most of my examples are drawn, are characteristic of hundreds of novels which fit into four main categories: (1) the fewest, set in contemporary exotic arenas of the colonized world; (2) many more, which enact a kind of cultural imperialism by rewriting scenes from European history with identifiable (if anachronistic) Americanized heroes, from the fall of Rome to nineteenth-century Italy; (3) a number of others that similarly insert overt American heroes into the revision of a popular British genre set in mythical kingdoms, based on Stevenson's *Prince Otto* and Anthony Hope's *Prisoner of Zenda;* (4) a proliferation of romances about American history, largely revolutionary and colonial, but also including the Civil War and Reconstruction. The modern Western, initiated with Owen Wister's *The Virginian,* finds its immediate genealogy in this genre, which reclaims the American West through the course of overseas empire.[28]

The Disembodied Empire and the Closed Frontier

Not surprisingly, critics have viewed the historical romance primarily as a nostalgic retreat to a simplified past away from contemporary social strife at home and abroad. As Howells put it, "the tarraddidles of the historical romancers" offered "a relief from the facts of the odious present" (936).[29] To call these novels escapist, however, is to show not their avoidance of contemporary political discourse, but their reproduction of it. In the decade before the wars in Cuba and the Philippines, a politics of regulated escape was propounded by advocates of U.S. expansion, who believed that social and psychic pressures attendant upon the close of the frontier and the 1893 depression could be relieved by opening new frontiers abroad. Frederick Jackson Turner, for example, endorsed overseas expansion as an inevitable solution to "The Problem of the West":

> For nearly three hundred years the dominant fact in American life has been expansion. With the settlement of the Pacific Coast and the occupation of the free lands, this movement has come to a check. That these energies of expansion will no longer operate would be a rash prediction; and the demands for a vigorous foreign policy, for an oceanic canal, for a revival of our power upon the seas, and for the extension of American influence to outlying islands and adjoining countries, are indications that the movement will continue.[30]

Embedded in the discourse of closed space is the rhetoric of surplus energy that describes the overproduction of goods and the oversaving of capital as a physical pressure in need of release. Frank Norris compared this national surplus hemmed in by geographic boundaries to the undirected physical energy of "the boy shut indoors who finds his scope circumscribed and fills the whole place with the racket of his activity."[31] Such destructive excess found an outlet historically, according to Norris, only in the pursuit of more distant frontiers, either westward or in the eastern Crusades. The recent war in the Pacific and ensuing response to the Boxer Rebellion in China, he claimed, joined both trajectories in full circle around the globe.

Another ideologue of expansion, the Reverend Josiah Strong, revealed that American anxiety about the closed West may have had global dimensions that expressed fear of belatedness on the imperial stage, of the absence of those white spaces on the map impelling Marlow in *Heart of Darkness*. Strong warned that "there are no more new worlds. The unoccupied arable lands of the earth are limited and will soon be taken."[32] Yet in contrast to Lenin, who later foresaw international conflict as a result of a world that could only be "divided and subdivided," Strong turned crowded space into empty space, as he proclaimed that the Anglo-Saxon race (in its highest form in the United States) would yet transcend this geographic obstacle and, "to impress its institutions upon mankind, will spread itself over the earth" through its religious, cultural, and economic institutions. According to Strong, an escape for the excess "energy" galvanizing the Anglo-Saxon race was still available for a world infinitely malleable, if geographically limited, to be remade in the image of the United States.

The new historical romance directly addressed this anxiety about a world closed to expansion by remapping the world overcrowded with contesting powers to create new worlds out of old, which offer themselves for the taking. Howells, in fact, compared the novelist to the empire-builder: "imaginary thrones, principalities and powers in a map of Europe which the novelist changed with more than Napoleonic ease, became the ready, the eager prey of English and American soldiers of fortune" (937). Most of these romances begin by announcing the close of the frontier in the temporal form of the hero's lament for the lack of opportunity for heroic adventure. This lament introduces the second Crusade of *Via Crucis,* for example, which, in its commercialism and lack of nobility, seems a pale shadow of the first. This same complaint is directed against the Quaker father of Hugh Wynne, whose commercial bent, timid uprightness, and pacifism suffocates the young man, who welcomes the American Revolution as a return to the heroic valor of his Welsh ancestors. Even a novel set in colonial Jamestown starts with a sense of closed frontier as the hero daydreams of the good old days of Dale's laws, starvation, and bloody Indian battles. The present, by contrast, is hemmed in by peace with the Indians and the threat of domestication, in the form of a boatload of female settlers imported from England for marriage.[33] If the novels as a genre offered a nostalgic retreat from the late nineteenth-century United States, they each open by reenacting this retreat, rendering the present of the novel as a closed space, longing for boundlessness in the form of an even more distant virile past.

The most popular American version of this theme, *Graustark,* starts on a train home to the nation's capital from the clearly unromantic West. The upper-class hero, bored with his routine life in Washington, has failed to find excitement in a world where duels are outlawed and a stagecoach ride to save the heroine from missing her train devolves into a botched chivalric deed that appears to him as a parody of a dime novel. Only his pursuit of a mysterious Germanic princess reopens the possibilities of adventure foreclosed in the West. One of the first things Lorry learns upon arriving in Graustark, from another footloose American, is that the native men "fought like Sam Patch" (100); that they act like real cowboys on horseback. This sounds like the real

West, rather than the self-conscious parody which, as Frank Norris noted, the American West had become.

Part of the criticism of these romances as escapist is that they reflect America's provincial lack of interest in geopolitics.[34] The novels, however, often present the same critique, and thus offer themselves as corrective lessons in world geography. Lorry, a world traveler, initially flaunts his ignorance of other lands: "his ideas of geography were jumbled and vague—as if he had got them by studying labels on his hatbox" (13). This myopia, however, impedes his pursuit of the mysterious princess, when he tries to follow her to "one of those many infernal little kingdoms and principalities" somewhere east of Paris (91). After he finally locates Graustark on a Baedeker map, he is dismayed yet tantalized to find it "away off to the east," for "one would think barbarians existed there and not such people" as those "refined, cultivated, smart, rich" ones he met on the train (95). But such a duality is precisely the allure of Graustark, which in its medieval setting—complete with castle, tower, and dungeon—turns out to be attractively backward, with swarthy peasants in turbans, riding on horseback and brandishing swords. Yet like Twain's Camelot, Graustark also has the grace of an aristocratic civilization in its "air of antiquity," and its "guys are great on gallantry" (103).

The mythical kingdom of Graustark is typical of the settings of the historical romance, and, as an escape from the geopolitics of the 1890s, reveals the triadic structure shaping Americans' cognitive map of the world. Graustark has the overcivilized qualities of the European powers with which the United States was competing and the barbaric characteristics of the peoples it was trying to save and subdue. The romance conflates and makes exotic the threatening poles in contemporary political rhetoric, of Old World "tyranny"—empire—and New World "anarchy"—revolution—against which the United States intervenes and defines itself as unique. In this respect the monarchy of Graustark resembles the republic of Olancho, "one of those little republics down there" in South America, in Richard Harding Davis's *Soldiers of Fortune*. In Olancho a gallant young Englishman dies defending his Spanish lady—the wife of the would-be dictator—against rebellious Olanchan nationalists. As these noble but pathetic residues of the Spanish and English empires move offstage, the American hero, Clay, a civil engineer and abundantly decorated mercenary, single-handedly defeats the revolutionaries. The historical romance thus remaps a new world out of the ruins of a decayed empire and a thwarted revolution, and often merges the two in a single threat, as in the federation of Indian tribes referred to as a "Southern Empire" in the colonial Virginia of *To Have and To Hold*.

To rebuild these ruins, the American hero is offered the antiquated position of dictator or king, a job he laughingly declines, thus signifying the excess rather than absence of power. By marrying the heroine and bringing her home, he asserts a less direct and more complete control over the realm he has liberated. Lorry abandons the throne of Graustark to return to Washington; yet, in a gesture anticipating Woodrow Wilson, he bestows a democratic future on the monarchy by having its ancient noblemen vote to allow the princess to marry him; they conclude that in the absence of a masculine scion of the noble family, "why not the bold, progressive, rich American" (396). After similarly declining the dictatorship of Olancho, Clay marries the daughter of the owner of the American mining company who employed him, on whose behalf he preserved the republic. *Soldiers of Fortune* ends on board ship, with the hero returning to become a respectable "engineering expert." Triumphant, he points out lights on the distant horizon to his fiancée: "over there is the coast of Africa." In both cases, by refusing direct political power in favor of marriage, the heroes secure an even stronger hold overseas as they return home to the commercial corporate world they seemed to escape in foreign adventures.

Just as political power is reinforced abroad by being renounced, the main character can best prove his masculinity outside his national boundaries. The hero of *Soldiers of Fortune* becomes the ideal American man by virtue of his homelessness; his sentimental attachment to a home is really to the grave of his filibustering father. He divides the work months of the year between construction (as engineer) and destruction (as mercenary) in the outposts of the European empires, and then takes his vacation in Vienna, where he goes to imbibe high civilization. When Clay is saluted by an American marine at the end, he says proudly, "I have worn several uniforms since I was a boy, but never that of my own country" (335). It is striking that this representative American never lives there. Yet this absence, this refusal of national dress or place, makes him more authentically American than the uniformed marine by rendering his nation's qualities universal and self-evident in his own body. The male hero's escape from domesticity makes the entire world a potential home and quells its menacing foreignness. In these novels of the 1890s, masculinity has a function similar to the "manifest domesticity" we saw in Chapter 1. The self-contained white male body is delineated by its rejection of feminization and racial otherness, but it is mobile and flexible enough to make itself at home anywhere in the world.

Only in the release from geographic bounds can the United States secure the borders of its own identity. And this escape to a distant frontier is nostalgic in that it allows the American man to return home by becoming more fully himself. If Olancho and Graustark are escapes, they magically reopen that world which Strong sees closing down, a composite world of old and new, of barbarism and civilization, an "expectant world," in Canby's words, awaiting an influx of U.S. might. Fantasies indeed, these novels enact the desire for infinite expansion without colonial annexation, total control through the abdication of political rule, the detachment of national power from geographical boundaries.

The Embodied Man and the New Woman

Masculinity freed of national boundaries at first glance appears a purely corporeal identity, materialized through the immersion in primal violence, as Jackson Lears has argued.[35] The heroes' actions in these novels, however, juxtapose violent demonstrations of brute strength and a chivalric dedication to women, a commitment that sometimes leads to the renunciation of fighting in favor of love. When the hero of *Soldiers of Fortune* rides off with his beloved during a battle, he remarks, "I had forgotten. They have been having a revolution here" (306). He asserts his manliness through this nonchalance toward the male sphere of war, just as he asserts his Americanness by disavowing a uniform. Furthermore, this renunciation enhances his control by rendering the indigenous revolution as insignificant background to his declaration of love.

Many of these novels implicitly tell the story of defeating a nationalist revolution by displacing this conflict onto the more overt plot of rescue, in which the hero saves the heroine from her own environment. The romance splits the subjects of imperial power into gendered positions in which the heroine plays the part of the good Indian, siding with the forces of progress, while her male counterparts resist as brutal savages. In fact, the measure of their barbarism, like that of the ancient Hawaiians in Twain's writing, lies in their mistreatment of women. Both the backwardness and the allure of exotic cultures stem from their worship of women as objects of chivalric adoration on the one hand, and the women's role as chattel to be married off for political alliances on the other. The liberator frees the heroine from her outdated role as item of exchange for a barbaric institution that makes "marriageable women but commodities in statecraft," as Major put it (148). The hero undermines the feudal order and supplants it with his own chivalry by liberating the heroine from this bondage. He enacts the point Theodore Roosevelt made in 1910, for example, when he lectured to Egyptian Moslems about the Christian respect for women as a mark of superior civilization.[36] Roosevelt was echoing a long-standing imperial trope we saw voiced by Sarah Josepha Hale as well, that civilization—or its absence—can be measured by the domestic status accorded women.

The women who are liberated in these novels have already in a sense saved themselves; by virtue of their love for the hero they have proven themselves ahead of their time. Cast in the role of the New Woman—independent, self-reliant, and adventurous—they often disguise themselves as men to plot the escape scenes, which the heroes obediently act out. The heroine of *Richard Carvel* saves the hero from death in a British prison by disguising herself as a beggar. Even the heroine of *The Virginian,* a New England schoolmarm, rescues the self-reliant hero from the wilderness, where he is left wounded after a fight with Indians. The heroine's strong-willed passion, individualism, and activism show her out of place in her feudal or genteel environment. Mary Tudor of *Knighthood* is described similarly as a self-willed "girl pitted against a body of brutal men, two of them rulers of the two greatest nations on earth—rather heavy odds, for one woman" (137). But Mary does beat the odds and marries Brandon through her own machinations, with which he passively complies. Yet rather than run away together to New Spain, as she had planned, her male disguise is exposed, and this "sweet willful Mary" voluntarily "dropped out of history; a sure token that her heart was her husband's throne; her soul his empire; her every wish his subject, and her will, so masterful with others, the meek and lowly servant of her strong but gentle lord and master" (248). Marriage is described here not simply in the rhetoric of political conquest, as we might expect, but in the language of political collaboration, the language of desire. Voluntarily chosen by the woman, rather than forcibly imposed, marriage represents the modern alternative to both empire and revolution.

The New Woman thus becomes a figure for imperial subjects of the New Empire. The heroines prove their own modernity by at once freeing themselves from traditional hierarchies and voluntarily subduing themselves to some "real live man," just as imperial subjects, like the loyal Olanchan general in *Soldiers of Fortune,* prove their capacity for liberation through their alliance with American power. The romance heroine plays a role like that described by Frantz Fanon: "In the colonialist program, it was the woman who was given the historic mission of shaking up the Algerian man."[37] The romance heroines go one step further in imperialist fantasy; they eclipse and supplant their colonized male counterparts.

In American mythology, this female role replays the Pocahontas myth, which was undergoing a revival in the popular culture of the 1890s.[38] In *To Have and To Hold,* Pocahontas is a constant allusive presence (after her death); her husband, Rolfe, is a companion of the hero, and her brother, a noble savage gracefully embracing his own doom, aids the British settlers in the final destruction of Indian resistance and thus the founding of the colony. In the figures of Pocahontas and the white heroines, these novels represent the female desire to be liberated from feudal and traditional bonds as the desire to be subjugated to modern power. The 1899 Schurman Commission in the Philippines noted a similar desire in eroticized terms: "The very thing they yearn for is what of all others our Government will naturally desire to give them."[39] Such a perfect fit is imagined between conqueror and conquered to erase any trace of conflict. Yet in the novels, this female desire to be liberated contains a potential threat to the man who saves her. "Such a woman as Mary" in *Knighthood* is called "dangerous, except in a state of complete subjection—but she was bound hand and foot in the silken meshes of her own weaving" (248). If these meshes are self-designed, can they be torn at will? That is the lurking threat in this fantasy of imperial collaboration; the position of the hero as chivalrous rescuer makes him curiously dependent on maintaining the desire of his female subject.

The heroine, as a composite figure, has at least a double function: she feminizes colonial subjects and masculinizes American women. In the first case, the plot of rescue may shed light on a phenomenon often noted by historians, the abrupt shift in the American image of the Cubans and, to a lesser extent, the Filipinos, from heroic revolutionaries (before the U.S. entry into the war against Spain) to bedraggled "unmanly" bandits unworthy of their American allies.[40] When gender is taken into account in the narrative of rescue, this shift seems less extreme. Tales abounded in the popular press of outrages perpetrated by the Spanish against Cuban women, as in the alleged strip searches on the U.S. ship, *Olivette,* or in the celebrated case of Evangelina Cosio y Cisneros, the "Cuban Joan of Arc," a member of a prominent Cuban family who was imprisoned on suspicion of aiding the revolutionaries.[41] The press virtually scripted the case as a romance novel, claiming that she had been imprisoned for resisting the lustful advances of a Spanish officer. Hearst's *New York Journal* launched an extensive letter-writing campaign on her behalf and then sent reporter Karl Decker, in the role of knight errant, to rescue her (he staged it as a prison break, but accomplished it behind the scenes through bribes). This case enlisted the support of many readers from women's organizations; one wrote to the *Journal* that the episode reminded her "of the chivalry of the knights of old, who rescued damsels in distress."[42] As the *Journal* noted in its book-length history of the case, "As in old Romances, there is no uncertainty as to which way our sympathies should turn."[43] The rescue of a captive Cuban woman served as a symbol for the entire Cuban nation—a connection made explicitly in the press: "We have freed one Cuban girl—when shall we free Cuba?"[44]

If the entry into the war was viewed as a chivalric rescue mission, then it is unsurprising that the Cubans and Filipinos could not be represented as men acting with autonomous agency or that they were viewed by Americans as lacking the "qualities which make for manhood."[45] Not only did the conditions of guerrilla warfare shatter the image of the heroic soldier Americans expected to find, as historians have argued, but the feminized view of the Cubans as welcoming damsels in distress did not allow the Americans to represent them as subjects acting on their own behalf. In a related context, President McKinley justified the war against the Filipinos by chastising them for not acquiescing to the role of the rescued: "It is not a good time for the liberator to submit important questions concerning liberty and government to the liberated while they are engaged in shooting down their rescuers."[46] To be liberated, according to McKinley, meant, as it does in romances, to submit to being rescued, not to make claims for self-government.

While the heroine is an ideal imperial subject by virtue of her combined rebellion against tradition and submissiveness to the modern order, she is similarly a model New Woman. Many of the novels position the heroine against a more domestic or genteel counterpart, who, though attractive, is clearly an outdated and unsuitable match for the hero. Yet the "newness" of the heroine is often represented as a return to a more primitive and heroic past, as it is also for the hero. Even Thompson, who applauded the historical romance as a masculine revival of an older epic mode against the domestic novel, starts *Alice of Old Vincennes* with a prototypical New Woman represented as a type from hardier frontier days. Several novels, such as *Janice Meredith*, open with heroines reading romances illicitly, not to debunk a Bovary-like romanticism, but to fulfill their dreams with even more romantic adventures. The evidence of a female readership may prove Howells correct in his view that just as women were entering the arena of athletics and spectator sports, the romance was claiming the field of imperial adventure for women as readers.

The appeal of the historical romance to both female and male readers may suggest a way of reconsidering the representation of gender relations at the turn of the century. Advocates of masculine rejuvenation, such as Roosevelt, usually responded to the threat of the New Woman by urging a concomitant return of women to their traditional roles as homemakers and childbearers. In "The Strenuous Life" Roosevelt called not only for men to be more manly, but also for women to be more womanly by resuming their allegedly feared and rejected work of motherhood.[47] These novels suggest a more complex pattern of recuperation—namely, that women are invited to imagine themselves participating in the adventures of empire as a means of rejecting traditional roles. The novels elicit the desire for liberation from domestic constraints through adventure and athletic activity, even as they channel that desire into the support of imperial conquest. By concluding with marriage, these works suggest that the home too can be recuperated by the empire, which channels women's dissent into reaffiliating them with their male counterparts. Roosevelt and his peers may have wished to send the New Woman straight home to bear more Anglo-Saxon children, but the romance offers a more circuitous—and perhaps more efficacious—route, via the course of overseas empire.[48]

The Spectacle of Masculinity

In the chivalric rescue narrative, the hero must violently subdue a barbaric oppressor, whether treacherous Indians, British loyalists, Eastern Cossacks, or Latin American revolutionaries. Violence in the romance, however, is always framed by the theatrical display of the hero in conspicuously staged scenes, where the heroine serves as the chief spectator. On this fictional new frontier, renewal does not emerge from bloody contests with a native other; the novels instead offer regeneration through a spectacle before the female gaze. This performance engineers the final defeat of the native insurgent by effacing his contesting agency.

Most violent acts in the novels are self-consciously performed for a female audience. The opening duel of *Knighthood*, the last act of violence in the book, focuses less on purgative bloodletting than on Mary's love-struck stare. Even the climactic battle against the infidels in the remote Holy Land of *Via Crucis* takes place in front of female Crusaders, whose queen declares to her knight, in the midst of the fray, "Oh what a man you are! What a man."[49] Both cases relegate conflict with an enemy to a backdrop for the woman's act of witness, one that validates the hero's virility.

In some cases, the spectacle of masculinity preempts and displaces the necessity to engage directly in violence. Although Lorry leaves Washington exhausted and neurasthenic, he and his friend arrive in Graustark magically transformed into "two handsome, smooth-faced young Americans [who] were as men from another world, so utterly unlike their companions were they in personal appearance. They were taller, broader, and more powerfully built than the swarthy-faced men about them, and it was no wonder that the women allowed admiration to show in their eyes. . . . The two strangers were over six feet tall, broad-shouldered and athletic. They looked like giants among these Graustark men" (106–107). Without any physical exertion, the American men automatically recover their primal virility in a relation of difference, in contrast to the native men around them. This difference, however, is realized not through conflict with those men, but through the observation of the native women "who were eyeing them and commenting quite freely." At the end of the novel, Lorry luckily avoids a climactic duel (the one he was disappointed not to find out West), as his barbaric enemies conveniently plunge knives into one another. But he still saves the kingdom by unveiling the plots of conspiracies and declaring his love in a verbal pageant before a packed court.[50]

The theatrical quality of primitive nostalgia permeated other areas of contemporary physical culture as well. In "Modern Survivals of Prowess" Thorstein Veblen described (quite sardonically) not just the atavistic qualities of sportsmanship, but also its marked histrionic appeal, the extravagant gestures of the white man hunting in his return to wilderness, where make-believe and performance before a real or imagined audience become the focal point, rather than the kill itself.[51] Theatricalized chivalry was in fact advocated by G. Stanley Hall, a psychologist and educator. For him, one of the most important elements of athletics for adolescents was the attention of female spectators: "The presence of the fair sex gives tonicity to youth's muscles and tension to his arteries to a degree of which he is rarely conscious."[52] The youth exerts himself physically through contest with his peers in response to a teenage girl, "who performs her best service in the true role of sympathetic spectator rather than as fellow player" (104). The female spectator unleashes the brute in the man yet holds him in check. In Lew Wallace's immensely popular novel *Ben-Hur*, dramatized on stage and in lavish outdoor spectacles, Ben Hur's beloved also figures as the audience for whom primitive violence is performed. She resists turning away from the chariot fight when she realizes: "An idea of joy there is in doing an heroic deed under the eyes of a multitude came to her, and she understood ever after how, at such times, the souls of men, in the frenzy of performance, laugh at death or forget it utterly."[53] The performative quality—rather than immersion in primitive violence—saves the actor from the fear of death, and redeems his masculinity, and the mass audience before whom he performs is represented by the female spectator.

"Jingoism is merely the lust of the spectator," wrote J. A. Hobson, in one of the first major studies of imperialism.[54] He compared the emotions of the spectator aroused at a sporting event to those of the jingoist. The athletic arena, in which Veblen, Hall, and Wallace viewed the spectacle of masculinity, was often interchangeable with the imperial battlefield in contemporary discourse. The historical romance appealed to what Hobson called "spectatorial lust" by positioning women in the role of the jingoist. When the heroines of these novels are not actively rescuing the hero, they are watching him fight or perform. By turning women into spectators, the romance posits an additional collaborative relation with women in the constitution of masculinity and the establishment of empire. Moreover, if the heroine/spectator is a figure for the female reader, she suggests a redefinition of domesticity in relation to imperialism, from a retreat from public space to a window or lens focused on masculine exploits abroad.[55] Furthermore, the presence of domestic viewers in the romance links these mass-marketed bestsellers to the strategic role of the mass-circulation newspapers in the culture of imperialism. By circulating imperial adventures into the American home, the novels incorporate domestic space into that imperial network and work with the press, which, according to Josiah Strong, "transforms the earth into an audience room."[56]

In addition, these novels enact not just the lust of the spectator but the lust for a spectator, as described by Stephen Crane, another journalist of turn-of-the-century imperial warfare. "When they go away to the fighting-ground," he wrote, "out of the sight, out of the hearing of the world known to them and are eager to perform feats of war in this new place they feel an absolute longing for a spectator. . . . None wanted to conceal from his left hand that his right hand was performing a manly and valiant thing."[57] The reference to hands splits the fighting male subject in two—the actor and the spectator, who takes the form of the journalist, as panderer in the arousal of spectatorial lust: "The war correspondent arises, then, to become a sort of cheap telescope for the people at home; further still, there have been fights where the eyes of a solitary man were the eyes of the world; one spectator whose business it was to transfer, according to his ability, his visual impressions to other minds."[58] The focus of this passage shifts from the soldier and his enemy on the battlefield to the audience at home. While manliness may be performed against the backdrop of remote frontiers, this spectacle does not fully materialize until it is broadcast by the media to a domestic audience.

This "absolute longing for a spectator" is dramatized in *Soldiers of Fortune* during the full-scale battle against the revolutionaries, which takes place, significantly, in the national theater. There a young American college boy's first experience of war reveals the importance of spectatorship on the battlefield. Although he first approaches the battle as an amusing collegiate football game, when he finds himself out front, "he felt neglected and very much alone. . . . [I]t struck him as being most absurd that strangers should stand up and try to kill one another, men who had so little in common that they did not even know one another's names. The soldiers who were fighting on his own side were equally unknown to him" (326). Rather than release the buried "predatory Viking" in the heat of the battle, his dislocation and loss of identity are mirrored in the anonymity of the soldiers on both sides. When the American enters into the thick of fire, he is described as "continually winking and dodging, as though he were being taken by a flash-light photograph" (327). The fantasy of turning gunfire into the flash of a photograph recuperates his masculine identity, which is threatened by the violent, inscrutable political affiliations of the imperial battlefield. Like Hall's adolescent athlete, whose muscles are strengthened by the gaze of his girlfriend, this soldier's sensation of being "shot" in a photograph recomposes a reassuring position as a fighting subject.

This heightened dependence of the imperial adventurer on his domestic audience—the jingo—both enables and undercuts the image of the self-reliant white man alone in the wilderness, by divorcing and sheltering him from the context in which he is fighting. Hobson notes a blindness in the spectator, who gloats "over the perils, pains, and slaughter of fellow-men whom he does not know, but whose destruction he desires in a blind and artificially stimulated passion of hatred and revenge. In the Jingo all is concentrated on the hazard and blind fury of the fray."[59] Hobson's repetition of the word "blind" emphasizes (albeit in a romanticized view of fighting) that "respect for the personality of the enemies whose courage he must admit and whom he comes to realize as fellow-beings" is eliminated. Thus "spectatorial lust" effaces the agency of the enemy in battle by reorienting the terms of the conflict from the political struggle on the imperial battlefield to the relation between the imperial soldier and his domestic audience.

The spotlight on the spectacle of American masculinity triangulated with the reporter and the domestic audience denies the existence of political resistance to imperialism, even in the act of war against those resisters. An oft-heard complaint in newspapers about the battlefields of Cuba and the Philippines was the invisibility of indigenous soldiers—both allies and enemies—who were literally hidden from view by their "unconventional" guerrilla tactics. This invisibility also had to be produced ideologically, to deny Cubans and Filipinos representation as equal contestants in political struggle. The romance suggests that the spectacle of American masculinity in the eyes of the female spectator contributes to the disembodiment of the colonized soldier, by denying him political agency and, by extension, masculinity. His invisibility is also produced, paradoxically, by incorporating him as actor into the spectacle of combat.

The theatricalization of the chivalric warrior in these romantic novels was in some sense literally enacted on the battlefields of Cuba and the Philippines. In a scene that marked the end of the battle with Spain for Manila and the beginning of the three-year war against the Filipinos, the Americans faced a dilemma of how to enter the city. The issue was not how best to fight the forces of Spain, whom they had already defeated at sea, but how to occupy Manila without having to share the fruits of victory with Aguinaldo's forces, who had been battling the Spanish for years and had joined with the Americans in expectation of independence. So the U.S. officer in command arranged secretly with the Spanish government of Manila to stage a mock battle, complete with the raising of the white flag (to be postponed in case of bad weather), in which the Spanish would surrender and the Americans would march into the city unaccompanied by their Filipino allies. As a military essayist explained, "our reason for this elaborate stage management seems obvious. It would keep the insurgents out of the city."[60] The Americans and Spanish colluded (as they did in the entry to Santiago, Cuba) in a theater of conquest and capitulation to exclude the Filipinos, who had been fighting for independence. Here the theatricalization of U.S. power worked to render ineffectual Filipino opposition to Spain and the United States. Yet an ironic consequence was that several Filipino troops "mistook" the theater for a real battle, and their shots generated rounds of shooting on both sides that gave unexpected reality to the "Battle of Manila." No wonder then that a reporter noted with surprise that the Filipino insurgents got their parts wrong, that they threw up trenches opposite the American outposts and "acted as if they were besieging us instead of being our 'friends.'"[61]

The historical romance exposes the desire for unlimited control motivating such scenes of staged conquests, which are disrupted by the actions of imperial subjects who do not voluntarily adopt their allotted roles. The novels enact the U.S. fantasy of global conquest without colonial annexation, what Albert Memmi called the ultimate imperial desire for a colony rid of the colonized.[62] This disembodied empire projects imperial conflict as the dramatization of the male self before a domestic audience without the challenge of a military or political contest. It strives to reimagine conquest by effacing any element of conflict.

If the spectacle of American manhood has the political import of denying national agency to the conquered, this repression can never be complete, for the theater itself is open to contest, to improvisation, as it was in Manila. Homi Bhabha has attributed a quality of mimicry to the colonized subject, which leads him to imitate his conquerors, yet yields a space for maneuver and mockery to subvert that identity.[63] In the Battle of Manila, the Filipinos indeed mimicked their assigned theatrical roles by playing them for real. The imperialist agent, however, also engages in a form of mimicry in which he does not retrieve an embodied primal self but assumes shifting theatrical roles which undermine his own agency. His need to turn gunfire into flashing camera lights fixes, destabilizes, and resocializes the identity of the "real live man," by making him contingent on the willing collaboration of the native actor playing a supporting role, and of the domestic spectator validating his image. With the close of the Western frontier, American masculinity turned to the New Empire to recuperate its Anglo-Saxon origins. But this same arena undermined that identity and retrieved the embodied male not in the longed-for primitive wholeness, but through fragmented spectacles in the gaze of the domestic audience. Thus the sight of Theodore Roosevelt on San Juan Hill may be viewed as a highly theatrical and contingent spectacle produced by modern weapons and mass media, both more effective and more vulnerable for that dependence on the technologies the Anglo-Saxon warriors were meant to escape.[64]

Back to the Future

The spectacle's effacement of imperial subjects in the 1890s meant more specifically the denial of their revolutionary agency and national aspirations. The United States belatedly entered the international imperial arena on a double front: against European competitors and the revolutionary anticolonial nationalists in Latin America, the Pacific, and China. The revival of the romance registered this complex historical moment by culminating in a proliferation of novels about the American Revolution, which revive the notion of the anticolonial origins of the republic as the birth of future empire. Furthermore, they redefine and delimit the meaning of revolution to make it inaccessible to others. The historical romances of the 1890s "de-revolutionize" the Revolution, in Michael Kammen's terms, not only to mitigate social conflict at home, as he argues, but also to repossess and neutralize the symbols of the American Revolution that served as a usable past for contemporary revolutions abroad.[65] The novels render revolution on the part of nonwhite people as anarchy in need of imperial salvation.

Before the United States intervened in the Cuban War of Independence, one of the major rhetorical figures deployed by Americans and Cubans to enlist support for the uprising against Spain was the analogy with the American Revolution. The Cuba Libre movement was legitimated as a reenactment of the American Revolution, as its general, Maximo Gomez, was compared to Washington, and its diplomat, Tomas Estrada Palma, to Ben Franklin. In the words of Congressman Sulzer, "Why they are just like us!" in emulating our Revolution.[66] In the immediate reaffiliations during and following the war, this analogy was rapidly dismantled in the United States, where it became more pressing to emphasize difference and show that "they," unlike "us," were incapable of self-government to which revolution aspires. After the war, only anti-imperialists compared Aguinaldo of the Philippines to George Washington, a trope tantamount to treason in its betrayal of the American past, according to imperialists like Senator Beveridge.

Thus if the historical novels addressed an internal crisis of "cultural in-direction" and social conflict, as Kammen argues, they also entered a contested terrain in international political culture, to dispossess other national movements of the language of revolutionary aspirations.

A major tool in this effort of dispossession was the representation of race.[67] While politicians ridiculed the notion of a black or brown George Washington, as did Mark Twain in Hawaii, the novels white-washed the Revolution as an indisputably Anglo-Saxon heritage. In novels by Winston Churchill and S. Weir Mitchell, Washington makes cameo appearances as the epitome of natural aristocracy and virility (demonstrated in one novel through his beating of a black slave out of spontaneous passion and anger). Yet more effective a weapon than the direct representation of race in these novels is the nostalgic narrative of Revolution as return to a fundamental Anglo-Saxon past. Revolu-tion is recast as devolution, a recovery of origins in the figure of the masculine hero rather than a radical break with the past. These ro-mances revile the British less for their tyrannical government than for their degenerate profligacy, and the few glimpses of alternative politi-cal struggles—such as the Indian rebellion in *To Have and To Hold,* or Latin American revolution in *Soldiers of Fortune*—are always conflated with the degeneracy of the British or Spanish empires. Thus revolu-tionary Americans are represented as simply restoring a purer Anglo-Saxon family strain that stays clear of the twinned taints of tyranny and anarchy.

The culmination of the American Revolution in some novels results in the restoration of an inheritance. In *Richard Carvel,* for example, the hero retrieves his father's estate in Maryland. In *Hugh Wynne,* how-ever, the problematic ownership of the ancestral estate in Wales—with which the novel opens—is never resolved; the question of land is made secondary to the recovery of manhood—Hugh Wynne's true heri-tage—from his commercial and pacifist Quaker father and degenerate British cousin. The Revolution as recovered heritage is thus at once di-vorced from European notions of landed inheritance and invested in the American man as the natural aristocrat. Revolution, in these nov-els, thus becomes a uniquely American heritage lodged firmly in the past, safe from the grasp of minorities and immigrants at home and anticolonial nationalists abroad.

If the historical romance rewrites the American Revolution through the lens of nostalgia for primitive origins, its recuperative potential is most fully realized in the figure of the Western cowboy. In his essay "The Evolution of the Cow-Puncher," Owen Wister portrays this quintessential American male as the atavistic reawakening of "slumbering untamed Saxon."[68] Contrary to his title, Wister traces no evolution but instead a return to an essential identity, as "the knight and the cowboy are nothing but the same Saxon of different environments" (81). In this essay, originally entitled "The Course of Empire," Wister draws a continuous line between the knight and the cowboy, as well as between the West, now on the decline, and the dawning American interests in the Pacific. Wister finds the same kernel of the Saxon man, who "has ruled the waves with his ship from that Viking time until yesterday at Samoa . . . from the tournament at Camelot to the round-up at Abilene" (81). When Wister wrote *The Virginian* seven years later, the hero's lineage was already in place.[69]

The modern Western—initiated by *The Virginian* in 1902—has an immediate genealogy in the popular historical novels of the 1890s and their romance of empire. By imagining contemporary American imperialism as the return to an original virile past, the historical romance reopens the closed frontier and reinvents the West as a space for fictional representation. Wister in his introduction explicitly labels his novel a "colonial romance," compares it to *Hugh Wynne,* and introduces it as a more realistic colonial romance than the frillier ones with their "Chippendale Settees" (ix). Moreover, *The Virginian* recapitulates each feature of the romance delineated in this essay, substituting the Wyoming frontier for the mythical Graustark, the Latin American Olancho, or the Holy Land of the Crusaders. Wister's romance opens with its own nostalgia for the closed frontier, a "vanished world" where the world-weary Eastern narrator seeks rejuvenation. There the homeless and nameless Virginian embodies the national essence in his muscular beauty and animal prowess. Yet as Lee Mitchell has pointed out, this hero does not engage in the sharp-shooting violence we have come to expect from the genre.[70] Rather, he defeats a rebellion in a staged theatrical performance before an Eastern audience of travelers, and his physical vigor is composed in the narrator's feminized gaze.

The Virginian also asserts his virility through his chivalrous attention to Molly, the genteel Vermont schoolteacher, who, like the other heroines, proves herself both as spectator and actor, rescuing the hero from Indians. In choosing the Virginian for a mate, she liberates herself from the traditional morality expecting her to marry to save her family financially, and she thereby proves herself worthy of her own more ancient revolutionary heritage. Her older aunt knowingly explains the heroine's attraction to the American hero, defining him tautologically, as does Senator Beveridge: "She wants a man that is a man" (163). The Western neither banishes the woman from a rugged male terrain, nor simply tames her;[71] rather it co-opts her desires and includes her in its pleasures of romancing the empire.

If the historical romance starts with a nostalgic lament for the closed frontier, the revival of the genre collectively reopens that space of the West. Soon after the publication of *The Virginian,* the revival was on the wane, though not without injecting life into the modern Western. We are accustomed to think of certain ways in which the Western frontier was violently exported to the New Empire in Cuba and the Philippines (and in later imperial wars of the twentieth century): in the form of soldiers (many of whom were veterans of Indian wars); as social policy (the resettlement of native Filipinos according to the plans of Indian reservations); and in vibrant symbols—Roosevelt's Rough Riders. Just as important, however, has been the way in which American imperialism reclaimed and galvanized the meaning of the West as the site of origins. The quintessential twentieth-century symbol of American nationhood—the lone self-reliant cowboy on the frontier—has endured parasitically by feeding on new outposts of the American empire. As the precursor of the modern Western, the historical novel of the 1890s romances the empire with a potent nostalgia that renders imperial conquest and the struggle for power over others as nothing more than the return home to the embodied American man.

CHAPTER 4

Black and Blue on San Juan Hill

If the historical romance reopened the Western frontier through the route of overseas empire, the same genre also contributed to bringing the South back into the new imperial nation. In novels about the Civil War and Reconstruction, medieval kingdoms abroad were replaced by the phantom tyranny of freed slaves at home, from which chivalric Southern heroes rescued their white heroines. Through sentimental marriage plots, these novels enacted the reconciliation of North and South in what Nina Silber has called the "romance of reunion."[1] In some of these romances, the resolution of the domestic plot relies on the pivotal eruption of a foreign war. In one popular example, Thomas Dixon's *The Leopard's Spots: A Romance of the White Man's Burden,* the Spanish-American War intervenes like a *deus ex machina* to unify white men in chivalrous rescue of white women from black men and of the white nation from black Reconstruction.[2]

For Dixon, the war against Spain finally puts to rest the question repeated like an anxious refrain throughout the novel: "Shall the future American be an Anglo-Saxon or a mulatto?" The answer is provided by two climactic events: the alleged rape of a white girl by a black man, and U.S. intervention in the Cuban Independence War. The war does for the entire nation what the imagined rape does for the small town: "in a moment the white race had fused into one homogeneous mass" out of former secessionists and unionists, rich and poor, Protestant and Catholic" (368). According to Dixon, "almost every problem of national life had been illumined and made more hopeful by the searchlight of war—save one—the irrepressible conflict between the African and the Anglo-Saxon in the development of our civilization. The glare of the war only made the blackness of the question the more apparent" (506). Yet the war also provides a white answer, when the menacing presence of armed black soldiers—the final affront of Reconstruction—provokes and empowers the white men of the town to declare their second Independence (the town's name)—this time from black occupation.

Dixon casts the imperial war as a new war of independence, fought not by Cubans and Filipinos, but by Southern whites against a black empire. Freed from federal control, the whites banish all politically powerful blacks and use the threat of lynching to subdue the rest to pre-Civil War submissiveness. The domestic consequence of the foreign war in *The Leopard's Spots* is that the "Anglo-Saxon race had been reunited. The Negro was no longer the ward of the Republic" (407). In the climactic chapter entitled "The New American," the war with Spain transforms white supremacy overnight from an outdated regional identity to a definition of modern American nationhood in the global arena.

What Virginia Woolf wrote of books, that they "continue each other," can also be said of wars: wars continue each other.[3] Wars generate and accumulate symbolic value by reenacting, reinterpreting, and transposing the cultural meanings of prior wars. *The Leopard's Spots* dramatizes a popular representation of the Spanish-American War as a continuation and resolution of the Civil War, as its purgative final battle. Politicians and journalists represented the war with Spain as a nostalgic recovery of the heroism of an earlier generation, and as an antidote that could heal the wounds and divisiveness of the internecine war. If the hundred-day brevity of the later conflict counteracted the interminable length of the earlier one, the international war also promised to reunify the nation by bringing together the North and the South against a common external enemy. Moreover, new battlefields abroad reputedly restored health and vigor to the male body, so massively dismembered in the war between the states. As the preface to a Civil War novel published in 1898 states: "on the heights of Santiago we see men of the South standing shoulder to shoulder with men of the North, mingling their blood victoriously under the old Flag, while the world looks on with admiration not unmixed with fear."[4] The male body became the symbolic medium for national restoration, as "the heritage of American manhood" represented the common ground between previously warring factions.

As Dixon's romance makes evident, in order to continue fighting the Civil War on the "road to reunion" as the final destination, representations of the Spanish-American War had to collapse the thirty-year history separating the two conflicts by waging a discursive battle against Reconstruction.[5] The imagined continuity between the two wars was disrupted by Reconstruction's conflicted legacy: by the former slaves' struggle for freedom and full citizenship on the one hand, and on the other by the white supremacist reaction that imposed disfranchisement, legal segregation, and lynching as a way of life in the South. During the era of Jim Crow, white supremacists did battle on two related fronts: the foreign wars against Spain and its colonies aspiring for national independence, and the domestic struggle against African Americans fighting to achieve civil and political rights. What then is the position of African Americans in relation to the Union reconfigured by the Spanish-American War and to the newly colonized subjects of the U.S. empire? Would these Cubans, Puerto Ricans, and Filipinos be assimilated into a post-Reconstruction model of race relations at home, and would the empire abroad facilitate the subjugation of blacks as colonized subjects at home? Would African Americans identify the fight for civil rights and national identity at home with anticolonial struggles for national independence abroad? Or would they fight for citizenship at home by aligning themselves with the U.S. imperial project abroad?

These questions were addressed in 1899 by African American author Sutton Griggs in his romance, *Imperium in Imperio: A Study of the Negro Problem*.[6] While the Spanish-American War ties together Dixon's plot of national reconciliation, the eruption of that same war in *Imperium* unravels the narrative of black national unity and leaves African Americans homeless, in a no-man's-land between nation and empire. Griggs tells the story of the creation of an underground black nation, the Imperium, founded to redress the gaps in the American Constitution to protect and enfranchise African Americans and to "unite all Negroes in a body." At the height of the Imperium's organizational success, two events radically disrupt it: the sinking of the *Maine,* and the lynching of a federally appointed postmaster and his family in

South Carolina (based on the actual mob murder of Postmaster Frazier Baker in 1898). These two crises throw the Imperium into discord about whether or not to join the United States in the fight for Cuban independence, which most members saw as a black movement, "as the Cubans were in a large measure Negro" (210). The radical voice of the founder prevails and convinces the Imperium to side with the foreign enemies of the United States in order to seize the state of Texas as a separate black nation. The heinous lynching fuels his characterization of African Americans as colonial subjects within the United States, where the "Negro finds himself an unprotected foreigner in his own home" (182) and where whites "have chosen our race as an empire, and each Anglo-Saxon regards himself as a petty King and some gang or community of Negroes for his subjects" (218). The more moderate President of the Imperium rejects this revolutionary course, however, and urges his constituency to remain within the Union to fight for full citizenship and equal rights. The President demonstrates his double allegiance to the "imperium in imperio" by willingly submitting to his own execution for the treason he committed by rejecting the decision of the Imperium to secede, and by wanting to be buried with an American flag. The narrator of the book, we later discover, is one of the executioners, who, horrified by the possibility of an unleashed race war, betrays the Imperium in the interest of peace and lives long enough to tell the tale as a "traitor," the first word of the book.

Thus for Griggs and Dixon alike, the advent of an imperial war abroad narrowly averts another civil war at home, this time a race war between whites and blacks. In this trade-off, African Americans serve as the medium of exchange to pay the cost of national reunion: in Dixon's novel by their expulsion and subordination, and in Griggs's by their paralyzing and unresolved double allegiance in which patriotism and treason are intertwined.

In these fictional fantasies, the representation of empire functions both as an external catalyst that intensifies domestic racial conflicts and as a medium for their resolution. A similar dynamic is at work in popular journalistic accounts of the U.S. role in the Cuban War for Independence. Focusing on conflicting accounts of the famous battle of San Juan Hill, I argue that the spectacle of imperial masculinity was challenged by the presence and writings of African American soldiers, who troubled the racial divisions between colonizer and colonized and the assumed identification between race and nationhood. When writing about Cuba in *The Rough Riders,* Theodore Roosevelt anxiously differentiated his image of American masculinity not only from Cubans and Spaniards, but also from African American troops who were fighting alongside him. In letters to the black press, African American soldiers criticized the export of Jim Crow segregation to imperial outposts abroad, and also saw these sites as opportunities to claim a form of imperial citizenship and militant manhood at home. In projecting U.S. racial anxieties onto the battlefield of Cuba, writers fought multiple skirmishes over the claims of nonwhite peoples for self-government at home and abroad. The triumphal narrative of national reunion was predicated on the anarchy of empire: on the dissolution of the boundaries between the foreign and the domestic that imperial battlefields were meant to reinforce.

The Showdown

The charge up San Juan Hill can easily be debunked or demystified, and it has been since the earliest reports of the war: it was not heroic, but a military fiasco; not a massive orderly charge, but a straggling line of desperate soldiers, pitilessly exposed to enemy fire; not even the romantic San Juan Hill, but the more mundane "Kettle Hill" (itself an apocryphal name). By now it is more useful to understand how the battle of San Juan Hill was produced as an icon, precisely because it processed, contained, and crystallized multivalent and contradictory political meanings into a monumental frieze. In looking closely at the representations of this legendary battle in the white and black press accounts of the time, we can see a battle raging over the interconnected representations of race, manhood, nation, and empire.

No American has remained more visible and virile in the iconography of San Juan Hill than Theodore Roosevelt, leading his Rough Riders. In Richard Harding Davis's words, "he was without doubt, the most conspicuous figure in the charge . . . mounted high on horseback, and charging the rifle-pits at a gallop and quite alone, [he] made you feel that you would like to cheer."[7] In contrast to his own conspicuousness, in his account of the battle (which first appeared in

Scribner's in April 1899 and later in *The Rough Riders*), Roosevelt commented that it was "astonishing what a limited area of vision and experience one has in the hurly-burly of a battle."[8] In fact, so limited was his vision that he only killed one Spanish soldier, whom he could see at point-blank. He did it with a revolver from the sunken battleship *Maine,* given to him by a brother-in-law in the navy.

In marked contrast to this blurred vision is the remarkable clarity with which Roosevelt notes the presence of black American soldiers, "completely intermingled" with his own troops. "Such mixing," he explains, "was inevitable in making repeated charges through thick jungle," but was in need of "reforming" under his command (135). As the U.S. troops entrenched themselves on the top of San Juan Hill, Roosevelt's narrative retrenched along racial lines. The battle concluded without a cathartic shootout with Spanish soldiers, but with a sustained confrontation with African American soldiers that caps the horizontal narrative, throughout the report, of the increasing intermingling of blacks and whites. An emblem of this happening is the figure of the color sergeant of the black Tenth Regiment, who ended up bearing his own colors and those of the white Third Regiment as well (whose flag bearer was killed).

Toward the end of the battle, Roosevelt notes that neither white regulars nor volunteers were weakening, in contrast to the "strain of the colored infantrymen" whose white officers had been killed, and who were left as masterless men in vague affiliation with Roosevelt's troops. When the black soldiers started to drift to the rear to join their own regiment or transport the wounded, Roosevelt perceives them as "depleting my line" and confronts them violently and theatrically: "So I jumped up, and walking a few yards to the rear, drew my revolver, halted the retreating soldiers, and called out to them that I appreciated the gallantry with which they had fought and would be sorry to hurt them, but that I should shoot the first man, who on any pretense whatever went to the rear" (138). When he vows to keep his word, all of his men watched with "utmost interest"; his "cow-punchers, hunters, and miners solemnly nodded their heads and commented in chorus, exactly as if in a comic opera, 'He always does, he always does!'" (138). Roosevelt claims that his show worked when the black soldiers, the "'smoked Yankees'—as the Spaniards called them," played their own minstrel parts. They "flashed their white teeth at one another, as they broke into broad grins, and I had no more trouble with them" (139). Roosevelt concludes this confrontation with a paean to racial harmony and national unity: "they seem[ed] to accept me as one of their officers," and the Rough Riders, with their "strong color prejudice, grew to accept them with hearty good-will as comrades, and were entirely willing, in their own phrase, 'to drink out of the same canteen'" (139). At this point in the narrative, with racial trenches dug deeply and national unity thus affirmed, Roosevelt can return to the battle in a roll call that named and praised the gallantry of the individual Rough Riders, as though their individual integrity had been protected by his confrontation with African American troops.

This showdown on San Juan Hill, which serves as both the climax to and digression from the narrative of the battle, raises several interesting questions. Why did the presence of African American soldiers loom so large to Roosevelt as to disrupt the uphill thrust against the Spanish troops, and why the counter-narrative about the racial intermixing of American soldiers? Why did the potential absence of the African Americans in returning to their regiments appear even more disturbing? In addition, why is the scene at once so startlingly violent and yet so comically theatrical?

There is a familiar trope in war fiction and journalism of dislocation and loss of vision on the battlefield, in response to which a visual anchor must be found—a comrade, a flag, a feature of the landscape—to reorient the soldier and reader. For Roosevelt, black and white intermingling provided an emblem of chaos as well as a familiar footing or anchor. Roosevelt's confrontation with the black troops reestablished the reassuring order of the domestic color line in a foreign terrain, as their heightened visibility displaced and compensated for the occluded vision of the Cuban political landscape. Intermixing was not the only challenge to Roosevelt's order, posed by black soldiers in blue uniforms. Their presence raised white fear of armed insurrection and of national self-representation, which African American soldiers pursued in their printed rebuttals of Roosevelt's account. This double threat of revolt and representation resonated with the struggle for independence of the Cuban revolutionaries, whom the U.S. soldiers were sent to liberate and to subdue at the same time. While the United

States sought the unification of a white nation in the clearly demarcated lines of the imperial battlefield, Roosevelt instead found evidence of anarchy in the blurring of racial boundaries.

"Alone in Cuba"[9]

This scene of domestic racial confrontation in *The Rough Riders* cannot be separated from its international context of shifting alliances and conflicts between Americans and Cubans. The United States entered a war in which the Spanish colonial regime was losing ground before the Cuban insurgent army that had been fighting the War for Independence since 1895. This war was the culmination of three anticolonial wars that had started in 1868. One of the turning points of the most recent war occurred at the end of 1895, when the insurgent army, which had been more powerful in the east, succeeded in invading the western provinces of Cuba, with the help of many of the civilian inhabitants. A major factor in the success of the insurrection, according to Ada Ferrer, was the widespread acceptance of a multiracial army—fifteen years after the abolition of slavery—as the agent and symbol of Cuban nationhood. The white Cubans' fears of black insurrection in a slave-holding society had doomed the earlier anticolonial struggles for independence.[10] Although the army remained ridden with racial and class conflicts and tensions that would inform the new nation as well, the reality and image of men of all races fighting together were crucial to the military and political movements for Cuban independence. The United States entered the war not only to "liberate" Cuba from Spain, but also to have control over what happened in Cuba in the aftermath of that war. In tandem with the military and political maneuvering to exclude Cuban soldiers from participating in the surrender of Spain in Santiago, race became a major tool in representing them as unmanly and cowardly, and Cuba itself as incapable of self-government and national sovereignty.

In their reports of the war, U.S. journalists were remapping the political coordinates of the Cuban battlefield to erase and supplant Cuban narratives of their long revolutionary struggle against Spain. A repeated theme that emerges from the reports of the Cuban battlefield is the contrast between the invisibility of the Cuban allies and Spanish enemy, and the almost suicidal conspicuousness of the U.S.

troops. As many reporters commented, in contrast to the Spanish who hid in trenches or sniped from behind trees, and the Cuban insurgents who cowered behind their putative liberators, the American soldiers marched out into clear view. They offered an inviting target made even more obvious by their outdated smoking guns, in contrast to the modern smokeless weapons of the Spaniards. In addition, reporters noted the large lumbering observation balloon sent up ahead of the troops, which proved not only impotent in surveying enemy positions, but even worse, drew dramatic attention to the position of the U.S. soldiers and turned them into open targets.[11]

The lack of overarching surveillance presented a problem of representation as well as of military strategy. As one photographer for *Harper's Weekly* explained, "Although I was thus on the first firing line, and many men were wounded and killed all about me, as you will see by my photographs. . . . I found it impossible to make any actual 'battle scenes,' for many reasons—the distance at which the fighting is conducted, the area which is covered, but chiefly the long grasses and thickly wooded country."[12] This absence of a "scene," a framed context for the wounded bodies, is due to more than the hindrance of the landscape; it is the result also of a kind of political myopia. Whereas Elaine Scarry has argued that wounded bodies in warfare give meaning to an otherwise abstract political conflict, I would suggest the reverse here; the spotlight on wounded bodies effaces the political context by fetishizing those bodies as the only meaningful focal point.[13] In other words, the conspicuousness of American bodies and the corresponding invisibility of all other combatants had to be produced ideologically as subject positions, not just perceived as military maneuvers. The positions were plotted in part by a narrative that located the U.S. entry into the war as the point of historical origin and effaced all prior history of the Cuban struggle against Spain.

Although the exposure of the U.S. soldier was lamented as strategically suicidal, it had the important discursive effect of defining American masculinity itself. Report after report praised officers for needlessly yet gallantly standing up in full view under fire, and the charge was portrayed as a kind of grandstanding conspicuousness of sheer bodies hurling themselves up the hill against impregnable trenches. Pictorial representations depict the battle from the point of view of the artist looking up the hill behind the troops and drawing their backs.

But a figure usually breaks this perspective by turning around frontally to the spectator, even when he is shooting ahead of him. Rather than confront the enemy, he turns to pose for an audience at home.[14]

The spectacle of the American male body remapped the coordinates of the battlefield to wrest away political agency from the Cubans fighting for independence, a process put in motion as soon as the U.S. troops landed in Cuba. Roosevelt's first impression of the insurgents was that of a "crew of as utter tatterdemalions as human eyes ever looked on, armed with every kind of rifle in all stages of dilapidation." Their appearance did not lead him and many others to think of the dire material context in which the Cuban insurgents had been fighting for three years, only to expect "that they would be no use in serious fighting, but it was hoped that they might be of service in scouting" (71). When the battle began, however, Roosevelt was disappointed (but not surprised) to find that the Cuban guide at the head of the column ran away at the first sign of fighting. He contrasts this figure with two Americans who remained, "who though noncombatants—newspaper correspondents—showed as much gallantry as any soldier in the field" (82). The replacement of Cuban scouts with U.S. newspaper reporters is apt; better guides in remapping the coordinates of the battlefield to foreground the spectacle of American manhood, they supplant the Cuban map of the complex political terrain that antedated U.S. intervention. This triangulation of the soldier with the journalist and domestic audience recuperates an image of American masculinity by denying masculinity and political agency to the Cubans, whose long revolutionary struggle is made to disappear.[15]

The imperial desire to write out the role of Cubans in their own revolution may explain the importance of journalistic heroics in the cultural representations of what had been dubbed "The Correspondents' War." Earlier, the yellow press of Hearst and Pulitzer captured the public eye by its sensationalist coverage of Spanish atrocities and its call for U.S. intervention. The papers became known for staging many of the spectacles they reported, as in the famous apocryphal story about Frederick Remington and Randolph Hearst. When in 1896 the illustrator complained that nothing was happening in Cuba, Hearst reportedly responded, "You furnish the pictures and I'll furnish the war." The pivotal western invasion by the Cuban insurgent forces apparently did not fit the bill of "war." To keep his promise of selling the "journalism that acted," Hearst filled his front pages with Spanish atrocities at the same time that he started the modern sports age. Both Hearst and Pulitzer made the news they reported by sending reporters on special spy missions, by leading rescue campaigns of Cuban ladies (as we saw in the Cisneros case), or by using their own yachts—transporting their journalists—to capture Spanish refugees. These spectacles often featured the reporter himself as the chief actor, at a time when international imperial warfare gave birth to the "foreign correspondent" as a professional writer with a public persona. Bylines changed "from our own correspondent" to personal names, and headlines sometimes included the name of the reporter as a celebrity; for instance, "Stephen Crane at the Front for the World." Reporters often made themselves or their colleagues the heroes of their stories, and depicted the act of reporting as the main plot. This focus turned writing into a strenuous activity, and the reporter into a virile figure who rivaled the soldiers. By dramatizing the exploits of the reporters, newspapers transformed complex political and military conflicts with long histories into romantic adventures in exotic landscapes.

This displacement is starkly visible in the case of Stephen Crane, who both played and parodied the heroic correspondent by theatrically exposing himself to bullets under fire and by "capturing" a Puerto Rican town in a mock invasion.[16] His own report of the battle for San Juan Hill, aptly titled "Stephen Crane's Vivid Story of the Battle of San Juan," works to remove Cuban participants from the fight he turns into a spectacle of American virility.[17] Crane represents the charge as a sporting event, referring to the absent audience who "would give an arm to get the thrill of patriotic insanity that coursed through us," as well as to the international audience of foreign diplomats who were shocked and impressed by such foolish gallantry (158). On a populist note, Crane also views the fight as a "grand popular movement" led by the "gallantry of the American private soldier" whose officers were left behind (155). Yet when the Americans reach the top of the hill to entrench themselves for the night, Crane abruptly interrupts his narrative and shifts from the upward battle for Santiago to the horizontal struggle with U.S. allies, the Cuban insurgents. "It becomes necessary to speak of the men's opinion of the Cubans," pauses Crane. "To put it shortly, both officers and privates have the most lively contempt for the Cubans" (163). Class divisions within the U.S. army between privates and officers—which Crane previously celebrated—are healed in their common disdain for their allies.

Crane's article never returns to the continuation of the battle, but instead backtracks to review the same events in terms of Cuban non-participation. While the Americans "sprinkled a thousand bodies in the grass," not a single Cuban was visible. Once an "efficient body," the insurgents have now become "no more useless body of men anywhere," demoralized and emasculated by American aid (163). While the Americans fight, the Cubans are only interested in stuffing themselves with U.S. rations. Thus the end of Crane's narrative of the charge up San Juan Hill is neither the conquest of Santiago nor combat with Spanish soldiers, but the appropriation of the Cuban uprising as a North American popular movement and the displacement of lazy, inefficient, hungry Cubans with the spectacle of aggressive American manhood.

Crane's report has the effect of excising the Cubans from the battle in which their fighting was essential.[18] Although the U.S. army command forcibly excluded the Cuban command from participating in the decisive events and decisions of the war, the journalistic representations of the Cubans as cowardly, undisciplined, and unsoldierly—in short, unmanly—blamed them for their disappearance from the scene. Even Crane's depiction of Cubans and North Americans fighting side by side in an earlier battle undermines their alliance by turning the Cubans into a backdrop or foil against which the erect "strong figures" of the Americans are composed. In contrast to the "business-like" marines, for example, the Cubans are described as "a hard-bitten, under-sized lot, most of them Negroes, and with the stoop and gait of men who had at one time labored at the soil. They were in short peasants—hardy, tireless, uncomplaining peasants—and they viewed in utter calm these early morning preparations for battle."[19] While these peasants show no capacity to reflect on their position, "contrary to the Cubans, the bronze faces of the Americans were not stolid at all" (135). When they fight, Crane comments on the "rock-like beautiful poise" of the marines taking aim, which "one noticed the more on account of the Cubans who used the Lee as if it were a squirt gun." In the midst of fighting, "toiling, sweating marines" stand out against "shrill jumping Cubans" (138). Finally, when a Cuban is hit, he is described as "a great hulking Negro" who "seemed in no pain; it seemed as if he were senseless before he fell." And when a fellow soldier carries him, they appear not as comrades in arms, but "the procession that moved off resembled a grotesque wheelbarrow" (138). Thus while the overt narrative trajectory of these reports pits the U.S. army against the Spanish, the detailed representation pits American bodies against Cuban ones to disaffiliate them as allies. Whether stolid or hysterical, the Cubans relinquish control to the U.S. troops and become a passive yardstick for measuring their prowess. By the end of the battle for San Juan Hill, Crane sees the dependency of the Cuban on the American as a de facto abdication of his right to independence: "If he stupidly drowsily remains out of these fights, what weight is his voice to have later in the final adjustments?" The Cubans themselves are "the worst thing for the cause of an independent Cuba that could possibly exist" (164).

In a battle showcasing American masculinity, the Cubans forfeit their identity as men in the eyes of U.S. journalists: "the more our commanding officers see of the Cubans the less they appear to think of them as soldiers or as men."[20] The pivot for this differentiation is often linked to their perceived racial identity, as another reporter notes: "I have seen degradation in Negro slaves, but never have I seen such degradation as a Cuban exhibits in everything that means manhood."[21] It is a short leap from their absence from the front line to their insufficiency as men, to their racial identity as Negro (which visually looms large for Crane), to the impossibility of their nationhood. As one correspondent concludes, "I ask where is the Cuban nation. There is no Cuba. There is no Cuban people. There are no freemen here to whom we could deliver this marvelous land."[22] In reporting on the war, U.S. journalists mobilized the post-Reconstruction discourse of race to represent the multiracial insurrection force of Cuba as not only incapable of self-government, but as incapable of even fighting for independence in the first place.[23]

Racing the Empire

We can now juxtapose the climax of Crane's narrative atop San Juan Hill—the disaffiliation from the Cubans—with that of Roosevelt's story—disciplining African American troops. In both cases, the narrative shifts from conflict with an external enemy, Spain, to internal struggles with reputed allies. These breaks signal a disruption not only in political alliances but also in the links among representations of national, racial, and gendered identities. If Crane's narrative renders Cubans invisible as military political agents, in what ways might Roosevelt have displaced them with the heightened visibility of African American troops in need of control? Roosevelt, after all, claims that he forced the "smoked Yankees" not to run away as the Cubans did, but to stay and be men under his command. Yet if Cubans are dismissed as unmanly and incapable of nationhood partly on the basis of racial identity, how might the black soldiers in blue uniforms reinforce, undermine, or further complicate this dismissal? And what does their presence mean for the constitution of U.S. nationhood in the male body? What then is the relationship between the forced abdication of Cubans from the military and political battlefields and the representation and forced placement of African American soldiers in the front line under Roosevelt's command?

Consider that Roosevelt did not simply relate a tale of battle but that he was implicitly engaged in unspoken debate with counter-narratives in several overlapping contexts. Though published less than a year after the war, Roosevelt's narrative was one of the documents involved in a struggle over writing the history of that war, a struggle in part against an African American narrative of black heroism that had gained some currency. For a brief moment after the war, black regiments were acknowledged for their heroism by the black and white press, homecoming parades, and congressional medals, evidence which African Americans used to bolster the case for black commissioned officers.[24] Accounts of several battles took on legendary stature in which black troops preceded the Rough Riders up San Juan Hill by cutting through barbed wire, rescued the Rough Riders from a Spanish ambush, and launched the charge with the shout of a black trooper. Even a member of the Rough Riders conceded, "if it had not been for the Negro Cavalry, the Rough Riders would have been exterminated."[25]

These stories first circulated in the black press through the publication of letters from black soldiers serving as foreign correspondents, whom African American newspapers could not afford to hire. The letters often aimed at correcting the omissions or distortions of the white press. An unsigned letter to the *Illinois Record*, for example, contends that "it was never mentioned how at the famous charge of the 10th

Cav. and the rescue of the Rough Riders at San Juan Hill, the yell was started by a single trooper of C Troop, 10th Cavalry and was carried down the line . . . Will it ever be known how Sgt. Thomas Griffith of Troop C cut the wire fence along the line so the 10th Cav. and Rough Riders could go through?"[26] Other letters contrasted the heroic fight at San Juan Hill waged by black and white troops together, with the "hellish" treatment of black troops at home: "Both were under the same flag, both wore the blue, and yet these black boys, heroes of our country, were not allowed to stand at the counters of restaurants and eat a sandwich and drink a cup of coffee, while the white soldiers were welcomed and invited to sit down at tables and eat free of cost." Black soldiers also related the current war to the Civil War, less to emphasize sectional reunion than to continue the battle for freedom at home and claim the legacy of black militancy, to show that "the coolness and bravery that characterized our fathers in the 60s have been handed down to their sons of the 90s."[27]

African American newspapers repeatedly lambasted the white press for never mentioning the names of individual black soldiers and for ignoring their contributions. Roosevelt's account of San Juan Hill raised special outrage for its blatant distortions of accomplishments that had entered the public limelight. African American soldiers and correspondents regarded Roosevelt's account, and the white press coverage in general, as a national conflict over the public narration of history, a conflict with as vital political consequences at home as those of the international war abroad. As John R. Conn underscored in the ending of his letter on the battle to *The Evening Star*, "the sword rested while the pen fought."[28] Presley Holliday, a member of the Tenth Cavalry, ended his detailed rebuttal of Roosevelt's account in a letter to the *New York Age*: "I could give many other incidents of our men's devotion to duty, of their determination to stay until death, but what's the use? Colonel Roosevelt has said they shirked, and the reading public will take the Colonel at his word."[29] Holliday thus situates Roosevelt's account in a rigged contest over public words, in which Roosevelt's narrative overrides the words with which Holliday ends his letter: "No officers, no soldiers."[30]

One political stake in this struggle was the campaign for the appointment of African American commissioned officers, a cause which the military successes of the black regiments were used to bolster.[31]

Roosevelt's account explicitly contributed to the argument against black officers, which he based on common stereotypes: the natural servitude of blacks, their lack of discipline, and their incapacity for self-governance. Describing his "mixed force" on the San Juan heights, which included black infantrymen without white officers, Roosevelt insisted at length that the troops were "peculiarly dependent on their white officers" (137); in contrast to the white regulars and his Rough Riders, who could fight on their own even if their officers were killed, "with the colored troops," he asserted, "there should always be some of their own officers" (137). After the showdown with the "smoked Yankees," he praised the white officers of the Ninth and Tenth, under whose leadership "the colored troops did as well as any soldiers could possibly do" (139). In an unsigned letter a black soldier insisted, on the contrary, that the white Southern officer of the Tenth never led his regiment, for which he only showed racist contempt, but instead stayed behind while they faced death. In the correspondent's words, "who showed cowardice, the gallant colonel or his regiment?"[32] Roosevelt's threat to shoot the black troops thus forced them into a submissive role to prove his point retrospectively, since in fact many of the white officers were either killed or lagged behind and the black soldiers did indeed fight independently. The initiative taken by white privates ahead of their officers, which Crane praised as a popular movement, Roosevelt found intolerable on the part of black privates. They must have conjured up the anarchic specter of armed blacks out of control, of racial intermixing as political insurrection, an image equally incendiary at home and abroad.

   In establishing himself as their accepted officer, Roosevelt implicitly linked the political fate of African Americans in the United States to that of Cuban nationalists. An argument similar to that about the need for white officers to discipline black soldiers was made about the need for U.S. government to discipline the Cubans by radically circumscribing their sovereignty as a nation. The Platt Amendment, forced on the Cuban constitution in 1901, gave the United States unlimited right to intervene in the new nation, militarily and economically. As the military Commander Leonard Wood wrote to his friend Roosevelt, "There is, of course, little or no independence left Cuba under the Platt Amendment."[33] The Cubans' perceived racial identity as Negro was used as an argument about their incapacity for self-government and their need for supervision. Recognizing this link between racism at home and abroad, the African American press protested Wood's imposition of Jim Crow segregation on Cuba. Filipinos at the same time were similarly portrayed as stereotypically "Negroid" in popular writing and political cartoons, and their racial inferiority was used as an argument for annexation.[34]

This interchangeability of colonized subjects marked by homologous racial identity became a contested signifier, however, open to conflicting political interpretations. As in the 1848 argument against annexing Mexico, Southern Democrats deployed their belief in the unfitness of inferior races for self-government as an argument against colonial annexation of the Philippines, to keep these nonwhites out of the republic.[35] This negative identification of Cubans, African Americans, and Filipinos as "colored" found contradictory political interpretations among African Americans. Some argued for the efficacy of incorporating black Americans into the imperial project because of their ability to mediate between the United States and its nonwhite colonies. Several African American soldiers wrote from Cuba and the Philippines encouraging blacks to emigrate there and take advantage of economic opportunities relatively free of the color prejudice entrenched at home.[36] More often, this identification contributed to an adamant political position against American imperialism. Many editorials in the black press took the side of the "men of our own hue and color" and decried the exportation of post-Reconstruction disfranchisement, segregation laws, and the resurgence of violence and virulent racism to the new outposts of empire.[37] The *Washington Bee*, for example, excoriated Wood's effort to limit suffrage in municipal elections in Cuba as worthy of the most racist politicians in Mississippi and Louisiana:

> In other words, the men who have furnished the brawn and sinew of the many wars which have been fought for Cuban independence must accept under the benign influence of American policy to be relegated to the rear and denied the privilege of participating in a government to secure that which cost the blacks so many lives that they had to offer upon the sacred altar of liberty. The excuse that the blacks are illiterate is the same blarney that comes from the South today.[38]

This editorial mobilizes images of black heroism for an anti-imperialist argument on behalf of Cuban independence, which echoes the claims made for the full rights of citizenship earned by black soldiers from the United States. The links between disfranchisement in occupied Cuba and the Jim Crow South point to imperialism as the exporter of the domestic color line and recontextualize racism at home as part of a global imperial strategy of rule.

When Roosevelt published his account almost a year after the battle, the events on San Juan Hill had already become less important than their refraction through the lenses of their consequences: the postwar debates about the viability of U.S. imperialism and the fitness of non-whites at home and abroad for self-government. Roosevelt's account was published during the U.S. war against Filipino nationalists, whom he viewed as no more capable of nationhood than were black troops capable of fighting alone. While confronting and subordinating African Americans within the national body, Roosevelt was simultaneously making a place for newly colonized subjects in the disembodied U.S. empire.

It would be historically inaccurate and theoretically simplistic to collapse the relations of the imperial United States to Filipinos, Cubans, Puerto Ricans, Hawaiians, and African Americans into a monolithic model of colonized and colonizer. Such a model not only assumes a false coherence in the identity of the colonizer, but also ignores the historical and global differences among colonized subjects and their relation to empire. Roosevelt, for instance, suffered a double vision: on the one hand identifying African Americans with, and on the other hand differentiating them from, the imagined unassimilable Cubans, Filipinos, and Puerto Ricans. If the Cubans could be "given" nominal independence, Puerto Ricans relegated to "disembodied shades," and the Philippines annexed as a colony, African Americans posed more of a problem for the Republican Roosevelt. He had to represent them within the national body, a problem magnified by their presence in uniform abroad.

In its anarchic mixture of races, the imperial battlefield may have mirrored to Roosevelt the domestic urban site he had recently left as police commissioner of New York City, and he would have brought his experience with non-Anglo-Saxon immigrants from the city to bear on the heights of San Juan Hill. In a revealing letter to Frederick Jackson Turner, Roosevelt complained he did not have time to work on his history of the West because of his duties as police commissioner.[39] His duties at that time included a controversial and ultimately unsuccessful effort to enforce the excise tax and blue laws in a struggle against Tammany Hall, which would have shut down saloons on Sunday and regulated drinking laws in the immigrant communities—especially the German and Irish. For Roosevelt these laws would have accomplished what the frontier did, according to Turner: create individual Americans. Blue laws would have contributed to the Americanization of immigrants by restricting their cultural practice of gathering at the beer garden or the pub. In disciplining African American troops on San Juan Hill, Roosevelt was exercising the regulatory power of Americanization that eluded his grasp on the streets of New York. (Politically, he would have viewed Tammany Hall as formidable opposition and African Americans as traditional clients of the Republican Party.) Roosevelt's narrative on San Juan Hill disciplined African American troops in a subordinated integration to deny them the autonomy and equality they sought within the army. He forced them into the body politic at gun point, and Americanized them by keeping them in their place—simultaneously in the line of fire and in the color line.

In a rebuttal of Roosevelt in *The New York Age*, Presley Holliday of the Tenth Cavalry explained that the African American soldiers who broke the line found racial "intermingling" intimidating because it already embodied the hierarchical social order Roosevelt was trying to assert:

> It is a well known fact, that in this country most persons of color feel out of place when they are by force compelled to mingle with white persons, especially strangers. . . . Some of our men (and these were all recruits with less than six months' service) felt so much out of place that when firing lulled, often showed their desire to be with their commands . . . White soldiers do not as a rule, share this feeling with colored soldiers. The fact that a white man knows how well he can make a place for himself among colored people need not be discussed here.[40]

What Holliday omits from the discussion points to the violent effort in making this "place" for the white man by subduing the potential of autonomous black agency. Roosevelt was trying to incorporate and to Americanize black soldiers in a racially "mixed lot" by forcing them to stay within the national line of defense, reasserting the color line at the same time to forge the bond of national unity. According to him, only by remaining in line, under white command, could black troops achieve entry into the ranks of American nationhood.

In positioning African Americans in a nationalist hierarchy, Roosevelt was also constructing what Holliday called the unique place of the white man among nonwhites, to protect the special connection between white manhood and American nationhood. The phrase "smoked Yankees" implicitly defines "real Yankees" as Anglo-Saxon and contributes to the popular understanding of that term in its double meaning as a biological racial category and a political historical category, denoting the exclusive originating power and present capacity for self-government. The designation "smoked Yankees" aligns the volunteer Rough Riders, often derided in the press for their theatrical playacting, with the white regulars, professional soldiers, against the black regulars of the Tenth Cavalry, who had gained the nickname Buffalo Soldiers for their fighting in the Indian wars. The visual image of "smoked Yankees" suggests whites fighting in blackface and implicitly relegates these professional soldiers to the role of comic actors, mimics, or masked performers with no agency of their own. In *A New Negro*, Booker T. Washington speculated that Roosevelt was anxious about having his Rough Riders linked with black troops by the press, which was most interested in the novelty of how both the "colored" troops and Roosevelt's flamboyant volunteers would perform under fire.[41] Roosevelt's fear that the amateur Rough Riders would not be taken seriously as soldiers is projected onto the theatrical image of the grinning blackface soldiers. In this realignment, which makes black regulars dependent on white volunteers, Roosevelt also defends the virile image of the Rough Riders against the stories circulating about black troops rescuing the Riders from ambush or abetting their charge. Such narratives would have severely compromised the image of the Rough Riders' autonomy—cowboys on a new frontier—as well as their role as chivalric liberators of the Cubans; in fact, they would then play the passive feminized role of the rescued to the active male role of the black troops.

The role of the chivalric rescuer, used so pervasively in imperial discourse, was itself subject to contested meanings. African American soldiers not only deployed the chivalric mode in writing of their military experience in relation to the Cubans or to their fellow soldiers; they also brought that image back home to the South. Soldiers encamped in the Southern bases took a chivalric attitude toward local

African Americans; soldiers cut down trees where blacks had been lynched, protected local communities from white brutality, and defied Jim Crow laws with the force of their numbers, arms, and authority of their blue uniforms. Lauded in the black press, these incidents were decried in the white press as forms of anarchic misrule, of black men out of control.[42]

In the contest over the uses of chivalry, Roosevelt can be seen as attempting to rescue the chivalric mode itself from black counter-narratives and preserve it as an exclusively Anglo-Saxon possession. In Cuba Roosevelt may have rediscovered the Western frontier he abandoned in the city; yet the nostalgia motivating the Rough Riders to act like cowboys and seek new Indians in a Wild West abroad was realized in confrontation with African Americans in a foreign terrain where black and white threatened "to intermix." In *Rough Riders,* it is only after his confrontation with "smoked Yankees" that Roosevelt goes on to summarize his account of the battle, naming his individual men and their gallant deeds as though he has rescued their image as soldiers from some kind of male miscegenation.

Reuniting the Nation

Roosevelt's protection of the white male subject contributed to the purgative discourse with which this chapter opens, of the Spanish-American War as the final antidote to Reconstruction, healing the conflicts of the Civil War by bringing together blue and gray on distant shores. The Rough Riders have been understood as a unifying cultural symbol—between North and South, West and East, working class and patrician, cowboy and Indian, and this unity is grounded in the notion of manliness, in the physicality of the male body that transcends or underlies social difference. In the words of a popular poem about the Rough Riders,

> Let them know there in the ditches
> Blood-stained by the swells in the van
> And know that a chap may have riches
> And still be a man.[43]

Common graves, common streams of blood, bodies strewn in the Cuban grasses all sanctify a democracy of manhood to which some were even willing to add African Americans. As Lieutenant Pershing, officer of a black regiment, stated: "White regiments, black regiments, regulars and Rough Riders, representing the young manhood of the North and South, fought shoulder to shoulder, unmindful of race or color, unmindful of whether commanded by an ex-Confederate or not and mindful only of their common duty as Americans."[44] Roosevelt's confrontation on San Juan Hill baldly exposes the ground of hierarchy and violence in which this national unity was embedded.

Although white and black regiments could be seen to merge in their "common duty as Americans," black and white male bodies had different symbolic resonance, a different signifying function in the political landscape. One of the rationales for organizing federal regiments of African American volunteers (when many individual states balked at organizing militias) was the Lamarckian argument that they were immune to the diseases of the tropical environment. These troops came to be known as the Immune Regiments, as though they were physically closer to the terrain, more like "natives" than like white Americans. This attribution allowed them to be assigned the most loathsome duties, but also positioned them ideologically. Immune, they could serve as a buffer between the white soldiers and the contagious environment and allow the restored white male body to emerge unscathed from foreign physical and political perils. This recuperation was especially important given the pervasive presence at home of dismembered veterans of the Civil War and, more immediately, given that more men died of dysentery, malaria, and food poisoning from army rations in Cuba than they did fighting on the battlefield. The presence of the black body, immersed in yet allegedly invulnerable to the physical contagion of the battlefield, elevates the figure of the white male to the level of political abstraction, but makes him dependent on that very presence.

The foundation for the construction of the white male body as a figure for American nationhood lies in the subjugation of black male bodies at home and abroad. Consider the following passage by Richard Harding Davis, describing an early stage of the battle for San Juan Hill. Davis was outspoken in his support of African American soldiers and their contribution to the war effort and in his harsh criticism of the U.S. command in its inept conduct of the war:

> I came across Lieutenant Roberts of the Tenth Cavalry, lying under the roots of a tree beside the stream with three of his colored troopers

stretched around him. He was shot through the intestines, and each of the three men with him was shot in the arm or leg. They had been overlooked or forgotten, and we stumbled upon them only by the accident of losing our way. They had no knowledge as to how the battle was going or where their comrades were, or where the enemy was. At any moment, for all they knew, the Spaniards might break through the bushes about them. It was a most lonely picture, the young lieutenant, half naked, and wet with his own blood, sitting upright beside the empty stream, and his three followers crouching at his feet like three faithful watch-dogs, each wearing his red badge of courage, with his black skin tanned to a haggard gray, and with his eyes fixed patiently on the white lips of his officer. When the white soldiers with me offered to carry him back to the dressing station, the negroes resented it stiffly. "If the Lieutenant had been able to move, we would have carried him away long ago," said the sergeant, quite overlooking the fact that his arm was shattered. "Oh, don't bother the surgeons about me," Roberts added, cheerfully. "They must be very busy. I can wait."[45]

On the surface, this is a tableau of national consolidation between whites and blacks, bonded by shared wounds and self-sacrifice. In fact, the bloody wounds imaged through Crane's popular "red badge of courage" bleach everyone one shade whiter. The troopers turn less black, a "haggard grey," while the lieutenant turns even whiter, with his "white lips." Yet this tableau reinscribes the racial hierarchy out of which national unity is forged, not only in the explicit racist images of the blacks as "watch-dogs" or the fact that they, in contrast to the white officer, remain unnamed, but in the way in which the heroic white body is intimately constructed out of black bodies in several hybrid configurations. In describing immobilized bodies, Davis vividly invokes and quells the implicit sexual quality of racial "intermingling," which Roosevelt confronts in the upheaval of the battle. From one angle, they appear as one grotesque body—white on top and black on the bottom: the upright white lieutenant wounded in the middle is the torso and the black troopers form the limbs or lower body. Their common wounds join them together in a symbolic castration. From another angle, these figures are ambiguously sexualized and gendered, with the lieutenant an upright phallus and the black privates crouched ready to receive him. From yet another perspective, the black soldiers act as chivalric knights protecting their lady as they gaze lovingly at his lips. When they resent the interference of the white soldiers offering to touch their officer, they "stiffen" and thereby assert their virility, forgetting the symbolic castration inherent not only in their wounded limbs, but in their social inability to touch him, in their racial difference. These African American soldiers, wounded on the periphery of their own bodies, stand at the periphery of the body politic, or at the bottom of a representational hierarchy. They pledge their allegiance to their white officer; he, however, is capable of a higher allegiance to the cause, which he displays in his cheerful "don't mind me." They represent their officer, their master, while he represents the whole nation, America. The upright white male body, rooted in his black counterparts, also differentiates them, as he becomes a mediator between the crouched black masses—the unnamed soldiers—and the nation, which they cannot represent directly.

Thus Davis's tableau of unity on San Juan Hill has the same violently differentiating effect as Roosevelt's more overtly violent form of post-Reconstruction politics. Both are acting against the political and symbolic demands of black soldiers. Davis sheds light on the debate about African American officers, who might not only take on leadership roles and bear weapons, but also represent the nation directly, unmediated through their allegiance to white officers. The challenge of black officers to white authority lay in their capacity to represent American nationhood abroad, when society required that their blackness be subsumed into a white nation. Black officers would challenge the coherence of imperial boundaries that align masculinity, whiteness, and nationhood against the anarchy of black misrule. Just as Roosevelt and others supported the black troops as long as they were led and represented by white officers, the white male pictured alone in the wilderness of empire on San Juan Hill comes to displace, appropriate, and incorporate the agency of nonwhites in the empire and at home.

Black troops in blue on San Juan Hill threatened to destabilize this hierarchy, however, by occupying a range of possible positions. As Griggs's novel suggests, armed African American soldiers may betray the U.S. empire through their realignment with outside forces. Or even more destabilizing may be their challenge to the internal coherence of that empire by demanding participation and representation as equals. Many black soldiers in the aftermath of the Cuban campaign preferred to fight the war in the Philippines rather than face the racism encircling the army encampments of the South. In a few well-publicized cases, black soldiers switched sides to fight on behalf of Philippine independence.[46] Other soldiers sought imperial citizenship at home by fighting foreign wars. Black soldiers in blue uniforms raised the whites' fear that the imperial war meant to heal the rifts of the Civil War would continue to heighten that conflict by recasting it as a global race war. The threat of black soldiers in blue uniforms, like that of the "colored" color bearer, lies in their direct representation of American nationhood in lands defined as inhabited by those unfit for self-government, those who cannot represent themselves, and who are thus in need of the discipline of the American empire. As Roosevelt attests to on San Juan Hill, blacks in blue represent the fears and potential undoing of the anarchy of empire.

CHAPTER 5

Birth of an Empire

In a scene from *Citizen Kane* celebrating the success of the owner's newspaper, Kane twice poses a rhetorical question to his journalists: "Well gentlemen, are we going to declare war on Spain?" His friend Leland wryly responds: "*The Inquirer* already has," to which Kane retorts: "you long-faced, overdressed anarchist." During this repartee, Kane as the host welcomes in the evening entertainment: a chorus line of women spottily clad in stars and stripes and toting toy rifles, led by a marching band of black musicians. The shooting script of the film originally called for a longer debate between Leland and Kane about the impending U.S. intervention in Cuba.[1] Kane proposes sending Leland to Cuba as special correspondent to compete with Richard Harding Davis, but Leland rejects the offer and challenges the paper's commitment to warmongering. This debate was cut from the final version of the film when the setting was changed from a brothel to a banquet hall to pass the production code. In the final screen version, traces of war talk and illicit sexuality from the shooting script linger on the costumed female bodies of the chorus line.

This reference to conflict about the Spanish-American War links Orson Welles's landmark film of 1941 to the earliest history of cinema in the late 1890s. That war was one of the first to be shot on film, at a moment when the "moving picture" first emerged as a novel form of entertainment. Despite its participation in the birth of U.S. cinema, the war then disappeared as a subject from later films. No major films have chronicled the three-month-long war in Cuba or the subsequent

146

three-year-long war in the Philippines, although films have been made about virtually every other war in U.S. history.[2] This chapter is about that duality, about the formative presence and telling absence of this pivotal war in the history of U.S. cinema. Moving pictures about the war in Cuba and the Philippines were central to the organization of movie-making as a viable business and to the capacity of films to tell stories in the first decade of the twentieth century. If the Spanish-American War then disappeared from the screen, its evocation of an American empire continued to inform the genealogy of American cinema. Veiled allusions to the war inform D. W. Griffith's landmark film, *The Birth of a Nation* (1915), and Oscar Micheaux's response, *Within Our Gates* (1920). The war is mentioned several times in *Citizen Kane* (1941), which was based on the career of William Randolph Hearst, the newspaper magnate who built his career on his incitement of war hysteria in the yellow press. References to the Spanish-American War, I argue, appeared both at moments of cinematic innovation and at threshold periods of international crisis, when the question of American involvement in European wars was under intense debate and the global role of the United States was hanging in the balance. *Birth of a Nation* came out at the beginning of World War I and *Citizen Kane* during World War II, as debates were raging about entering each war. If "race movies," as Michael Rogin argues, "provide the scaffolding for American film history,"[3] imperial films, I contend, provide the submerged foundation on international terrain for a history that charts not only the internal bonds of national unity but also the changing relations between the domestic and the foreign.

Imperial Mobility

As we have seen in the last two chapters, popular enthusiasm for the war against Spain has long been linked to the rise of the mass media in the United States and its power to mobilize public opinion, particularly to the yellow journalism of William Randolph Hearst and Joseph Pulitzer. The newfound popularity of "moving pictures" also played a significant, if less well known role in rousing support for the war and for the project of imperial expansion. During the Cuban War for Independence, before the U.S. declaration of war against Spain, cameramen for Edison and Biograph made their way to Florida where troops were amassing, and they joined Hearst's journalists on the yacht he dispatched from Key West to the Caribbean. In urban theaters and traveling exhibitions throughout the country in 1898 and 1899, crowds flocked to see the novelty of war scenes shot in Florida and Cuba. These brief films, less than a minute each, showed battleships at sea, the wreck of the *Maine* and the funeral of its victims, panoramas of Havana Harbor, troops in marching formation, soldiers embarking on trains and ships, the Rough Riders riding, generals in conference, and triumphant victory parades leaving Havana and welcoming Admiral Dewey home to New York and Washington. The films also captured the more informal moments of war—soldiers washing dishes, lounging in camps, digging paths, and loading their gear on trains and mules. There were views of battleships with laundry hanging from the decks, of troops disembarking offshore at Daiquiri, tossing their mules overboard to sink or swim, and digging roads through the brush.[4] Because of the weight and size of the cameras, "actuality" shots of battles were almost impossible to take, though some cameramen did try to cart their equipment to the battlefields of Cuba. Filmmakers compensated by staging famous battles in the New Jersey countryside and shooting naval conflicts that were fought in the harbors of Manila and Havana in bathtubs with toy ships and cigarette smoke. As soon as the war began between Americans and Filipinos, a repertoire of battles in the Philippines was enacted as well, though no American cameramen were present there.

Audiences were, for the most part, not troubled by the combination of "real" and "reenacted" films, a distinction we would make today, since both equally provided the thrill of immediacy in viewing the otherwise remote experience of war. The exhibition of war films provided public occasions for the expressions of nationalist sentiment, as viewers hissed the Spanish crown, cheered Dewey's victory, sang patriotic songs, and saluted the oft-repeated raising of the American flag against the painted scenery of Morro Castle in Havana Harbor. At the height of the war, these films were so popular that they were repeated every hour around the clock in urban theaters, where the spectacle of war was not contained on the screen but suffused every aspect of attending the theater. The projection machines, an early attraction in themselves, such as Edison's Kinescope, were renamed War-Graph, or Warscope. The Eden Musee was remodeled as the interior of an arsenal battleship for the celebration of Admiral Dewey's return in September. Soldiers disembarking in New York harbor would go to that theater both to watch themselves on screen and be hailed by spectators.[5]

These early war films seem to fulfill J. A. Hobson's observation (see Chapter 3) that "jingoism is the lust of the spectator," wherein the desire to observe the spectacle of war with the immediacy of a sporting event overtakes any interest in the political context or narrative.[6] This notion of jingoism as spectatorial lust dovetails interestingly with Thomas Gunning's analysis of early film as a "cinema of attractions." Early films, he argues, exhibited their power as spectacle to surprise, shock, and delight the curious spectators, with no attempt to subordinate the spectacle to a coherent narrative.[7] These audiences had more in common with crowds at a fair or carnival than with the later voyeuristic spectator of classical film.[8] The war films indeed highlighted the experience of spectatorship, by placing the viewers in the position of the crowds watching parades of soldiers and waving to them as they embarked on ships, or in the position of mourners and curiosity seekers as the coffins of the *Maine* victims rolled by on carts. In battle scenes, the audience watched Rough Riders rushing at them or soldiers shooting toward them, as the actors faced the camera head on, or the audience was positioned behind the American soldiers following the flag and marching directly into enemy fire. In an Edison catalogue for exhibitors entitled "War Extra," the "magnificent spectacle" of a warship was enhanced by the sense that "her death-dealing guns seem to point directly at our camera."[9] Some theaters heightened the immediacy of war with the accompanying sound of guns and filling the theater with smoke. As on the pages of the historical romances and newspaper reports, the charged visual relation on screen appeared to be primarily not that between U.S. troops and their enemies or their allies, but one that took place between the spectacle of American troops abroad and their domestic audience at home. As Paul Virilio notes about the intimate connection between war and cinema, "War can never break free from the magical spectacle because its very purpose is to *produce* that spectacle."[10]

One of the major attractions of these war films lay in the exhibition of American mobility itself, rather than in the rarely visible display of foreign lands and peoples. A majority of films showed Americans in motion: marching, riding, sailing, embarking on ships, and returning home. Anchored warships could even be made to appear in motion, as the camera mounted on a smaller vessel circled the larger ship for a panoramic view. Whether the movement is of men, horses, vehicles, or ships, the act of moving matters more than either the point of departure or arrival. Scholars have associated the development of early cinema with modern transformations of the experience of motion through space and time, and have thus linked the rise of film to railroad travel and to the experience of walking through the modern metropolis.[11] Ella Shohat has suggested that early film also developed hand in hand with imperial expansion around the globe.[12] The spectacle of the battleship, rather than the railroad, may best represent this imperial mobility. If shots of trains dramatized the camera's mastery of continental travel, the pictures of ships at sea enacted global mobility. The year before the war broke out, cameramen for Edison embarked on a Pacific journey through the routes of American political and commercial interests: Mexico, Japan, Hong Kong, Hawaii, and Manila. Traveling on warships and merchant vessels, and underwritten financially by American transportation companies, the cameramen contributed to opening the world to the export of American commerce and military might.

Moving pictures helped make the world accessible to American power abroad and to the gaze of audiences at home by exhibiting the reach of the camera itself. The films both enacted and celebrated the capacity of military power and the ability of the camera to encompass the globe. As U.S. militarism and commerce subjected new arenas to imperial intervention, film had a complementary goal as a force that opened the world to the survey of the American gaze. The mobility of film was a fitting accomplice to the disembodied discourse of American imperialism, in which territories abroad were viewed as stepping stones to further expansion divorced from bounded spaces, rather than as desirable ends in themselves (see Chapter 3). As foreign sites became more accessible to the camera's eye and thus visible to the audience at home, these sites became paradoxically blurred and unreal; mere interchangeable settings for the exercise of American power.

If, as Virilio claims, "weapons are tools not just of destruction but also of perception," then the reverse may also be true, that cameras are not just tools of perception but also of destruction. There was an intimate connection between arms and cameras, one which Virilo dates to World War I, but that can be seen in the origins of film in the 1890s: "the history of battle is primarily the history of radically changing fields of perception."[13] The emergence of film as a new field of perception went hand in hand with the most extensive period of European and American expansion in what has been called the Age of Empire. Films about the Spanish-American War can be seen as part of the arsenal of the new American empire. The association of the moving picture with the mobility of men and weapons, however, was by no means a uniquely American phenomenon. In fact, the early film industry was international in scope, in its production and marketing. Before 1898, U.S. audiences would have likely seen the Lumière films, which portrayed tourist scenes from around the world, as well as shots of military troops from different countries marching, charging, and enacting battles. Americans were also not the only ones to make films about the Spanish-American War: Georges Méliès made several films of the explosion of the battleship *Maine*, along with other imperial themes. Also popular among U.S. audiences were films about the Boer War and the Boxer Rebellion in China.[14]

Well before the U.S. declaration of war against Spain, films advertised the power of the medium to mobilize men and images. Edison's *War Correspondents,* for example, displayed newspaper correspondents in Key West racing to the telegraph office.[15] The film dramatized the speed with which journalists could transport the news but also implied that the new medium of film could compete with and supersede the newspaper in terms of verisimilitude. To advertise a panoramic view of Morro Castle/Havana Harbor, the *War Extra* from the Edison Company's catalog noted that "in view of probable bombardment, when the old fashioned masonry will melt away like butter under the fire of 13-inch guns, the view is of historic value."[16] "Historic" because the filming anticipates and almost precipitates the destruction that the actual bombardment would wreak. Shooting film here precedes shooting guns and thereby creates "historic value."

The mobility of American men was also enhanced by the contrast with immobilizing shots of Cubans and Spaniards. Several films show Cubans standing or squatting passively in line waiting for rations from the American army, a common stereotype of Cuban dependency and lack of self-reliance.[17] One popular reenactment, *Shooting Captured In-*

surgents, shows blindfolded Cubans standing to be shot by a firing squad, and in *Cuban Ambush,* the Cubans remain hidden while attention is drawn to the heroic death of a Spanish soldier.[18] Depiction of Cuban inertia echoes the depiction of African American boys and men standing by idly and watching white soldiers march and work. A *War Extra* describes *Cruiser Marblehead* as a "busy scene" on the docked ship, which had bombarded San Juan, Puerto Rico: "coal passers, stevedores, sailors and officers all seem imbued with a spirit of hustle. All except the coons on the wharf, watching the work. One of them slowly gets up, stretches and yawns."[19] This juxtaposition implicitly associates American mobility with whiteness, in contrast to both Cubans abroad and African Americans at home. In one of the few films of black soldiers, *Colored Troops Disembarking,* the *War Extra* glosses: "it is laughable to see the extreme caution displayed by the soldiers clambering down. The commanding officer struts on the wharf urging them to hurry."[20] Shots of white soldiers disembarking just as slowly appear in many films with no comment. The textual cues here seem necessary to distinguish the movement of black troops as missteps—"clambering" or "strutting," a racialized distinction not clearly visible on the screen.

While these examples suggest how films may have boosted the war effort, film historians have also shown that the war played a crucial role in boosting the business of film. The popularity of the war films financially revived a fledgling industry whose initial novelty was beginning to fade. In addition, the serious appeal of the content helped to make films more palatable to religious and genteel middle-class groups throughout the country who were suspicious of film as a lower-class form of amusement.[21] As an early reporter on film wrote, "An elaborate argument could be based on the premise that the only important contribution of the Spanish-American War to the history of the United States lay in the impetus it gave to the work of Smith and Blackton in placing the foundation blocks for the motion picture industry."[22] As in accounts of yellow journalism, acknowledging the importance of the media downplays the importance of their ideological content and the political context of the war. While recent film historians would not agree with this exaggerated assessment, they have implicitly followed a similar line of argument. Many historians routinely refer to the Spanish-American "war film craze" as the main attraction of the pre-nickelodeon era and as a key catalyst in the development of early cinema: "no genre of programming could be developed to match the consistent drawing power of the images of the Spanish-American War."[23] Yet most scholars take the patriotic attraction of these films for granted and treat them as a catalyst for other cinematic developments, without fully exploring how the films worked to produce patriotism in a particular historical context.

Charles Musser has argued that the exhibition of war films played a pivotal role in the development of narrative in film. Before the war, moving pictures were for the most part displayed in a vaudeville format of disparate subjects interspersed with other entertainment acts, with little attempt at thematic unity or narrative continuity. While exhibitors also included Spanish-American War films in this format, accompanied by songs, slides, and lectures, now for the first time they organized the films around a unifying theme and followed the chronological narrative of the progress of the war. They might start, for example, with the staged explosion of the *Maine,* go on to divers in the wreck, to the on-site funeral for its victims, and then move on to scenes of troops embarking for Cuba, a staged battle for the American flag, a victorious bombardment of Havana Harbor, and end with the raising of the American flag. Or they might have a segment solely on the battles at sea in the Pacific, culminating with Dewey's homecoming parade. This singular focus was advertised outside the theater or traveling exhibition as "War Show." Such thematic and chronological coherence, suggests Musser, contributed to the development of the story film, which would become the dominant mode of classic Hollywood cinema.[24]

Thus the capacity of films to tell stories arose as much from a political desire to project national narratives of imperial conquest and geographic mobility as from technological or aesthetic innovation. To understand this connection between story films and war, it is not enough to assume that the exhibitors and spectators could draw on a straightforward military teleology of combat, victory, defeat, treaty-signing, and the ceding of territory. These linear narratives were constructed out of fields of contention, subject to conflicting interpretations, as were the meanings of the multiple wars of 1898 and their political results in Cuba, Puerto Rico, and the Philippines. The celebration of Dewey's uncontested victory over the Spanish fleet in Manila Bay, for example, and the official closure his homecoming gave to the war, detracted public attention from the beginning of a vicious American ground war against the Filipinos' struggle for national independence. If the changing scope of imperial warfare did not fit a closed narrative structure, neither did patriotism or jingoism provide automatic sources of affective cohesion. Jingoism does not simply express a preexisting unity, just as visual images are not transparently legible references. Both forge moments of public unity by mobilizing multiple and often conflicted fantasies and anxieties. Narrative construction of the war's meaning as well as of the new experience of viewing films had to be exerted through an abundance of interpretive materials that accompanied the films, such as catalogs, lectures, advertising, and newspaper notices. Together, these schooled an audience in how to see imperial warfare in foreign arenas newly visible on screen.

How then do spectacles of foreign wars and imperial mobility on film become stories with recognizable plots? How at this early moment of cinematic history did film start to narrate imperial warfare, and how did war provide an opportunity for film to tell stories? Spectacles of foreign warfare became stories in relation to the domestic sphere and to the creation of a "home front." Films framed the foreign war in relation to domestic space to make American viewers feel at home abroad. By "domestic" I refer to the double meaning of the term as the mutually defining spheres of the household and the nation (see Chapter 1). These early films of men marching and fighting abroad were not only about wars overseas but also about redrawing the boundaries between home and abroad, between the domestic and the foreign, boundaries that were both threatened and reconstructed by imperial expansion. The new medium of film contributed to the cultural process of negotiating these boundaries, to make distant lands both accessible and "foreign in a domestic sense." Just as film brought the world into the domestic space of the theater, representations of American mobility abroad were intimately involved in reconfiguring the nation as home.[25]

One early story film set during the war in the Philippines suggests how film mobilized the trope of domesticity to generate a narrative of imperial conquest. Billy Bitzer made *The American Soldier in Love and War* in the Biograph studio, and it was released in 1903 (the same year as Edwin Porter's *Uncle Tom's Cabin* and *The Great Train Robbery*).[26] According to the *Biograph Bulletin,* the film was set in the Philippines at a time when American colonial rule was being established there, at the end of a brutal three-year war of conquest. The brutality of American troops at the time was openly debated in congressional investigations, testimony of soldiers, and the pages of newspapers, which even printed images of massacred Filipinos. *The American Soldier* conveyed a very different view of the war. While the title refers to separate female and male spheres of the home and the battlefield, the film does more than send the soldier away from his love at home to fight a foreign war. It further enlists the female sphere of domesticity to project a colonial regime overseas and to tell the story of empire.

The Biograph Company marketed this three-scene film, along with two other war films in its catalog, with a clear concern about creating a narrative out of disparate footage:

> These three scenes are to be used in connection with war views, to make a *complete story* in one film for projection. The first scene shows the young American officer parting with his sweetheart and starting for the Philippines. The second shows the regiment leaving its post to embark on a transport—then comes a fight in the brush, then the wounding of the young officer; his capture and rescue by a Filipino girl, and finally his meeting the sweetheart and her father in the Filipino hut, where he has been nursed back to life.[27]

Rather than simply describe the film, the bulletin instructs the exhibitor how to display the disparate scenes as a continuous and coherent story. This narrative weaves together four heterogeneous spatial registers: moving from a three-dimensional theatrical bourgeois interior to actual footage of real soldiers, to a reenacted battle scene (both filmed outdoors), and to two patently unreal two-dimensional exotic backdrops. These juxtapositions implicitly contrast the home as real and the foreign as artificial and unreal spaces, bridged by the presence of the American soldier and by the experience of the viewer.[28] The *Bulletin* relates a narrative that would be familiar to its audience and was soon to become dominant in early story films—the tale of a rescue. The film enacts the popular narrative of the war as a rescue mission, at the hands of a virile American man, of Cubans from decadent Spaniards, and Filipinos from their own barbarism. Yet this film, like the contemporary historical romances, suggests a counter-narrative that turns imperial adventure into the rescue of American masculinity.

Scene one opens with a white, well-dressed woman seated in a three-dimensional set of a middle-class drawing room. A soldier enters and embraces the woman in a repeated tearful farewell. The realistic bourgeois interior represents the domestic sphere of female sentiment that correlates with the subjectivity of the crying woman, who is comforted by the soldier. Although war enters the home as a disruption of domestic relations, the domestic sphere also appears as the site from which the war is launched. In a film made by Edison in 1899, *Love and War,* the family in a similar interior is reading the newspaper and following the course of the war.[29] This film ends with Red Cross nurses rushing into a field hospital to tend to the wounded son of the family. The home in both films thus appears analogous to the theater as the site for watching the spectacle of foreign wars, and the battlefield hospital appears as a venue for woman's sphere abroad.

According to the *Bulletin,* the next scene is an "actuality," that is, the real footage of men embarking for war. In fact this film was recycled from a shot of men embarking for Cuba from Governor's Island four years earlier, which makes the sites of empire interchangeable. The soldiers could presumably be marching anywhere in the world. The scene following that one is a reenacted practice battle, also in an unspecified location.[30]

Scene two is set in the proscenium of a stage against a painted two-dimensional "jungle" scene. The American soldier enters, falls to the ground, and is immediately assaulted by a generic "native" in blackface and black leotard. Just as the enemy is about to beat the soldier to death, a native woman appears, to grab the club and plead on her knees for the soldier's life.

This scene is interesting for its portrayal of race and masculinity. Advocates of empire saw the annexation of the Philippines as a crucible for restoring primal vigor to an enervated white masculinity by subduing primitive men (see Chapter 3).[31] Yet in this scene the American soldier falls immediately, with no visible prior struggle; only then does this caricature of a primitive man with a club prepare to kill him. The native demonstrates cowardliness by attacking an already fallen man. The native woman then proves herself more civilized than her male counterpart by rescuing the American in a gesture evocative of Pocahontas rescuing Captain John Smith (a popular figure in the 1890s). Her appearance splits the colonized subject into a feminized nurtur-

Figure 1. *The American Soldier in Love and War,* 1903, Museum of Modern Art/Film Stills Archive.

ing accepter of colonial rule, and a cowardly, brutish, aggressive male resister.

Scene three takes place against a painted backdrop of an unspecified tropical island. The soldier, with a bandage around his head, is sitting outside the hut, while the woman who saved him fans him, and a younger woman offers him a bowl of food. The white woman of the first film arrives with an older man sporting a pith helmet and white beard. She embraces the soldier and then gives her necklace to the native woman, while the old man shakes hands all around.

We return here from war to love, to a domestic frame, the exterior of a primitive hut, which contrasts with the opening bourgeois interior. Instead of the soldier returning home from war, the domesticity associated with the white woman goes abroad to rescue the white man from the proliferation of native women, who, in a harem-like setting, nurture and feed him. The second woman replaces the native man; the aggressor gives way to this twin image of the colonized as the female nurturer and server—the mammy figure—and the orientalized and eroticized younger woman. Like Pocahontas and the heroines of the historical romances, these female figures represent the desire to serve as the desire for subjugation. "The very thing they yearn for is what of all others our Government desires to give them,"[32] wrote the 1899 Commission on the Philippines in similarly eroticized language (see Chapter 3). This domestic frame, with a wounded soldier at its center, effaces any trace of the bloody conflict or conquest which brought the American soldier to the Philippines. He—rather than the Filipinos—is the wounded victim. Yet this portrayal of the soldier also conveys a destabilized and more vulnerable image of masculinity, as he never stands erect in the film but falls immediately and remains either prone or seated. The catalogue says that the soldier is "captured and rescued by the Filipino girl." The implicit threat may be one of the American soldier "going native" by taking a local concubine, both a reality and fear of colonial administrations. If Roosevelt found men of different races intermingling in the imperial battlefield, this film raises the fearful or enticing potential for miscegenation with native women. The symbolic threat carries through the logic of expansion; that is, the expansion of borders may undo the men sent abroad and ultimately challenge the racial coherence of national unity.

If the native woman rescues the American soldier from the native man, in the final scene the white sweetheart arrives to rescue the American soldier from a surfeit of native women. The family romance represents the restoration of order that is at once domestic and imperial, with the white couple reunited on foreign terrain. As the soldier remains immobilized, the white woman gives beads to the Filipina as a sign of gratitude but also bondage.[33] Then what is the old man doing there? The catalogue says he is the white woman's father, accompanying her as a chaperone. He would also be recognized from political cartoons as Uncle Sam. If the white woman rescues her man under the aegis of Uncle Sam, she may then leave the old man with the native women. In the coupling at the end, the ambiguous familial figure of "Uncle" replaces the native man among the native women. The film thus evokes, settles, but then revives the threat of imperial expansion as miscegenation: the incorporation of racial foreigners within the domestic nation.

The American Soldier in Love and War frames a foreign war in part through gender and racial anxieties at home. In a context in which Roosevelt advocated imperial conquest as the expansion of separate gendered spheres to global dimensions, that is, of women tending the home while men take up the white man's burden abroad, this film shows how those spheres become intertwined. Imperial conquest appears as the restoration of white American domesticity on foreign terrain. Biograph marketed the film along with other films about adultery, divorce, and women who kill their adulterous husbands. This film might be viewed as an instrument for putting the white New Woman under control by showing her the model of willing submissive native women and by leashing her new mobility to an imperial order.

The demarcation of the separate spaces of home and war is a gendered one. Feminist film historians, building on the work of Miriam Hansen, have shown that early cinema offered women access outside the home into an alternative public sphere, "a space where women were free to enjoy the pleasures of voyeurism and active spectatorship otherwise denied them."[34] Contemporaries were surprised that women made up a large portion of the audience for the popular moving picture of the Corbett-Fitzsimmons boxing match in 1897. These same venues welcomed women spectators to war films. One theater, for example, courted a female audience by offering souvenir pictures of the battleship *Maine*, specifically to the "ladies."[35] My point here can only be speculative—that women viewers, like women readers of romance novels, were welcomed into this public sphere of spectatorship, where the desire for freedom from domestic restraints could be satisfied and channeled through the routes of empire abroad. Viewing war films offered a release from domesticity and a reconfiguration of the domestic sphere into what Josiah Strong called an "audience room for the world." If the spectacle of war provided a safe way for women to enter a public sphere of global mobility, in turn the oppositional potential of this public sphere might have been harnessed and disciplined by the activity of watching war films.

In the portrayal of Filipino characters as generically "black" and primitive, we can also see how early imperial films mobilized marks of racial difference in an international arena. Although these figures would not be recognized ethnographically as Filipino, they would be identifiable from popular contemporary political cartoons that conflated Filipinos, Cubans, Puerto Ricans, and Hawaiians as stereotypically black. Blackness on the screen was a mobile signifier, transferable to a variety of different colonized groups. While film was put to use early on for ethnic documentation—to make primitive peoples more real and particular to the Western viewer—it also had the effect of making them generically interchangeable and thus unreal.[36] In a trade journal's anecdote about shooting the famous battle of San Juan Hill, for example, African Americans were hired to play the Spanish soldiers:

> A photographer for a moving picture machine had hard luck at Orange NJ, recently in his attempt to depict an engagement on San Juan Hill. He engaged eighteen Negroes to represent Spaniards . . . and costumed them appropriately. He paid the Negroes 75 cents each in advance, gave them some beer, in order that they might be in fighting trim, and then adjusted his photographic apparatus. When ready the Vitascope man found that the "Spaniards" had disappeared, taking with them 200 rounds of blank cartridges. The police found a number of the pseudo Spaniards later engaged in a game of craps, but as they fled no arrests were made.[37]

Here the threat of armed black men—some of whom actually fought on San Juan Hill—is evoked and ridiculed by costuming them as Spaniards. Their comic mutiny is associated with Spanish cowardice and decadence: both refuse to act like "real" men. But ultimately the photographer becomes the butt of the joke, when the black actors escape and he loses his vision behind the very apparatus meant to control this representation.

The Birth of a Nation at Home and Abroad

The first major war film in the history of American cinema is of course not about the Spanish-American War, but about the American Civil War: D. W. Griffith's landmark epic from 1915, *The Birth of a Nation*. In a movie about the Civil War and the rise of the Ku Klux Klan in the 1860s, the war of 1898 obviously cannot appear directly. But this absence, I argue, is a symptomatic one, as the film is informed by the Spanish-American War from at least two sources: the prior history of war on film, and the Thomas Dixon novels on which Griffith based his film, *The Clansman* (1905) and *The Leopard's Spots* (1902).

Scholars have suggested that Griffith's famous shots of the Civil War battlefields reproduced Mathew Brady's photographs. I would suggest that they were also shaped by the more recent mode of representing warfare on film. Billy Bitzer, Griffith's cameraman for *Birth of a Nation*, earlier had traveled on Hearst's yacht to shoot films of troops in Cuba. It was Bitzer too who made *The American Soldier in Love and War*. In *The Birth of a Nation*, views of the climactic ride of the Klan echo on a grander scale films made of the Rough Riders on their way to rescue Cuba. In addition, the shots of trench warfare in that film are staged quite similarly to the reenactments of battles in the Philippines (as well as those of another colonial war extensively filmed, the Boer War). In *The Birth of a Nation* the most striking scenes of visual menace on the screen are those of black soldiers in Federal uniforms exerting their authority as an occupying force. It was the Spanish-American War that most recently brought this threat to the visual foreground, in films, photographs, and stories of black soldiers in national uniforms (see Chapter 4).

This is not to say that Griffith and Bitzer directly copied or were influenced only by the Spanish-American War films. Yet when they came to stage and shoot historical battles from the Civil War, the representational field most immediately available to them and their audience would have included not only Brady's photos and European epic films, but also the only American war extensively and recently shot on film. Furthermore, the Spanish-American War was interpreted as a political and symbolic resolution to the domestic disunity of the Civil War, a solution which Griffith offered in the rise of the Klan. If Griffith claimed that the Klan gave birth to the "real nation [that] has only existed in the last 15 or twenty years," he placed its birth in the 1890s, in the era of Progressivism and its related movement of imperialism abroad.[38]

This connection between the domestic and foreign, the Civil War and the Spanish-American War, is explicitly drawn in a novel we have examined above, *The Leopard's Spots,* one of Dixon's novels on which Griffith based his film. In this novel, a black man's alleged rape of a white girl has the same unifying effect on a Southern community that the Spanish-American War has on the entire nation. Both events, the domestic and the foreign, cause "the white race" to "fuse into a homogeneous mass" out of different regions, classes, and religions.[39] Griffith portrayed this white fusion of the nation in the Klan in response to an imagined rape, hence a domestic tale, rather than in response to the overseas war. In fact, in revising Dixon's novels of Reconstruction, Griffith excises the war of 1898 and replaces it with the Civil War.

Yet imperialism is not absent from *The Birth of a Nation,* where Griffith, like Dixon, narrates the history of Reconstruction as a Northern occupation of the South. Silas Lynch, the Northern mulatto, tells the white woman he wants to marry, "I will build an empire and you will be my queen." The ride of the Klan, known as the "invisible empire," makes the men look like an insurgent force riding in rebellion against an African empire. The first shot in the film figures slavery as an invasion by blacks, an original threat to the proto-national unity of white Puritan settlers. The original version of the film ends with Lincoln's vision of sending all blacks to Africa, and the final version ends with a Christian God of peace defeating a god of war, who looks like an African icon. The Christian god thus purges the white nation of black soldiers, who have been collapsed into the figure of the black rapist.

Thus *The Birth of a Nation* takes place on a broader international terrain than the focus on the internal domestic conflict of the Civil War and racial violence overtly suggests. Viewers at the time understood part of this international implication: at the beginning of the war in Europe, the Klan riding to the rescue at the climax of the film offered a potential figure for the white American nation riding to the rescue of the world.[40] Not surprisingly, Griffith was the only civilian invited to the battlefields of the Great War to make a propaganda film urging U.S. entry. As Billy Bitzer explained, "the world's foremost director was the one man who could *tell a story* that all—Americans especially—would understand."[41]

One filmmaker did understand the relation of *The Birth of a Nation* to the Spanish-American War and to World War I: African American filmmaker Oscar Micheaux, whose 1920 melodrama, *Within Our Gates*, has been seen as a direct critique of the earlier film. Whereas in Griffith's film black men in uniform represent anarchy and the Klan order, in *Within Our Gates* the flashback to the lynching of the heroine's foster family shows a spectacle of chaos and personal trauma. This powerful lynching scene, in which a family is hanged and a bonfire built to burn them, cuts back and forth to the scene directly echoing the black man's threat to white women in the cabin of *The Birth of a Nation*. In Micheaux's film, though, a white man is trying to rape the black heroine, until he discovers through a mark on her body that he is her father.

The resolution of these threatened rapes is telling. The powerful flashback to the lynching is contained by cutting to the final scene of courtship of the heroine by a Northern mulatto doctor. In the intertitle, his first words in response to her visibly sad memories are not "marry me," but "We should never forget what our people did in Cuba under Roosevelt's command." He goes on to remind her of black participation on the battlefields of Mexico and World War I, and finally: "We were never immigrants. Be proud of our country always.—And you, Sylvia, have been thinking deeply about this, but your thoughts have been warped. In spite of your misfortunes, you will always be a patriot and a tender wife."[42]

And so she marries him. While Micheaux here claims that African Americans are more American than foreign immigrants, they can only prove their national identity as imperial citizens by their participation in wars abroad. The story of foreign warfare enters the domestic field as a marriage proposal, as the male suitor displaces the memory of white violence onto the woman's unhealthy obsession with the past. He asks her to forget that domestic violence by another kind of displacement, by remembering military ventures abroad and marrying into imperial citizenship. Cinematically, however, her flashbacks to domestic racial violence remain searing on the screen, overflowing the frame and final promise of a patriotic imperial marriage.[43]

Thus Micheaux in *Within Our Gates* reveals something disavowed yet implicit in Griffith's *The Birth of a Nation:* that the domestic unity of the nation depends on the violent subordination of blacks at home to forge a whiteness capacious enough to include immigrants; equally, it depends on the violent assertion of U.S. power abroad, a site from which Dixon and Griffith exclude African Americans, and which Micheaux, like black soldiers who fought in foreign wars, turns into an opportunity to achieve both domesticity and citizenship.[44]

Imperial Citizenship

A quarter of a century after *The Birth of a Nation,* references to the Spanish-American War appear in another landmark American film, Orson Welles's *Citizen Kane.* Although better known for its cinematic innovation than for its treatment of national identity, the title itself highlights the issue of citizenship, and Welles had thought of naming the film "The American." An early scene from Kane's childhood shows him playing at fighting a Civil War battle with snowballs, declaring, "the terms are unconditional surrender . . . The Union forever."[45] As in Griffith's film, the projection of national identity on the screen took on heightened dimensions from the international crisis of world war, at a time when the question of American entry into a European war had extreme urgency. In both films, allusions to the earlier imperial war of 1898 underscore the reconfiguration of America's global identity at these threshold moments of international conflict. I am not arguing for a reading of these films as veiled allegories or outright propaganda for foreign policy. Rather, I suggest that they both participate in and comment on the crucial work of film in creating and circulating images of American national identity at home and abroad, and they screen images of the foreign in order to domesticate them. In focusing on the life of William Randolph Hearst, Welles hearkens back to the intertwined histories of American media and American empire building at the turn of the twentieth century.

The name "Hearst" has long been identified with the word "empire." The film repeats the well-known story of Hearst pushing the United States into an imperial war in Cuba by whipping up public hysteria in his yellow press. Beyond his support for the war, Hearst's journalism syndicate and political aspirations are themselves often labeled a "media empire." The film reenacts one of the most famous apocryphal scenes from Hearst's career in the form of a telegraph exchange with a fictionalized Frederick Remington: "Food marvelous in Cuba—girls delightful—could send you prose poems about scenery. There's no war in Cuba," to which Kane responds, "You provide the prose poems—I'll provide the war." Welles links the building of Kane's media empire at home to his capacity to deploy these media to incite an intervention into a foreign war. In this view, Cuba is a tropical blank slate for the projection of Kane's imperial ambitions. The power of Kane's media to create reality—to "provide the war"—links him not only to Hearst but also to Welles's renowned showmanship and to the imperial power of film itself.

Orson Welles showed an interest in staging imperial dramas several years before making *Citizen Kane.* The radio show "War of the Worlds" enacted a colonial invasion of earth by beings from a foreign planet, and is famous for having immediately convinced listeners of the reality it simulated. Right before starting *Citizen Kane,* Welles embarked on an ambitious project (under contract to RKO), which he never completed, to make a film of Joseph Conrad's *Heart of Darkness.* Critics have explored the rich aesthetic connections between Conrad and Welles and between his plans for the incomplete film and his completed execution of *Citizen Kane.* Yet none have asked how Conrad's imperial narrative might have structured Welles's representation of America. Does *Citizen Kane* evoke a notion of imperial citizenship in which the 1890s of Conrad and Hearst resonate through the present of the film in 1940? In the search for the meaning of Kane's famously elusive final word "Rosebud," was Welles rewriting Kurtz's more resounding last words, "the horror, the horror"?

Formally, *Citizen Kane* is divided into two parts: the first focuses outward on Kane's highly public rising career, in which he uses the war as a major stepping stone, and the second turns inward to the domestic sphere and his collapsing marriage. James Naremore describes this shift as a turn "to private life rather than the public structuring of an empire."[46] The film blurs this distinction, however, as Kane's imperial qualities are reproduced in the domestic sphere of his marriage to a working-class singer. Domesticity becomes a site of empire-building, in the opera hall Kane builds for his wife's singing debut and in Xanadu, which he constructs as their home. These are fruits of Kane's empire in the outside world, as they both reproduce and unravel his imperial ambitions. Kane's creation of his wife's career out of nothing parallels his incitement of the Spanish-American War. She provides a mediocre talent; he provides the career. Kane crosses the gap between the male sphere of war and mass media and the female sphere of the home and high culture, for war and opera alike serve as testimonies to his imperial willfulness at home and abroad. In both cases, Leland, Kane's closest friend and colleague, objects to Kane's imperious projects. While in the film their first disagreement about the war is reduced to a brief lighthearted repartee, in the shooting script the argument concludes with Kane offering Leland a regular column to write his dissenting opinions about the war. Kane's empire at first seems capacious enough to contain even its opposition. In the final version, the two men come together to watch the spectacle of the female bodies dressed in the American flag and carrying guns. In the second half of the film, Leland's muted resistance to Kane's political empire emerges full-blown over the spectacle of a woman on stage, just one this time. At one of the turning points of the film, which shows the beginning of Kane's decline, Leland starts to write a negative review of Susan's opera debut, thereby refusing to endorse Kane's imperial ambitions in the domestic sphere. By completing and publishing the review himself, Kane gives Leland the voice of dissent he promised him about the war. Yet he also undermines the basis of his own domestic empire and in firing Leland from the newspaper, Kane weakens his media empire as well.

Kane's imperial project also shows up in his obsessive collecting of statues, art, buildings, and animals, first from Europe and then from "the loot of the world." He imports "the very stones of many other places from every corner of the earth." His voracious appetite for collection removes all objects from their contexts yet never even unpacks them from their crates. In the film we never see Kane abroad (except in the opening newsreel); instead, he mobilizes his power beyond U.S. borders to create the spectacle of global loot brought home. As Kane becomes physically immobilized in the orientalized domestic sphere of Xanadu, he brings fragments of the entire world into his home in a way that makes the home uncannily foreign and gothic. Ultimately the boundaries between private and public, domestic and foreign, collapse in the final scene of the film, as the intimate answer to the mystery of "Rosebud" appears on the pile of burning stuff along with the "loot of the world."

Michael Denning and Laura Mulvey have situated *Citizen Kane* in the political context of popular front struggles against fascism and New Deal arguments against American isolationism.[47] Both readings acknowledge the international dimensions of a film that appears almost claustrophobically enclosed within the domestic spheres of nation and home, yet both also overlook the complex relation of the film to American imperialism. Mulvey sees the references to the Spanish-American War as evidence merely of Kane's "willingness to play on vulgar jingoism."[48] Denning claims that in going from *Heart of Darkness* to *Citizen Kane,* Welles recast the imperial genre of civilization versus the jungle into an antifascist narrative of civilization versus fascism.[49] Yet that formulation preserves an imperial framework by equating fascism with the "uncivilized" colonized world. I suggest that the democratic Citizen Kane is inseparable from the Imperial Kane, as he aggressively pursues his representative American status by building empires in both the public and private spheres with the "loot"—news as well as objects—he appropriates from around the globe. The isolationism Mulvey sees in Kane goes hand in hand with his imperial desires.

As Denning has shown, Welles based Kane in part also on Henry Luce. Luce had built a modern media empire by founding *Life, Time,* and *Fortune* magazines and by promoting popular and innovative forms of photojournalism and newsreels, techniques that Welles drew on in his filmmaking. Welles also worked for Luce, and Denning has shown that Welles's progressive Mercury Theater had many ambivalent dealings with the Luce companies.[50] *Citizen Kane* opens with a newsreel of Kane's life narrated through the rhetoric of empire, in a parody of Luce's popular series, "The March of Time." Welles thus introduces his own cinematic in-depth investigation of Kane's life from multiple perspectives, by defining it against the official images and linear narrative of Luce's newsreels.

Through his control over the media, Luce became an influential ideologue in redefining an imperial global role for the United States, namely, to lead what he famously dubbed "The American Century." He published an essay under that title in *Life Magazine* several months before the release of *Citizen Kane*. Exhorting the United States to enter the war in Europe, Luce aimed also to control the terms of its representation, to "give this war its proper name," and to "bring forth a vision of America as a world power which is authentically American."[51] Such authenticity meant projecting a global power for the United States that would free it from geographic boundaries. Luce argued that territorial defense could not provide a strong enough rationale for entering the war, nor could appeals "to fight for dear old Danzig or dear old Dong Dang" (20). Equally dissatisfied with abstractions such as "Democracy and Freedom," he asked: "is there nothing between the absurd sound of distant cities and the brassy trumpeting of majestic words?" (21). His answer defined an "internationalism" that would make American interests synonymous with the "world environment in which she lives" (24) and that would efface the irritating otherness of foreign lands, peoples and cultures with strange names. Throughout the essay, Luce envisioned American world power as anti-imperial and deterritorialized, in direct contrast to the imperial dominions of Rome, the Vatican, Genghis Khan, the Chinese, and most recently the British. "American internationalism," in contrast, was already taking hold through the circulation of "American jazz, Hollywood movies, American slang, American machines and patented products [which] are in fact the only things that every community in the world, from Zanzibar to Hamburg, recognizes in common" (33). As opposed to the military and political domination by the Old World empires, the United States would use American culture and commerce—backed, of course, by weapons and the state—as the conduits and embodiments of its world power. Luce saw no tension between nationalism and internationalism; instead, American culture and consumer goods provided the only common ground or universal language across the globe. Indeed, his own media empire did much both to foster the omnipresence of American products and values and to bring home to a domestic audience a world stripped of its discomfiting foreignness.

Orson Welles later wrote that "if Luce's prediction of the American Century will come true, God help us all. It will make Germany's bid for world supremacy look like amateur night."[52] His theatrical metaphor used the terms of showmanship for the rivalry over global power; the American Century would offer a more professional and thorough performance of world supremacy than the amateurism of fascism. Although *Citizen Kane* was completed just before "The American Century" was published, it is possible to see the Kane character not only as a warning against isolationism and fascism, but also as a grotesque embodiment of Luce's internationalism—an enactment and a critique of imperial citizenship.

Welles's aesthetic innovations in *Citizen Kane* have been open to various political interpretations. André Bazin saw his acclaimed use of deep focus and the long take as democratic, in allowing freedom for the viewer to interpret the scene, while Denning has related Welles's showmanship and magician-like control to his turning of Nazi propaganda techniques against fascism.[53] It would be important to investigate further the relation between Welles's formal innovations and the imperial themes of his films. Bazin notes, for example, that Welles's use of low angles and ceilings makes us feel that "Kane's lust for power crushes us, but is itself crushed by the décor. Through the camera, we are capable in a way of perceiving Kane's failure at the same time we experience his power."[54] Might the innovative camera work, with its deep focus and showmanship, have created an imperial gaze for the American Century, in its capacity to penetrate deeply into unknown spaces and at the same time reflect back its own image? Would Welles both deploy and challenge this imperial gaze when he traveled to Brazil under the auspices of the Office of Inter-American Affairs to make *It's All True?* When he sailed his characters through the Panama Canal in *The Lady of Shanghai?* When he explored the violent imperial relations of the Mexican-United States border in *Touch of Evil?*

Welles's cinematic innovations combine facets of Luce's photojournalism with the earliest techniques of filmmaking before Griffith. *Citizen Kane,* in both form and content, hearkens back to the turn of the twentieth century, when the capacity of the new "moving pictures" to tell stories arose in part out of the imperative to narrate the spectacle of U.S. mobility and military power abroad. Griffith further developed this form of storytelling, which, I have argued, relied on enlisting the domestic sphere as a frame for empire building. Micheaux used this frame to reconfigure the relations of race, nationhood, and empire. Welles later challenged the relation between film's storytelling capacity and imperial narratives, while Henry Luce in "The American Century" was seeking the "proper name" for a partly new, partly old version of this story. The desire to tell this story has surfaced at key moments in the intersecting development of U.S. cinema and U.S. foreign policy to renegotiate the relation between the domestic and the foreign, between the nation at home and the nation abroad.

Like Luce in his project of internationalism, Kane re-creates the world in his own image, which is at once mobile and elastic, yet claustrophobic and immobilized. As Kane's empire implodes in the home, Welles's film exemplifies the anarchy of empire, the nightmare underlying Luce's dream of Americanization. If America sees reflections of itself everywhere and strives to encompass the globe, then it risks losing the boundaries between the domestic and the foreign that define the nation as home, as unique and separate from the outlying world. As Kane amasses the loot of the world, his own body appears engorged and distended with the objects he has ingested. He tries to turn the entire world into hollow references to his own power, while he becomes impotent and immured in the home he creates as his castle, Xanadu. In the character of Kane, the outward reach of imperialism and the self-enclosure of isolationism are twinned. The film depicts a grotesquely representative American citizen who so identifies himself with the "world environment" that he never has to leave his house, though his last words express nostalgia, the desire, in the etymological sense of *nostos,* to return home. In accumulating fragments of the outside world into the domestic sphere, Citizen Kane turns the space of his American home into something hauntingly foreign.

CHAPTER 6

The Imperial Cartography
of W. E. B. Du Bois

In 1915 W. E. B. Du Bois published his magisterial essay, "The African Roots of War." Through a seismic shift of geographic and historical perspectives, Du Bois located in Africa the origins of the war in Europe:

> There are those who would write world history and leave out this most marvelous of continents. Particularly today most men assume that Africa lies far afield from our present problem of World War. Yet in a very real sense Africa is the prime cause of this terrible overturning of civilization which we have lived to see; and these words seek to show how in the Dark Continent are hidden the roots, not simply of war to-day but of the menace of wars tomorrow.[1]

The essay moves Africa from geographic periphery and historical backwater into the central vantage point from which to rewrite the history of the present and remap the terrain of the "World War." The essay offers more than the causal economic argument for which it is known. By grounding his inquiry in Africa, Du Bois exposes the way the representations of space and time have been structured by imperial maps and narratives of the world, and from this location he draws alternative maps and writes new historical narratives.

The war did not originate in 1914 in the Balkans, argues Du Bois, but at least thirty years earlier in the violent "scramble" for Africa and the spiraling competition to "possess the materials and men of the darker world." The importance of rewriting this history lies in the future. World war can only conclude in a real peace, he predicts, by ending colonialism, for it is "directly in this outer circle of races, and not in the inner European household, that the real causes of the present European fighting are to be found" (103). Du Bois uses domestic language to overturn the divisions of inside and outside, home and abroad, and he offers a critique of nationalism not only as the cause of empire but also as its consequence.

That same year, closer to home, Du Bois was one of the few Americans to condemn the U.S. invasion of Haiti, which was largely eclipsed by news of the European war. On the pages of *The Crisis,* the magazine he edited for the National Association for the Advancement of Colored People, he refuted the rationale that internal chaos within Haiti warranted outside intervention: "The anarchy in Haiti is no worse than the anarchy in the United States at the time of Civil War, and not as great as the anarchy today in Europe. The lynching and murder in Port-au-Prince is no worse than, if as bad as, the lynching in Georgia. Haiti can and will work out her own destiny, and is more civilized today than is Texas."[2] The repetition of the word "anarchy" relocates Haiti from its status as an island isolated in its own discord onto a global map of imperial violence that extends from Europe and its colonies to the American South. From the perspective of Haiti, Du Bois overturns the conventional boundaries between civilization and barbarism, order and anarchy, the domestic and the foreign.

Alongside reports from Haiti that year in *The Crisis,* Du Bois published a running account of the NAACP protests against D. W. Griffith's *The Birth of a Nation.* Du Bois lambasted the film for rewriting the history of emancipation and Reconstruction as an "orgy of theft and degradation."[3] Looking back at 1915 in his autobiography, *Dusk of Dawn,* he linked the military invasion of Haiti to the film, which he called an even "more insidious and hurtful attack" because of its global scope. The film's racist spectacle, claimed Du Bois, "made great" the "new technique of the moving picture" and expanded its appeal throughout "America and the world."[4]

Movie theaters in the United States in 1915 may seem as far afield from colonial Africa as does the Caribbean republic of Haiti from the theaters of war in Europe. I argue, however, that Du Bois represented these arenas as inextricably linked by the anarchy of empire. The eruption of World War I exposed the violently shifting grounds on which he could remap the complex interconnections among such remote geographies and renarrate their intersecting histories. Du Bois saw these sites conjoined not only by economics and military might, but also by struggles over representation. The U.S. invasion of Haiti deployed on an international scale the national script of Griffith's film; they both rendered the struggle for black self-government as anarchic and destructive misrule. "The African Roots of War" offered a counter-narrative of American origins that located the birth of the modern nation in the anarchic dislocations of imperial exploitation.

Building on the insights of "African Roots" at the end of the war, Du Bois brought together these interconnected geographies and histories in a remarkable book, *Darkwater: Voices from Within the Veil* (1920). Although overlooked by later critics, *Darkwater* is one of Du Bois's most ambitious and formally innovative efforts to represent racial conflicts within the United States through transnational networks of imperial power. My chapter focuses on a reading of *Darkwater* as a linguistic form of imperial cartography that uses language to draw overlapping maps of the emerging postwar world. *Darkwater* expands the meaning of "world war" beyond the battlefields of Europe to encompass and interlink the colonization of Africa and Asia, the struggles of the post-Reconstruction United States, and the overseas propulsion of the U.S. empire. *Darkwater* also looks inward at the domestic spaces of the home, schoolroom, factory, and city, to place these apparently local spaces at the crossroads of movements of vast global change. Mapping social space involves a struggle over representation, to renarrate the histories inscribed in or erased from conventional maps of the world. As Du Bois's imperial cartography charts the way that the anarchy of empire dissolves the boundaries between the domestic and foreign, he also reimagines forms of transnational collectivity that go beyond the boundaries of colony and empire.

It is well known that Du Bois drew a powerful link between "segregation at home and colonialism abroad," and that he connected these spheres through the common denominator of the color line.[5] This double focus was encapsulated by the double trajectory of Du Bois's career: his national fight against racism in his leadership of the NAACP, and his international struggle against colonialism in his organization of the Pan-African movement. This formulation, however, runs the risk of separating as much as bringing together; it implicitly upholds a logic of American exceptionalism that projects imperialism as a foreign issue of European colonialism and thereby disavows the domestic reality of U.S. empire-building. By limiting Du Bois's treatment of empire to the European colonization of Africa, scholars of Du Bois often overlook the international role of the United States in demarcating and policing the global color line, as well as the way global imperial dynamics affect race relations within the United States. An analysis of Du Bois's complex representation of American imperialism, I contend, can enrich our understanding of how his internationalism deconstructs the bifurcation between racism at home and colonialism abroad.

Numerous scholars have studied Du Bois from multiple international perspectives: his involvement in the Pan-African movement, black nationalism, and international socialism, and, more recently, in the transnational contexts of the African Diaspora or the Black Atlantic.[6] These studies focus on Du Bois's political opposition to Western colonialism and racism and his transnational reconfiguration of black identities, yet they rarely take account of Du Bois's relation to American imperialism, especially in the first half of his career. Paul Gilroy posits a useful distinction between the notion of "roots" as an essentialist definition of identity anchored in a homeland, and "routes" as a fluid concept of hybrid identities and affiliations that emerge from travel and change.[7] I am interested in how Du Bois links these two meanings to imperial dynamics across the globe. "Roots" in "The African Roots of War" refers not simply to an organic ancient identity but to the historical crossroads of imperial conflict and violent dislocation.

Like Mark Twain, Du Bois remains one of America's most outspoken critics of imperialism worldwide. Yet in contrast to Twain, his anti-imperialism has been better known outside the United States and is still most often associated with the period of decolonization after World War I. In addition to Du Bois's overt condemnations of imperialism, I am interested in the way his writing, like Twain's, both charted and was embedded in the transnational routes and networks of imperial power. From his earliest writing at the turn of the century, a shifting conception of empire was central to his understanding of race relations within the United States. Du Bois saw U.S. imperialism not as an isolated phenomenon but as part of a broader global system. If he decried the imposition of imperial force on the world, he also saw the United States as a product of imperial relations acted upon by forces beyond its boundaries. For Du Bois, imperialism did more than propel U.S. domination abroad; it also struck at the heart of the domestic nation. Thus rather than just condemn the United States as a center of world power, Du Bois used the framework of empire to decenter American power and destabilize its national boundaries. Yet at times, as I will show, Du Bois also recentered his own international authority by enlisting the exceptionalist logic of American imperialism. Together, these complex—and often contradictory—views locate U.S. imperialism itself in a broader international framework that goes beyond the limits of national geographies and histories. *Darkwater* powerfully enacts for readers what World War I brought violently to the foreground for Du Bois: that "the U.S. was living not to itself, but as part of the strain and stress of the world."[8]

Empire and the Color Line

Before turning to *Darkwater,* it is useful to have a sense of Du Bois's representation of U.S. imperialism in his earlier writing. His global mapping of the color line follows the trajectories of empire. In 1906 he wrote that "the tendency of the great nations of the day is territorial, political and economic expansion, but in every case this has brought them in contact with darker people. . . . The policy of expansion then simply means the world problems of the Color Line. The question enters European imperial politics and floods our continents from Alaska to Patagonia."[9] A chief feature of his approach here is that he does not separate racism at home from colonialism abroad, but views both as part of a broader international dynamic of empire. In his earliest historical writing, Du Bois narrated U.S. history as a product of imperial forces. In his 1897 dissertation, "The Suppression of the African Slave-trade to the United States of America, 1638–1870," Du Bois recast the story of American origins within the sweeping narrative of European colonialism and the African slave trade. He also recast major events in American national history in a broader hemispheric context, by decentering the national framework in which history is written and retelling that story from the perspective of Haiti:

> The role which the great Negro Toussaint, called L'Ouverture played
> in the history of the United States has seldom been fully appreciated.
> Representing the age of revolution in America, he rose to the leader-

ship through a bloody terror, which contrived a Negro "problem" for the Western hemisphere, intensified and defined the anti-slavery movement, became one of the causes, and probably the prime one, which led Napoleon to sell Louisiana for a song, and finally through the interworking of all these effects, rendered more certain the final prohibition of the slave-trade by the United States in 1807.[10]

Key here is not simply the chain of a causal argument; as in "African Roots," it is the vast shift of geographic perspective that grounds the narrative of "the interworking of all these effects." Viewed from the vantage point of Haiti, the history of U.S. expansion does not arise from its self-generated compulsion—the "frontier," the "errand into the wilderness," or "manifest destiny"—but develops in relation to the anti-imperial and antislavery struggles of the Caribbean revolution. This perspective goes beyond the perimeter of national history to place the United States within a wider imperial network tied to Africa, Europe, and the Caribbean.

The multiple dimensions of empire are central to Du Bois's earliest articulation of his famous pronouncement: "the problem of the twentieth century is the problem of the color line,—the relation of the darker to the lighter races of men in Asia and Africa, in America and the islands of the sea." This statement is most often cited from the second chapter of *The Souls of Black Folk,* where it frames Du Bois's history of the Freedmen's Bureau during Reconstruction.[11] It is often noted that Du Bois first made this statement in a slightly different form at the meeting of the Pan-African Conference of 1900 in London, in his address "To the Nations of the World."[12] These two settings seem to exemplify his double vision of "racism at home and colonialism abroad." Few scholars note, however, that Du Bois also made this statement earlier that same year in Washington, D.C., in an address to the American Negro Academy, "The Present Outlook for the Dark Races of Mankind."[13] There he set forth his project to "consider with you the problem of the color line not simply as a national and personal question but rather in its larger world aspect in time and space" (73). He claimed that "yet a glance over the world at the dawn of the new century will convince us that this is just the beginning of the problem—that the color line belts the world and that the social problem of the twentieth century is to be the relation of the civilized world to the dark races of mankind" (73). As the essay sweeps worldwide from past to present, its pivotal point, where local and global meet, hinges on American empire-building started in 1898:

> But most significant of all at this period is the fact that the colored population of our land is, through the new imperial policy, about to be doubled by our own ownership of Porto [sic] Rico, and Hawaii, our protectorate of Cuba, and conquest of the Philippines. This is for us and for the nation the greatest event since the Civil War and demands attention and action on our part. What is to be our attitude toward these new lands and toward the masses of dark men and women who inhabit them? (77)

Thus in 1900, when Du Bois first articulated the "problem of the twentieth century," he spoke from two imperial centers, Washington, D.C., and London, and he mapped the global color line in relation to both European and American imperialism. In his answer to the question above, he deploys the discourse of American exceptionalism—empire for freedom, manifest destiny—as a strategy for eradicating the very color line that empire has constructed:

> Manifestly it must be an attitude of deepest sympathy and strongest alliance. We must stand ready to guard and guide them with our vote and our earnings. Negro and Filipino, Indian and Porto Rican, Cuban and Hawaiian, all must stand united under the stars and stripes for an America that knows no color line in the freedom of its opportunities. We must remember that the twentieth century will find nearly twenty millions of brown and black people under the protection of the American flag, a third of the nation, and that on the success and efficiency of the nine millions of our own number depends the ultimate destiny of Filipinos, Porto Ricans, Indian and Hawaiians, and that on us too depends in a large degree the attitude of Europe toward the teeming millions of Asia and Africa. (78)

Du Bois's evocation of 1898 has a double-edged effect. On the one hand, it decenters the U.S. "race question" as part of a global imperial context. On the other hand, it centers "we black men of America" as leaders of the darker world, for which the United States serves as a model. "No nation ever bore a heavier burden than we black men of America" (78). Du Bois turns the white man's burden into the black man's burden, and imagines within the American Empire an *imperium in imperio* as a utopian vision of world change. The question here is not whether Du Bois was for or against American imperialism. He both enlists its discourse and turns it against itself. If in previous chapters we noted racist arguments against imperial expansion, Du Bois here makes an imperial argument against racism: imperial expansion has the potential to break down national borders and racial divisions and to promote multiracial affiliations across the globe.

Du Bois imagined the utopian potential in imperial expansion for unraveling the boundaries of nations and colonies. From the anarchy of empire, he envisioned the rise of new forms of collectivity that overflow those borders. Imperialism in 1898, according to Du Bois, invited African Americans in Washington, D.C., to reimagine their future in relation to other nonwhite subjects of the American empire worldwide. A shared experience of empire brought a "congress of men and women of African blood" into "the metropolis of the modern world" in London in 1900. In *Souls* Du Bois also mapped this contradictory movement of empire to divide and unite, as he looked backward in time at the "shimmering swirl of waters" where the first slave ships arrived in Jamestown. From there, he envisioned the potential of a "new human unity, pulling the ends of the earth nearer, and all men, black, yellow, and white." When Du Bois came to frame his chapter on Reconstruction in *Souls* by the proposition that "the problem of the twentieth century is the problem of the color line," this statement resonated from the imperial capitals where he had first articulated the problematic in 1900. In *Souls* he thus introduced the uncompleted work of Reconstruction in America by linking it to imperial locations around the globe, as he projected into the immediate future the urgent need for new forms of reconstruction on a global scale.

Paris and Podunk

The eruption of World War I violently pulled "the ends of the earth nearer" by exposing the destructive foundation of European civilization in colonialism and by spurring the emergence of new anticolonial alliances. At the war's end Du Bois traveled to Paris, where the story has often been told of his organization of the Pan-African Congress. The Congress had a wide-ranging symbolic and political impact for years to come, but this meeting in 1919 was politically hampered by its dependence on French colonialism and by the fact that few African representatives attended.[14] While in Paris, Du Bois was equally concerned with another forum, the Peace Conference, where he wished to represent the "Negro world" and link the struggle for civil rights in the United States to the struggle for independence in postwar Africa. He tried futilely, however, to gain a hearing from Woodrow Wilson, and he also faced mounting skepticism from African Americans at home.

In May 1919 Du Bois wrote a letter to *The Crisis* in which he defended his presence in France in the immediate aftermath of World War I, at a time of escalating violence against African Americans in the United States:

> I went to Paris because to-day the destinies of mankind center there. Make no mistake as to this, my readers.
>
> Podunk may easily persuade itself that only Podunk matters and that nothing is going on in New York. The South Sea Islander may live ignorant and careless of London. Some Americans may think that Europe does not count, and a few Negroes may argue vociferously that the Negro problem is a domestic matter, to be settled in Richmond and New Orleans. But all these careless thinkers are wrong. The destinies of mankind for a hundred years to come are being settled to-day in a small room of the Hotel Crillon by four unobtrusive gentlemen who glance out speculatively now and then to Cleopatra's Needle on the Place de la Concorde.[15]

Du Bois insists on viewing the "domestic matter" of American racism in an international network of imperial relations. He describes the victors of the world war ironically as "unobtrusive gentlemen" ensconced in a deceptively small room. From this enclosed center they wield the power to redivide and remap the globe, buttressed, he writes, by their vast control of "armies and navies, the world supply of capital and the press." Du Bois gives a subtle gloss to the view outside their Paris hotel room. When they glance outside their window, their gaze is repeatedly drawn to a monument celebrating the colonial conquest of northern Africa. The towering obelisk in the busy streets of Paris dwarfs and accentuates the enclosure of the hotel room, while exposing it to the outside. Locating the colonial spoils of Africa in the heart of the European metropolis has the effect of collapsing the very boundaries that the participants in the peace conference were redrawing and reinforcing.

Like the needle of a compass, the obelisk points toward alternative perspectives and directions from which to remap the postwar world. Du Bois's letter goes on to list an extraordinary array of organizations in attendance representing nations, peoples, races, religions, labor and political groups from all over the world, as though proliferating the potential sites marked by Cleopatra's Needle. Given the global significance of this international gathering, he resents that "some American Negroes actually asked why I went to help represent the Negro world in Africa and America and the Islands of the sea?" (187). He answers hyperbolically, "if the Negroes of the world could have maintained during the entire sitting of the Peace Conference a central headquarters . . . they could have settled the future of Africa" (187). This rhetorical bravado indicates the importance to Du Bois—and his anxiety—of staking out literal and figurative space from which to map counter-geographies of the postwar world.

Completed after his return from Paris, during the summer of 1919, *Darkwater* is suffused with the turmoil Du Bois found there, of old empires, nations, and colonies crumbling in the midst of struggles over new configurations of social and political space around the globe. In *Darkwater* Du Bois appropriates and transforms the cartographic power he found concentrated in the hands of the imperial nations. In contrast to the centralized perspective of the imperial gaze, *Darkwater* maps the world from multiple decentered vantage points; not Paris, London, and Washington, but Congo, Port-au-Prince, and East St. Louis. Cartography does not just reflect established boundaries between fixed geopolitical units, but discursively produces new aggregates of social space that can be policed, contested, and transformed. *Darkwater* focuses on movement around the globe that destabilizes fixed borderlines; cartography is an activity where fantasy and power meet. *Darkwater* reconfigures the geographical terrain of "world war" beyond the battlefields of Europe, from the colonies of Africa and Asia to Jim Crow America to sites of U.S. intervention abroad. Cartography in *Darkwater* is inseparable from history and language. It is a strategic device through which Du Bois narrates those pasts that dominant world maps overlay and erase. He redefines the meaning of the word "war" to include conflicts over representations of space and time, and critiques the contemporary definition of peace as he imagines alternative futures. The Paris Peace Conference posed for him the question of how to represent a world that was becoming increasingly interconnected by centralized forms of imperial power. It posed the equally pressing question of defining anticolonial alliances and decentralized emerging collectivities.

If Du Bois's aspirations for the Peace Conference filled the pages of *Darkwater*, the work also bore the marks of his controversial endorsement of the U.S. war effort. The war had catapulted Du Bois into one of the most controversial and contradictory periods of his career, where his national and international perspectives clashed and intermingled without resolution.[16] (The controversies resonate in the defensive tone of the letter from Paris.) In a notorious *Crisis* editorial of July 1918, "Close Ranks," he advocated that American blacks "forget our special grievances" to join the war effort in a segregated army with segregated training camps for officers.[17] In the tradition of imperial citizenship we have seen during the Spanish-American War and in Micheaux's film, Du Bois imagined black soldiers "standing shoulder to shoulder with our own white fellow citizens" in a militarized national body, ready through the medium of a common enemy abroad to "inaugurate the United States of the World." In this international context, Du Bois recuperated a vision of the United States as the "hope of mankind and of black mankind" by representing Germany as the embodiment of racial oppression. Only a year earlier he wrote that German colonialism was on a continuum with that of the French and English and with Southern racism in the United States.[18] Despite heated opposition from many African American quarters, Du Bois would never fully relinquish the position of "Close Ranks."[19] Throughout the war, Du Bois continued to advocate that African Americans pursue overseas what D. L. Lewis has called "citizenship through carnage," even though his "The African Roots of War" had decried the origins of that carnage in colonial oppression.[20] Yet during his trip to France at the war's end, Du Bois also documented both the power and dismal limits of imperial citizenship in his research for an uncompleted three-volume history of black troops in the war, which he planned to title "The Wounded World."[21]

From Paris Du Bois brought these uncompleted and controversial projects into the pages of *Darkwater*, where he turned the discourse of war from abroad to back home, as he did in another influential *Crisis* editorial, "Returning Soldiers." It concludes:

> *We return.*
> *We return from fighting.*
> *We return fighting.*
> Make way for Democracy! We saved it in France and
>   by the Great Jehovah, we will save it in the United States
>   of America or know the reason why.[22]

The conspicuous absence of the word "home" is supplanted by "fighting" to shatter the distinction between a foreign battlefield and a home front. The imperial discourse of the rescue mission abroad shifts direction into the heart of the undomestic nation. The "return fighting" from Europe and Pan-Africa to an unwelcoming home is one of the major narrative trajectories that inform *Darkwater.* Du Bois completed it during the "Red Summer" of 1919, a horrific nationwide conflagration of antiblack violence countered by the militancy of returning black soldiers. *Darkwater* can be read as Du Bois's contribution to that struggle, both as a weapon of war and a search for peace, which recasts domestic racial violence within a global imperial context.

It is tempting to understand the war as a watershed in Du Bois's career, when he turned from a nationalist and patriotic support of America's entry into the war to a more internationalist and antinationalist vision. Yet this narrative does not do justice to the multiple positions at play for Du Bois during the war, when he was simultaneously and contradictorily at his most national and international. These positions were by no means polar opposites with inherent political valences; instead, they were constitutive of one another. Du Bois was not simply choosing sides but engaged in implicit debates and dialogues with varieties of internationalism across the political spectrum: socialist revolution and pacifism, Wilson's League of Nations, Garvey's black nationalism, Pan-Africanism, All-Asia movements, anticolonial nationalism, the red scare in the United States that blamed black dissent on Bolshevik infiltration, and white supremacist panic about worldwide race war. This list of course cannot do justice to the range of movements and discourses engaged in remapping the world and in redrawing connections and boundaries between nations, colonies, and what Du Bois called the "inter-nation."

While Du Bois tried fruitlessly to achieve a meeting with Woodrow Wilson in Paris, others did pay attention. White Supremacist Lothrop Stoddard in *The Rising Tide of Color* quoted Du Bois's "African Roots" as dangerous evidence that the nonwhite world, from Japan to America to India, saw the war as an occasion for worldwide uprisings to seize power from the white world. Stoddard too had a cartographic imagination, starting with an atlas of the world in 1914 and including multicolored maps of the world along racial lines, with one next to his quotation of Du Bois, "The Distribution of the Primary Races."[23] While *Darkwater* does not include actual maps, it performs a similar act of cartography in imaging a globe encircled by "dark waters" of black migrations around the world. Stoddard was not the only one to criticize Du Bois. Marcus Garvey in a speech in 1920 declared, "You cannot advocate 'close ranks' today and talk 'dark water' tomorrow."[24] But Du Bois did just that in *Darkwater*. He did not stake out a single international position but put in play multiple maps that collide, merge, and compete with one another in dizzying combinations.

Darkwater

Marketed as a companion to *The Souls of Black Folk* and resembling it in form and content, *Darkwater* was widely reviewed and read as one of Du Bois's most important books at the time.[25] Yet while *Souls* has achieved a canonical literary status, critics have neglected *Darkwater*.[26] Both are composite multigenre texts that bring together essays, autobiography, poems, and parables, often in elusive combinations. *Darkwater* moves through an even more jarring juxtaposition of discontinuous spaces, divergent histories, and clashing literary styles. It can be read as an internationalist revision of *Souls*. The two books share a similar three-part structure, starting with autobiography and moving to the history of war—Civil War in one and World War in the other, then postwar Reconstruction and the question of black leadership. The first four chapters of *Darkwater* leap breathlessly from Du Bois's New England birthplace to the battlefields of Europe to the postwar settlement of Africa to industrial East St. Louis. The next four chapters turn to social conditions in the United States, focusing on the home, the status of black women, labor, the franchise, and education. In each case these putatively domestic spheres open up to vast movements of global change. The third part of the book looks to the future through more lyrical and personal pieces, which are also more global in sweep. The elegy for young black men at the end of *Souls* is echoed by the chapter "The Immortal Child" about the African-British composer, Samuel Coleridge-Taylor, best known for his operatic version of *Hiawatha*. The book ends with an apocalyptic science fiction fable in which New York City is destroyed by a comet. Most of the chapters start with an autobiographical fragment, and in place of the double epigraphs of *Souls*, Du Bois punctuates each chapter with a highly condensed poem or parable drawing on the mythology of Ethiopianism or the figure of a black Christ.

In spite of these formal similarities, *Darkwater* diverges from *Souls* significantly in abandoning the latter's well-known national paradigm of double-consciousness—"One ever feels his twoness, an American, a Negro."[27] Instead, the transnational scope of *Darkwater* explores multiple forms of consciousness, not delineated solely by nation and race though informed by both, and routed instead through the dispersed locations and dislocations of empire. While *Souls* enacts a journey on a North/South axis of the United States, the journey of *Darkwater* takes place through worldwide networks that encompass Europe, Africa, the industrial United States, and the "colonies that belt the globe." *Darkwater* collapses far-flung distances into jarring proximity, and bursts open the enclosed space of home and factory to far-ranging global trajectories. Even the lyrical interludes between chapters blur the boundaries between heaven and earth, cosmology and history.

Whereas *The Souls of Black Folk* has found a major place in the literary canon, *Darkwater* has remained curiously overlooked by critics of American and African American literature, even though several chapters have been repeatedly anthologized. I think this neglect has two sources: *Darkwater* does not neatly fit into the narratives of Du Bois's career, nor into dominant literary categories of modernist aesthetics and African American writing. Scholars have often followed Du Bois's own account of his intellectual autobiography in *Dusk of Dawn*, where he saw himself progressing toward an enlightened international view of empire through a Marxian perspective on labor and capital. The chapter "Science and Empire" traces with irony his own ignorance of imperialism as he lived through it, and he concludes that only in retrospect did "empire" provide a conceptual framework for writing the "history of our day": "That history may be epitomized in one word—Empire; the domination of white Europe over black Africa and yellow Asia, through political power built on the economic control of labor, income and ideas. The echo of this industrial imperialism in America was the expulsion of black men from American democracy, their subjection to caste control and wage slavery."[28] This framework of "Empire" in *Dusk of Dawn,* however, has its own blind spots. For one, it includes the United States in a world system only by relegating racial oppression at home to an "echo" of the dominant model of European imperialism. Furthermore, throughout *Dusk of Dawn,* empire appears as a totalizing and monolithic system that ultimately explains everything—a horizon of all social knowledge that remains elusive and static in itself and in the last instance defies definition.

Darkwater, by contrast, offers a multidimensional and multivocal account of what Du Bois calls on its last page "the Anarchy of Empire." In contrast to "Empire" in *Dusk,* "the Anarchy of Empire" cannot be summarized in one word or categorized as a coherent system or political theory, but instead emerges through experiments with form. The disjunctive qualities of the text in time and space, its vertiginous motion, jarring and fragmented juxtapositions, and cacophonous dialogues, all of which seem to have no rational connections, together chart the anarchic routes and irrational workings of empire.

If *Darkwater* does not fit neatly into narratives of Du Bois's career, neither does it fit major paradigms of literary modernism.[29] Building on the work of Raymond Williams, Edward Said and Fredric Jameson have argued that the formal elements we associate with European modernism register the severance of the metropolis from its colonies.[30] This rupture materially informs the lived experience of European modernity, for which the production of everyday life takes place in faraway colonies. These critics view the formal innovations of modernism—fragmentation, encyclopedic mapping, primitivism—as aesthetic strategies that embody, cloak, or compensate for this deep fissure and sense of loss and dislocation resulting from the sense that reality is always elsewhere. *Darkwater,* in contrast, deploys modernist forms of incongruity, fragmentation, and discontinuity for the opposite effect: to collapse distances and overturn the hierarchy between metropolis and periphery. In *Darkwater* the modernist discontinuities and disjointed textual effects work to map the interconnectedness of these bifurcated spheres, to show how distant locations collide with one another and enclosed spaces are wrenched apart by the imperial movements of capital, persons, weapons, and ideology. Rather than striving to reconstitute a lost wholeness at the heart of Euro-American modernity, Du Bois in his modernist aesthetics imagines alternative modernities from multiple vantages along the color line that "belts the world."

A guide to the modernist aesthetics of *Darkwater* can be found in one of the most elusive chapters of the book, "Of Beauty and Death." Du Bois opens with a dialogue between an autobiographical persona and a white friend who claims that Du Bois is too sensitive to racial insults and exaggerates them out of fear. He tries fruitlessly to explain how acts of racial discrimination cannot be quantified in time and place but occur "now and then—now seldom, now, sudden; now after a week, now in a chain of awful minutes; not everywhere, but anywhere—in Boston, in Atlanta. That's the hell of it."[31] For example, at a movie theater showing a Charlie Chaplin film, he is forced to buy a ticket to the smoking gallery. In choosing to protest, he experiences a range of emotions, from militant pride in fighting for the future of "unborn children" to humiliation at elevating a "cheap and tawdry" entertainment into a battleground for rights. In a search for an alternative form of beauty and pleasure, the author then presents a cinematic montage that breathlessly juxtaposes scenes from black participation and discrimination in the war, descriptions of sublime natural beauty (from the Maine coast to a Jamaican sunset to the Grand Canyon), scenes of Jim Crow trains in the South, ships returning from Europe to New York Harbor, and street scenes in Harlem. This montage presents the mobile composition of *Darkwater* as alternative to the fixed claustrophobia of the movie theater. In Chapter 5 above we saw how the cinematic eye developed out of an imperial gaze that could survey the world and compose it into an imperial narrative. Du Bois may be seen as appropriating the power of cinematic mobility for an alternative aesthetic. In "The African Roots" he notes that "in the minds of yellow, brown, and black men, the brutal truth is clearing: a white man is privileged to go to any land where advantage beckons and behave as he pleases: the black or colored man is being more and more confined to these parts of the world where life for climatic, historical, economic and political reasons is most difficult to live and most easily dominated by Europe."[32] This privilege of white men is the mobility of empire, which Du Bois sees as a question of representation as well. The white man is able to manipulate the camera's gaze and immobilize black men in its frame and also to redirect the black gaze. Du Bois in *Darkwater* was seeking a counter-mobility—modes of representation that could compete with the mobile containment of film.

Transient Tenants

Like many of Du Bois's books, *Darkwater* starts with autobiography to legitimate the narrative that follows. Written on his fiftieth birthday, the first chapter, "The Shadow of Years," presents a family epic that sweeps across continents from past to present. It opens with a description of his childhood home in rural Massachusetts. It was a conventional domestic abode: "quaint, with clapboard running up and down, neatly trimmed, and there were five rooms, a tiny porch, a rosy front yard, and unbelievably delicious strawberries in the rear" (485–86). This idyll of domestic stability totters, however, in the next line, where we read that "a South Carolinian, lately come to the Berkshire Hills owned all this," which made the Du Bois family "transient tenants for the time." The trope of "transient tenants" resonates throughout *Darkwater;* it uproots the organic meaning of home and links it to movement through time and space, exposing its foundation in unequal economic transactions. Du Bois then narrates his family genealogy; it connects generations less through place than through transit, even though he traces his ancestry to this same locale for two hundred years. Du Bois recounts Tom Burghardt's arrival in the region; brought as a slave by his Dutch "captor," he achieved freedom by fighting for the Revolution and had a son who fought in the war of 1812. While Tom's Bantu wife clung to her memories of Africa and "never became reconciled to this strange land" (486), Tom established a lineage of militant manhood that turned servitude into freedom through military service to the nation (a legacy that may reflect Du Bois's choice in World War I). On the other side of his family, he charts the routes of transient tenants from France and the Bahamas to his grandfather's move from Connecticut to Haiti, from there to work on a passenger boat in New York, and finally to retire in the port of New Bedford. Du Bois even romanticizes his absent father as the "Beloved Vagabond" (487).

He summarizes his family history with a mock epic flourish: "So with some circumstance having finally gotten myself born, with a flood of Negro blood, a strain of French, a bit of Dutch, but, thank God! no 'Anglo-Saxon,' I come to the days of my childhood" (488). Much scholarly debate has taken place about Du Bois's reliance on biological definitions of race.[33] Here his references to blood have a comically ironic effect; the imprecise measurements of "flood," "strain," "bit" parody the scientific and legal discourse of his time in which "one drop of blood" determined racialized identity, as well as the white supremacist hysteria about the "rising tide of color." In contrast, Du Bois narrates a genealogy composed not of bloodlines but of vectors of transnational migrations. This narrative fashions an international self at the confluence of routes that tie the landlocked New England town of his birth to sites in Africa, Europe, the Caribbean, and the American South; locations or dislocations on the map of what Paul Gilroy has called the Black Atlantic.

In fact, the title *Darkwater* extends more widely on a global scale beyond the Black Atlantic. "Dark" includes colonized peoples around the world, and water relates to moving, turbulent, and fluid bodies circulating around the globe, what Du Bois calls "the human sea" that beats against and changes the shores of continents, colonies, and nations while it is contained by them. *Darkwater* also refers to the turbulent movements of empire around the globe. The title implicitly comments on the liquid metaphors of racial mobility employed by white supremacist hysterics, as Du Bois turns on its head the discourse of "the rising tide of color" from the threat of world destruction to a utopian potential for world peace.

In his first chapter, Du Bois proceeds to narrate his education as a form of transient tenancy that challenges the discreet boundaries of town, region, and nation, and the way these localities are traditionally linked to communal and individual identity. When he graduates from high school with the goal of attending Harvard, he finds instead that white town leaders have arranged a scholarship for him at Fisk University. On his journey into the South, he notes the "curious irony by which I was not looked upon as a real citizen of my birthtown with a future and a career, and instead was being sent to a far land among strangers who were regarded as (and in truth were) 'mine own people'" (490). This irony relies on several inversions that divorce citizenship from habitation, as Du Bois becomes foreign to his own birthplace and finds a collective identity with strangers in a foreign place. His overuse of lexicographic marks in this passage to name "mine own people" both underscores this sense of connection and points to the linguistic work necessary to construct a sense of peoplehood, rather than just discover a preordained natural affinity.

This movement away, wherein the domestic becomes foreign and Du Bois finds himself at home abroad, is repeated in his trip to Europe after college. He travels there on a Dutch ship, reversing the route of his ancestor Tom. An ocean away from the United States, he finds another formulation of collective identity that redefines "mine own people" and overturns the geographic contrast of Old World constriction and New World boundlessness. At a time when Woodrow Wilson touted "America" as the universal standard of freedom and democracy, Du Bois remapped this space of American "boundlessness" as an enclosed sphere of "narrowness and color prejudice." Europe in contrast becomes an open space, where "Negro" refers not only to a particularized racial identity but also to a "greater, broader sense of humanity and world-fellowship" (491).

Thus the first chapter of *Darkwater* poses a challenge to the text that follows: to dislodge the fixed borders of local domestic spaces (home, town, region, nation) and to remap them as transient sites traversed by global movements of people, power, and capital. This first chapter links autobiography to cartography, a connection that continues through the autobiographical fragments that frame most of the chapters in the book. These fragments, selected from different arenas of Du Bois's private and public life, do not progress in chronological order to build a coherent representative self. Instead, they construct a porous self in motion that accretes dissonant layers of identity from disparate times and places. Autobiography in *Darkwater* fashions an international self linked to the trajectories of transient tenants that wind their way across the globe and the text: from Africans struggling for independence, to southern black migrants seeking industrial work in East St. Louis, to an African-British composer seeking inspiration in Negro spirituals and Longfellow's poems, to African American soldiers seeking U.S. citizenship on the far-flung battlefields of France. The trope of transient tenants does not celebrate mobility and hybridity against fixed identities, but instead charts the struggle to transform both forced movement and confinement into movements for social change.

America's Belgium

The eruption of World War dramatically alters the geography of *Darkwater*'s opening chapter. From tracing the movement of transient tenants across geopolitical borders, the author registers, in the next three chapters, tectonic upheavals that shift from the European battlefields to the postwar reconstruction of Africa to the race riots of East St. Louis in 1917. In repeating his youthful journey from America to Europe, Du Bois no longer seeks a civilized escape from American racism but instead yokes the continents together in the construction of imperial whiteness. The poem "Litany for Atlanta" bridges his autobiographical introduction to the triptych of war chapters. The poem decries God's silence about lynching as "white terror," and it serves as a segue from America to Europe through the international circuits of racial violence.

In the chapter ironically entitled "The Souls of White Folk," Du Bois transforms the dislocation of transient tenants into multiple vantage points from which to make visible the imperial and racial dimensions of the world war that are omitted from European and American maps. Though whiteness is the ostensible subject of this chapter, it focuses on the international emergence of a black anticolonial gaze, which renders whiteness visible. Emphasizing the act of seeing as much as the object seen, Du Bois explores the construction of race, both black and white, from points of view that are geographically embedded in locations of imperial conflict, what he calls in a 1924 essay an "external vantage ground—or, better, ground of disadvantage."[34]

The chapter opens with the figure of Du Bois in a tower high above the "human sea." From there, he wields a kind of imperial overview that telescopes into an intimate view of "the souls of white folk":

Of them I am singularly clairvoyant. I see in and through them. I view them from unusual points of vantage. Not as a foreigner do I come, for

I am native, not foreign, bone of their thought and flesh of their language. Mine is not the knowledge of the traveler or the colonial composite of dear memories, words and wonder. Nor yet is my knowledge that which servants have of masters, or mass of class, or capitalist of artisan. Rather I see these souls undressed and from the back and side. I see the working of their entrails. I know their thoughts and they know that I know. This knowledge makes them now embarrassed, now furious. They deny my right to live and be and call me misbirth! My word is to them mere bitterness and my soul, pessimism. And yet as they preach and strut and shout and threaten, crouching as they clutch at rags of facts and fancies to hide their nakedness they go twisting, flying by my tired eyes and I see them ever stripped,—ugly, human. (497)

In this passage, Du Bois appropriates colonial discourse to dismantle the hierarchy that renders the colonizer as the knowing and all-seeing subject and the colonized as a corporeal object devoid of reflection. A clairvoyant has the gift of seeing the invisible. If whiteness entails the privilege of disembodiment, as current theories hold, the clairvoyant gaze reembodies whiteness to make it hypervisible and grotesque. Du Bois insists that his "unusual points of vantage" cannot be reduced to the binary oppositions of known social hierarchies. In repeating that he is not "foreign" but "native," he challenges the distinction between near and far, home and abroad, and renders whiteness as foreign. "Native" in this context implicitly links the African American claim to citizenship at home to a colonized people's struggle for independence from a foreign rule. In the allusion to the Garden of Eden, Du Bois offers a counter-myth of origins, as the corporeal black body is aligned with Eve's. Instead of being created out of Adam's rib, however, blackness becomes a projection of his "thought and language." As white souls are cast out of their colonial paradise, they try to cover their exposed bodies with myths of superiority. In a parallel to the colonial trope of conquest as penetration, the clairvoyant gaze does not just passively observe but actively strips souls and pierces the skin to peer into "the working of their entrails." In his appropriation of colonial discourse, Du Bois turns the act of seeing into a power struggle that takes place in spaces of intimate proximity and also expands across the globe.

As Du Bois descends from his tower, he allies his sole clairvoyant gaze with a collective international anticolonial gaze. The text moves rapidly from scenes of lynching and racial hatred "right here in America" to the carnage of World War I. As his focus shifts, he changes his use of pronouns significantly. He starts by sharing his vision with racially unmarked Americans: "We have seen, you and I, city after city drunk and furious with ungovernable lust of blood." He suddenly turns on "you," who becomes visible as white in this unanswered question: "ask your own soul what it would say if the next census were to report that half of black America was dead and the other half dying" (499). Du Bois then moves beyond the national borders depopulated by this imaginary census. Expanding the meaning of "mine own people" of the first chapter, here he changes the referent of "we" to "the Darker world" and refers to himself for the first time in the book as "I in my blackness": "In the awful cataclysm of World War, where from beating, slandering and murdering us the white world turned temporarily aside to kill each other, we of the Darker Peoples looked on in mild amaze" (500). They gaze at a scene of vast destruction that echoes Du Bois's clairvoyant vision of the "entrails" of white souls: "As we saw the dead dimly through rifts of battle-smoke and heard faintly the cursings and accusations of blood brothers, we darker men said: 'This is not Europe gone mad, this is not aberration or insanity; this *is* Europe; this seeming Terrible is the real soul of white culture—back of all culture,—stripped and visible today'" (502). The power of the dark gaze to strip the skin of white souls is here magnified on global dimensions to pierce the veneer of European civilization. "The Great War is the lie unveiled," Du Bois wrote in the *Crisis; Darkwater* shows how the cataclysm of war opened prospects for anticolonial alliances that could further undo the lie that white culture was the source of civilization. This lie, Du Bois claims further, conceals the foundation of European civilization not only in its colonial violence, but also in the appropriation of earlier, flourishing nonwhite civilizations.

From the vantage of the "darker world that watches" (507), Du Bois argues historically that whiteness is a recent social phenomenon with origins in imperialism: "the discovery of personal whiteness among the world's peoples is a very modern thing—a nineteenth and twentieth century matter, indeed" (497). Inverting the discourse of colonial exploration, he contends that Europeans did not "discover" ancient darker peoples, but instead invented their own identity as white.

Throughout the chapter, Du Bois repeatedly emphasizes the modernity of whiteness, a temporality that is inseparable from the vast geographic span of empire: "the imperial width of the thing,—the heaven defying audacity—makes its modern newness" (504). He calls whiteness a "new religion" that unites America and Europe in a belief that "whiteness is the ownership of the earth forever and ever, Amen!" (498).

Contemporary studies of whiteness have been heavily influenced by David Roediger's *Wages of Whiteness,* a concept taken from Du Bois's *Black Reconstruction* (1935).[35] Roediger argues that nineteenth-century working classes in the antebellum United States adopted the privileges of whiteness to distinguish them from degraded black labor and thus align themselves with capital. Yet Roediger overlooks the international context in which Du Bois formulated this argument at least twenty years earlier, when he analyzed the racial formation of class in America as part of the global anarchy of empire. Skilled workers in both Europe and the United States, argued Du Bois, embraced the economic, social, and ideological benefits of whiteness, which were made possible only through imperial exploitation at home and abroad: "The white workingman has been asked to share the spoil of exploiting 'chinks and niggers.' It is no longer simply the merchant prince, or the aristocratic monopoly, or even the employing class, that is exploiting the world: it is the nation; a new democratic nation composed of united capital and labor."[36] In this imperial crucible of economics and race, Du Bois found not only the roots of war but also the birth of the modern nation: "such nations it is that rule the modern world. Their national bond is no mere sentimental patriotism, loyalty or ancestor worship."[37] The same colonial spoils that allow for the formation of the modern nation lead to violent competition over the colonies in world war. The exclusion and exploitation of dark labor worldwide explains the paradox at home: that the advance of democracy goes hand in hand with lynching and violent racism in post-Reconstruction America. This international triangle that unites labor and capital through the bond of whiteness against dark labor at home and abroad connects America to other imperial nations, rather than position it as an exception to them.

In the cartography of *Darkwater,* the extended lines of this triangle lead in two interrelated directions, represented respectively in the next two chapters. Chapter three, "The Hands of Ethiopia," focuses on the postwar settlement of Africa, where Du Bois foresees the ominous import of new kinds of industrial slavery. The next chapter, "Of Work and Wealth," moves back to the wartime industrialization of East St. Louis, where white workers battled against black migrant labor and thereby aligned themselves with the industrialists against whom they were striking. For Du Bois, such alliances cast ironic light on the internationalist claims of the socialist movements in the United States as well as Germany, whose members, he argues, have been bribed by the promises of empire: "Were they not lordly whites and should they not share in the spoils of rape? High wages in the United States and England might be the skillfully manipulated result of slavery in Africa and of peonage in Asia" (507). Du Bois contends that the wages of whiteness are paid from an international economic system that consolidates the modern nation and conjoins post-Reconstruction America to the African roots of war.

The international perspective on whiteness in *Darkwater* is inextricably tied to its imperial cartography. In remapping global geography from the "unusual points of vantage" of an emerging anticolonial gaze, Du Bois also challenges the meaning of language and the writing of history to show how language perpetuates and reflects the injustices and oppressions inscribed in the lines of maps. Just as he redefines the meaning of race and the modern nation from the vantage of the colonies, geographic shifts throughout *Darkwater* entail redefining the available lexicon for describing the international scene, through such basic words as "world," "war," and "peace." The wages of whiteness also include the right to own and circumscribe this vocabulary. As Toni Morrison writes, "definitions belong to the definers—not the defined."[38] We have already seen how Du Bois amply expands the meaning of the "world" in world war. From the vantage of Africa, the "world" does not stop at the battlefields of Europe, but takes root in a global struggle to control colonies that "belt the world"—in "Hong Kong and Anam, in Borneo and Rhodesia, in Sierra Leone and Nigeria, in Panama and Havana" (505–6). This redefinition of the "world" expands outward to encompass the earth, and inward to include black labor within the United States.

In charting the perimeters of the world, Du Bois also redefines and expands the meaning of war. He condemns pacifists for limiting their protests to battles involving white Europeans. Has war "just become horrible, in these last days," he asks,

> when under essentially equal conditions, equal armaments, and equal waste of wealth, white men are fighting white men, with surgeons and nurses hovering near? Think of the wars through which we have lived in the last decade: in German Africa, in British Nigeria, in French and Spanish Morocco, in China, in Persia, in the Balkans, in Tripoli, in Mexico, and in a dozen lesser places—were not these horrible too? Mind you, there were for most of these wars no Red Cross funds. (502)

Excluded from the nomenclature of "war," brutal military incursions become invisible from the perspective of Europe and the United States. In withholding the use of the word "war" from violent colonial conflicts worldwide, pacifists efface both the agency of colonial combatants and the longer history of conquest that, according to Du Bois, caused the Great War in Europe.

Darkwater rewrites the past to expose the imperial histories embedded in yet deleted from European and American versions of the world. This geographic, linguistic, and historical remapping converges in his repeated references to Belgium. From the vantage of Europe, Belgium stood at the center of the war; the "rape of Belgium" was a rallying cry against German invasion of a neutral country. This metaphor rendered Belgium female and put the Allies in the role of chivalric rescuers. Du Bois turns this rhetoric of rape against Belgium itself, by examining it from the vantage of King Leopold's Belgian Congo. He turns an enclosed national space inside out by undoing the historical amnesia about the economic foundation of Belgium's civilization: "Behold little Belgium and her pitiable plight, but has the world forgotten Congo? What Belgium now suffers is not half, not even a tenth, of what she has done to black Congo since Stanley's great dream of 1880" (502). A target of German aggression when viewed from within Europe, Belgium becomes aligned with Germany as agents of aggressive expansion and violent exploitation of Africa.

Du Bois further extends the boundaries of Belgium beyond the dyadic relation between Europe and its African colonies, to locate Belgium metaphorically in the cities of the United States:

Conceive this nation, of all human peoples, engaged in a crusade to make the "World Safe for Democracy"! Can you imagine the United States protesting against Turkish atrocities in Armenia, while the Turks are silent about mobs in Chicago and St. Louis; what is Louvain compared with Memphis, Waco, Washington, Dyersburg, and Estill Springs? In short, what is the black man but America's Belgium, and how could America condemn in Germany that which she commits, just as brutally, within her own borders? (500)

The rape of Belgium here becomes a figure for the lynched black bodies hanging throughout the cities of the United States that not only redefines the meaning of Belgium, but also radically undermines the position of America in the world. The detailed naming of American cities draws a counter-map of the United States through lines that connect the locales where the atrocities against black people were committed, and Du Bois rewrites the history of the present from that perspective. No longer a moral arbiter of other nations, the United States is judged by the dark world it professes to lead. Thus Du Bois collapses the physical and moral distances that appear to separate America, Germany, Belgium, and the Congo to show how they are inextricably intermeshed. In *Darkwater* he shows that nations as well as colonies are not autonomous entities limited by territorial boundaries, but are themselves transient tenants of sorts, formed by the networks of imperial violence and conflicts that traverse the globe.

In radically redefining the meaning of "world war" by means of its imperial scope, Du Bois similarly redefines the meaning of "peace." This involves a temporal shift that extends the war in time beyond the official armistice. Rather than call it the "war to end all wars," Du Bois recasts it as a "prelude to the armed and indignant protest of these despised and raped people" (507) who are preparing to revolt, from Japan to China, India to Africa, the West Indies to the United States. A war of competition over colonial exploitation cannot be resolved in the narrow space of a Paris hotel room, but rather "in this outer circle of races, and not in the inner European household," as he argues in "African Roots" (103). Redefining the meaning of war and peace involves collapsing the conceptual boundary that protects European nations as domestic spaces in contrast to foreign subjects of colonialism.

The threat of a truly worldwide war hovers over the entire text of *Darkwater* and fuels the urgency of its tone. Du Bois oscillates back and forth between drawing the color line to frame the new front of a global race war, and drawing it to delineate a site for the emergence of anticolonial alliances and the potential of "world fellowship."

African Routes

A comprehensive peace for Du Bois could only be negotiated from the vantage of Africa, the prime cause of world war. In the chapter on "The Hands of Ethiopia," Du Bois offers a plan for the postwar reconstruction of Africa that combines a revision of "African Roots" with proposals from the Pan-African Congress of 1919. This chapter has two uneasily related goals: to dismantle the colonial map of Africa and to avert the threat of a worldwide race war. It thus anxiously strives to contain the potential violence that this crumbling of old maps would unleash. Renarrating the history of the Great War opens urgent questions about the future. Hence Du Bois asks whether the reconstruction of Africa will lead toward independence and autonomy, or like post-Reconstruction America, to reenslavement by unfettered capitalism.

What was Africa to Du Bois at the time of writing *Darkwater*? Scholars have criticized Du Bois for romanticizing the continent in colonial exoticized images, both at the Pan-African Congress and on his trip to Liberia three years later.[39] Eric Sundquist sees *Darkwater* more positively as an anticolonial critique in which Africa becomes a psychic or spiritual homeland, an embodiment of a Pan-African Soul, or a "racial font of identity."[40] Yet both views overlook the more secular and modern dimension of Africa that serves as a critical leverage in Du Bois's writing. "Hands of Ethiopia," like "African Roots," starts with a quotation from Pliny, "*Semper novi quid ex Africa,* cried the Roman consul" [Something new always comes from Africa]. The newness of Africa paradoxically lies both in its antiquity, as the source of early civilization, and its modernity in relation to the history of empires: "Nearly every human empire that has arisen in the world, material and spiritual, has found some of its greatest crises on the continent of Africa, from Greece to Great Britain" (511). As this flash point of empire, Africa is where the anarchy of empire implodes and where something new can emerge. Du Bois thus links the modern crisis of war to Africa's antiquity, though not as a mythic space outside of time but as a geography that is historically embedded in empire and will be its undoing.

If in "Souls of White Folk" Du Bois adopts a global anti-colonial perspective from which to deconstruct whiteness, in "Hands of Ethiopia" he sets the imperial grounds on which to reconstruct postwar Africa. He condemns the ravages of European colonialism and presents a plan for African independence of "a new African World state, a Black Africa" (516). Yet he also maps Africa through a colonial grid as a backward continent in need of enlightened modernization, and he sees African Americans in the civilizing role of "missionaries of culture for their backward brethren in the new Africa" (518). In the rhetoric of colonial paternalism, Africa becomes an infant state in need of guidance and tutelage by the American black elite necessary to lead a program of modernization and to protect the land and populace from capitalism's imposition of industrial slavery on Africa. If the critical vantage of Africa exposes the war as the "lie of civilization," then Du Bois sees an enlightened modernization of Africa as a way to recuperate this same civilization.

Critics have connected Du Bois's Pan-Africanism to the civilizationist discourse of European colonialism.[41] Overlooked, however, is how Du Bois enlists, or is enlisted by, a specific logic of American imperialism. His vision of Pan-Africa uncannily resembles Woodrow Wilson's internationalist cartography in the aftermath of World War I. Wilson advocated an anticolonial imperialism in opposition to European colonialism, but even more vehemently he opposed anticolonial revolutionary movements as anarchic. It was this logic that underwrote his occupation of Haiti. In his internationalism he saw the United States not as a colonial power ruling specific territories, but as the redeemer, lawgiver, and model for a universal global system, the antecedent of Luce's American Century. He concluded his proposals for "Peace without Victory" in his resounding 1917 speech this way: "These are American principles, American policies. We could stand for no others. And they are also the principles and policies of forward looking men and women everywhere, of every modern nation, of every enlightened community. They are principles of mankind and must prevail."[42] For Wilson, U.S. nationalism was consonant with internationalism; to him American principles were universal and represented all of humanity.

Du Bois imagined African Americans in a similar representative and redemptive role in relation to Africa. In *Darkwater* he dismantles the colonialism that led to war, but conceives of peace under the mantle of American exceptionalism as an anticolonial force that can allay the double threat of rampant industrial exploitation and the revolutionary agency of African nationalism. His rhetoric of redemption also echoes Wilson's rhetoric of the redeemer nation. Du Bois figures educated American blacks as an international "talented tenth" working to uplift Africa. Africa thus becomes an inverse image of America—the lowliest rather than the most powerful, purged of imperial power and thus capable of uplifting the world.

In his journey to the concept of Pan-Africa, Du Bois appears at his most American. He implicitly reproduces the logic of imperial citizenship, though not as an African American soldier fighting abroad, but in close ranks nonetheless, standing shoulder to shoulder with other Americans to forward a peace plan for Africa. Thus what Africa is to Du Bois at this point of his career is inseparable from the question: what is America to Du Bois? He does not simply romanticize either Africa as homeland or the pomp and circumstance of French colonialism, as Lewis claims.[43] Instead, he implicitly engages in a romance of the American empire. Like the romance heroes we have seen in Chapter 3 of this book, the author of *Darkwater* can act with more agency and freedom abroad than he can at home, as he seeks to rescue his black brothers from the tyranny of industrial imperialism. His construction of Africa as a critical vantage also has some qualities of the imperial romance, wherein conflicts at home can be resolved more clearly abroad. The discourse of American imperialism as anticolonial redeemer of the world from the shackles of empire underwrites his vision of a redeemed and redeeming Africa as the site for projecting future world peace. Du Bois often represents Africa as passive; it must be freed by others and cannot quite redeem or represent itself. By omitting an autobiographical speaking voice in "Hands of Ethiopia," he adopts a kind of Wilsonian universalism in which America is the unlocatable and omnipresent prototype of world progress.[44]

Du Bois by no means backed Wilson's aim to rebuild the world on "American principles." After throwing his support behind Wilson for the election, he often turned the President's rhetoric against itself. Rather than hold America as a standard bearer for the rest of the world, Du Bois pointed out that the United States lagged behind the standards of countries it purported to lead: "Russia has abolished the ghetto—shall we restore it? India is overthrowing caste—shall we up-build it? China is establishing democracy—shall we strengthen our Southern oligarchy?. . . . No one that loves to lynch niggers can lead the hosts of the Almighty God."[45] Throughout his writing during the war he undermined the U.S. claims to "make the world safe for democracy": "Wilson may love the idea of democracy in Poland and Ireland, but for 12 million Negroes silence. Distance from Washington certainly adds enchantment to Democracy."[46] Overturning the Wilsonian map of the world—with the United States as a center of democracy emanating outward—Du Bois exposes how America makes democracy foreign at its center and can only fulfill its meaning by projecting it abroad. Like other anticolonial leaders of the time, Du Bois did not simply reject Wilson but wanted to take his rhetoric of self-determination to its logical extreme to expand it beyond the peoples of Europe.

Despite his direct critiques of Wilson's hypocritical policies, Du Bois's Pan-African map shares with Wilson a common framework of nationally sponsored internationalism. Africa, in Du Bois eyes, cannot redeem itself but must rely on higher powers of enlightened blacks, just as the self-determination of new nations relies on following an American model. If Du Bois's international perspective destabilizes and decenters American borders, at the same time he relies on America as a template for world government, for what he calls "supra-national power." His map of a reconstructed Africa coincides with an American desire for a borderless world, ruled by U.S. law and example, and supporting a world market. While Du Bois criticized Wilson at home, he continued into the 1920s to support the League of Nations as a forum that could turn his critique into practice; as a tribunal for racial injustice at home and abroad. At a time when many anticolonial leaders derided the League for its hypocrisy in relation to movements for "self-determination" by nonwhite peoples, Du Bois averred that "the worst inter-nation is better than the present anarchy."[47] Thus, on the one hand, Du Bois decentered Wilson's vision of America by locating the United States in the pantheon of imperial powers judged by the world's tribunal. On the other, even when he returned from war most disillusioned by Wilson's hypocrisy at home and abroad, his idea of the Pan-African leadership resembled Wilson's projection of the

United States as world savior. "The Hands of Ethiopia" thus holds out competing perspectives on the potentials of "world citizenship": a Wilsonian vision of "the United States of the World," and African routes emerging from the colonial "grounds of disadvantage."

Home Fronts

In chapter four of *Darkwater,* "Of Work and Wealth," Du Bois brings the "return fighting" scenes of world war to the streets of American cities, and calls for social change within the United States as part of the postwar global reconstruction. Fighting on the home front involves ranks of men and women who were not clothed in the uniforms of militant manhood: migrants, workers in factories, teachers and students in schoolrooms, servants in white homes, and black women in their communities. The fear of industrial slavery in postwar Africa erupts on the bloody streets of East St. Louis in 1917, and Du Bois's proposal to educate millions of Africans boils down to a single lesson in his classroom. The "penetrating" and "all seeing eyes" of his black students force him to question the ways that pedagogy can perpetuate the lies of progress and modernization. Under their gaze, he searches for an alternative to the "scholarly aloofness and academic calm of most white universities" (532). He changes his lesson to the "concrete social problem of which we all were parts" (524) and breaks down the walls of the classroom to relocate it in a global analysis of the violence that shapes the lives of his students.

Du Bois's alternative pedagogy similarly bursts open the domestic boundaries of an industrial city in the heartland of the United States. He teaches a "concrete social problem" by narrating in epic language a saga of modern industrial violence. Drawing on his earlier article for *The Crisis,* "The East St. Louis Massacre," he describes how whites went on a horrific citywide rampage, killing and lynching blacks who had migrated there from the South for jobs in the war-driven factories. The industries employed them at lower wages to break the strikes of white unions, which would not include them. In "Of Work and Wealth" Du Bois recasts the domestic racial strife as an international narrative and remaps East St. Louis as a juncture of far-reaching routes of global economic change. Both wartime Europe and postwar Africa converge in East St. Louis, "where mighty rivers meet," and Du Bois goes on to show how these rivers convey human migrations of capital, labor, and racial prejudice across the nation and across the globe. On the streets of East St. Louis he views scenes indistinguishable from the battlefields abroad: "yesterday I rode in this city past flame-swept walls and over gray ashes; in streets almost wet with blood and beside ruins, where the bones of dead men new-bleached peered out at me in sullen wonder" (525). The unblinking gaze of his students is matched by the mocking stare of the dead, which locates East St. Louis as a site in the "Wounded World," Du Bois's incomplete volume about black troops in the war. It is a short distance from fighting in East St. Louis to fighting in Europe: "we rush toward the Battle of Marne and the West, from this dread Battle of the East" (532).

Du Bois's account ties East St. Louis to Africa through many points of confluence; a shared racial identity takes shape through the parallel experience of violent dislocations and exploited labor in the economic and political cauldron of the anarchy of empire. The war in Europe, with its economic origins in Africa, halted immigration from Europe to U.S. factories, while it created the need for labor in a wartime economy. This international circuit spurred the black migration from the South for war work in northern factories. The race riots in East St. Louis cannot be seen only as a legacy of southern history and slavery, but as part of the world history of a global economic system. The violence of East St. Louis stemmed from the effort of white workers to maintain their international wages as part of the deadly birth of modern nations out of the exploitation of dark labor worldwide. When Du Bois retells the story here, he adds a scene of black men heroically fighting back, which did not appear in his earlier journalism. Though the race riot took place in 1917, he rescripts the story of East St. Louis from the vantage of the "return fighting" after the war. Here Du Bois can imagine a black militancy that he could not quite recognize on the part of Africans.

Just as Du Bois imagines the colonial devastation of Africa as an opportunity for future world peace, he projects a similar scenario emerging from the ruins of East St. Louis. After telling his students about this example of globalized racial violence, Du Bois concludes with the surprising lesson that "there are no races" but only global groupings relating to the international division of labor and capital. His students conclude with him that "disinherited darker peoples must either share in future industrial democracy or overturn the world" (534). To circumvent a future world war requires nothing less than the "reorganization of work and redistribution of wealth, not only in America, but in the world" (535). Du Bois and his students thus extend "world war" not only geographically via the color line to the colonies, but also economically to a redistribution of the wealth of the world.

In *Darkwater,* the battlefields of East St. Louis, Africa, and Europe lead inward to the home and the nation, as the violent upheaval of war leads to an analysis of everyday social issues of work, family, the franchise, and education. In exploring these traditional demarcations between home and factory, family and the ballot box, private and public, Du Bois breaks down these boundaries to map the domestic spaces of the home and the nation as crossroads of international movement and change. In the next chapter he reaches into the intimate recesses of the American home, where he finds an outdated form of domestic labor. "The Servant in the House" opens with the vignette of a white woman who asks Du Bois, after hearing his lecture on the franchise and politics, "Do you know where I can get a good colored cook?" (538). Du Bois counters this by looking into the inner workings of the bourgeois home through the eyes of a servant, in a way that echoes the "unusual vantage points" of the opening of "Souls of White Folk." Thereby he shatters the view of the middle-class home as a haven from the wider world. Instead, as in the earlier chapter, he looks into its entrails to find white domesticity founded on a "'manure' theory of social organization" (543). The home is not separate from the marketplace, but it relies on the labor of black women and men excluded from organized labor and forced into the "mudsill" as the "unskilled offal of a millionaire industrial system" (541). This labor undermines the distinction between private and public spheres, for bourgeois life is dependent upon black servitude as much in the most cherished intimacy of child-rearing as in the modern anonymity of Pullman cars. If the discourse of domesticity holds that the home shapes young citizens for democracy, Du Bois turns it around to show that democracy is built on the foundations of exclusion, the relegation of blacks to the realm of servants and noncitizens.

This "manure theory of social organization" implodes the home and links it to the world outside. In the next chapter, "Of the Ruling of Men," Du Bois seems to leap from the private domestic sphere to the public sphere of political governance to argue for extending the vote to women and blacks. But rather than simply include new members in a narrow definition of the political sphere, he extends this arena to the factories and beyond the border of the nation. Du Bois explains that a more inclusive franchise would not simply add new members to a pre-conceived social whole. Instead, each group would bring new knowledge from its own experience, needs and desires and "new points of view" that would radically reshape the social whole through "disarrangement and confusion to the older equilibrium" (556). Du Bois starts these far-reaching arguments literally close to home. Men, he argues, claim that women do not need the vote because their husbands and fathers can speak for them in the political sphere. He contests the notion that spatial and social proximity breeds knowledge; in fact it breeds distortion and silence, and only women can speak with knowledge of their own experience and interests. He extends this argument to Negroes of the South, who are similarly denied the vote on the grounds of proximate knowledge and paternalism. Proximity in the South does not lead to paternal benevolence: "instead of loving guardianship, we see anarchy and exploitation" (556). Du Bois rejects the domestic model of "benevolent guardianship for women, for the masses, for the Negroes," and sees it as no different from the colonial rationale in Kipling's claim that the white man must oversee "lesser breeds without the law" (553). Thus in arguing for an expanded franchise Du Bois does not stop at the borders of home, region, or nation, but covers the entire colonized world: "So, too, with the darker races of the world. No federation of the world, no true inter-nation—can exclude the black and brown and yellow races from its counsels" (556). Rather than see the home as a workable familial model for world governance, he links home, region, nation, and world through the disequilibrium of "new points of view."

If far-flung spaces around the globe converge in *Darkwater* through the turbulence of empire and war, domestic spaces are wrenched apart by the intimate upheavals of gender and race. Du Bois notes that "none have more persistently [and] dogmatically insisted upon the inherent inferiority of women than the men with whom they come in closest contact . . . So, too, it is those people who live in closest contact with black folk who have most unhesitatingly asserted the utter impossibility of living beside Negroes who are not industrial or political slaves or social pariahs. All this proves that none are so blind as those nearest the thing seen, while, on the other hand, the history of the world is the history of the discovery of the common humanity of human beings among steadily increasing circles of men" (557). "New points of view" from those excluded from the political sphere would counter the blindness supporting intimate systems of domination. Democracy and citizenship must spread beyond the perimeters of geographical proximity—home, town, region, nation. This echoes his opening autobiographical chapter, in which he confides that he was not recognized as a real "citizen of my birthtown" but had to travel far South to find "mine own people" and overseas to find "world fellowship." If a sense of belonging cannot be found close to home, it must be reconceived from a global perspective that reaches out in time as well as space. In time, "How astounded the future world-citizen will be to know that as late as 1918 great and civilized nations were making desperate endeavor to confine the development of ability and individuality to one sex,—that is, to one-half of the nation; and he will probably learn that similar effort to confine humanity to one race lasted a hundred years longer" (560). This utopian notion of future world citizenship depends on turning domestic spaces of the home and the nation inside out, as inadequate sites of social belonging, and positing the new perspective of an imagined global community.

Black women, claims Du Bois, are at the nexus of these "widening circles of humanity" that he charts from home to nation to "inter-nation," from women to Southern blacks to the colonized world. In "The Damnation of Women," black women provide the linchpin for the double movement of democracy beyond the nation, further out into the world and deeper into the home. This chapter poses the question: "What is today the message of these black women to America and to the world? The uplift of women is, next to the problem of the color line and the peace movement, our greatest modern cause. When, now, two of these movements—woman and color—combine in one, the combination has deep meaning" (574). The meaning is fraught and contradictory throughout *Darkwater*, as it expresses the disequilibrium out of which new viewpoints emerge. Du Bois represents the labor of black women as the inequitable foundation of domesticity, at the same time that their race excludes them from the privileges and fetters of domesticity, from the ideology of true womanhood. This double exclusion, according to Du Bois, gives the black woman a representational vantage—and advantage. Her labor challenges the boundaries between home and workplace. The necessity of her working outside the home gives her access to the modern economic system and facilitates a revolutionary stance.

"The Damnation of Women" echoes a poem in *Darkwater* that links the history of black women under American slavery to the violent history of colonization in Africa. "The Riddle of the Sphinx," strategically placed between the chapters "The Souls of White Folk" and "The Hands of Ethiopia," was first titled "The Burden of Black Women." A scathing critique of the "white man's burden," the poem exposes Kipling's justification of colonial rule as a cover for the rape of black women: "but the burden of white man bore her back / and the white world stifled her sighs" (509). Black women play a role in *Darkwater* similar to that of Africa. Just as Du Bois turns Africa, conventionally marginal to world events, into the central point from which to remap world geography, he turns the oppression of black women into the vantage from which to redefine the meaning of home and nation. Both Africa and black women are represented as the avatars of modernity and future social change. Yet in both cases Du Bois also expresses anxiety about their revolutionary agency and a need to control it through his assertion of militant manhood and by giving voice to their "stifled sighs."[48] While he shows that black women are violently excluded from the empire of the mother in the American home, he retrieves an empire for them in Africa and Haiti, cultures that he believed worshipped the figure of the black mother, "based on old African tribal ties and beneath it was the mother-idea" (567). He thereby links black women to an ancient, premodern status where they, like the continent of Africa, are in need of vigilant black American men to protect, lead, and uplift them. In contrast, Du Bois also represents women as soldiers "returning fighting" from the battlefield as they lead the fight on multiple home fronts.

The Anarchy of Empire

The domestic and international violence that pervades *Darkwater* erupts in the last chapter in a science fiction fable, "The Comet," which tells the story of the destruction of New York City by the impact of a comet releasing deadly gases. "The Comet" follows the chapter "Of Beauty and Death," which incorporates scenes of black soldiers fighting in the war in Europe and ends with their return to New York Harbor and Harlem. The light across the sky and the release of noxious gases conjure images of the battlefields of World War I. Externalized as a cosmic or natural disaster, the explosion represents the inner combustion of the social tensions and global conflicts that inform the anarchy of empire. This apocalyptic violence works as a metaphor that merges the carnage of European "civilization," the "Red Summer" across the United States, the militancy of the black soldiers who "return fighting," and the threat of anticolonial revolts at home and abroad. The comet brings the war home into the modern metropolis and into the heart of the black and white families.

The story starts with the chance survival of a black man, Jim, who works as a messenger at a bank; he escapes the destruction "in the bowels of the earth, under the world," in the underground vaults of the bank where he was sent to find missing documents (611). While driving through the rubble up to Harlem in search of his family, he finds a wealthy white woman, unnamed, who survived in the shelter of her darkroom developing pictures of the comet. Assuming everyone else in the world is dead, they are about to consummate their survival in a semi-mystical union between "primal woman; mighty mother of all" and "some mighty Pharaoh lived again" that promises the creation of a new human race. Suddenly the woman's fiancé and father arrive in a motor car. When she asks, "is the world gone?" they respond, "only New York," and then clamor to lynch the man for violating the white woman he had rescued (621). As a crowd amasses, Jim's fantasy of himself as an ancient king is debunked by the reimposition of Jim Crow reality, "well what do you think of that, of all New York, just a white girl and a nigger." He then escapes to find his own wife alive, cradling the corpse of their "dark baby" (622).

In his descent into the bowels of the earth, the black working man from Harlem evokes the work of colonial laborers and links them to the financial center of New York. In assuming the lineage of Ethiopian kings, he represents the darker world as a harbinger of the future. As a photographer, the white woman has access to culture, the tools of representation. The return of the father—the white banker—and the threat of a lynch mob restore Jim Crow order after the war to reconstruct New York City. In "The Comet" the Northern father and fiancé deploy a familiar Southern narrative that renders and punishes black agency as the rape of white women.

In his investigation of the treatment of black troops during the war, Du Bois documented the way the U.S. army exported this narrative to the battlefields of Europe, at the same time that it was screened as national history in Griffith's popular *The Birth of a Nation* (1915). In his reports for "The Wounded World," published in *The Crisis,* Du Bois singled out one of the most insidious pieces of U.S. propaganda against African American troops. The army published classified circulars warning the French to avoid black soldiers, who were alleged to rape white women; one officer referred to them as "the rapist division."[49] This official army policy recast a dominant national narrative as a weapon of international warfare to combat the struggle for black citizenship at home by exporting racism abroad. If black soldiers sought imperial citizenship by fighting foreign wars, the imperial nation opposed them by redrawing the lines of battle abroad. Du Bois explained that the army was responding to new possibilities for international affiliations encountered by black troops in Europe. He praised the warm gratitude of the French people toward black soldiers and the official recognition from their government. In France blacks found themselves standing not "shoulder to shoulder" with white Americans, as he encouraged in "Close Ranks," but rather alongside French soldiers as well as black Africans fighting in French colonial regiments.

Du Bois deploys a familiar chivalric narrative when he applauds the black troops for rescuing France in their heroic fight against the German invasion at the Marne.[50] The army propaganda attempts to transform black soldiers from agents of rescue to agents of rape. This is precisely what happens to the black man in "The Comet"; the white men immediately assume that he has violated the white woman, who corrects them: "He dared—all, to rescue me" (621). The woman, like the French people who reject this narrative on the basis of their own contact with black soldiers, remains powerless to change it for the national fathers.[51] Like the Klan riding in *Birth of a Nation,* the white northern banker returns in a motorcar from the suburbs to "rescue" his daughter. Contesting Griffith's dominant national narrative that renders equal contact between whites and blacks as the threat of rape, Du Bois reimagines the union between a black man and a white woman as the aborted conception of a new interracial inter-nation. In the parable of "The Comet," Du Bois implicitly places the national mythology of the black rapist in an international context where the metaphor of rape has contested political uses. Throughout *Darkwater* he turns the accusation of rape against the accusers: he redirects the battle cry of the "rape of Belgium" to the "rape of Ethiopia" as the central metaphor for the colonization of Africa. He redefines Kipling's "white man's burden" as the rape of black women within the United States and across the colonies, and represents the lynched black body as "America's Belgium."

Du Bois connects the army's designation of black soldiers in World War I to the history of black service in the Civil War, Reconstruction, and the Spanish-American War. Writing about black troops in Houston in 1917, who violently rebelled against their brutal treatment by white officers, he reminds us that "the nation, also, forgot the deep resentment mixed with the pale ghost of fear which Negro soldiers call up in the breasts of the white South. It is not so much that they fear that the Negro will strike if he gets the chance, but rather that they assume with curious unanimity that he has *reason* to strike, that any other person in his circumstance or treated as he is would rebel" (602). Du Bois suggests that precisely because of the white South's implicit acknowledgment of the right to rebel, lynching reconfigures the rational "reason to strike" as the irrational lust for white women.

"The Comet" concludes *Darkwater* with a question: what new social formations could arise from the destruction of the world? The reassertion of white supremacy through the threat of lynching raises dire questions about the future in the figure of a black child. Jim is joyfully reunited with his silent black wife, but they embrace across their baby's corpse. *Darkwater* earlier expresses urgency about the future of black children in "The Immortal Child" (581–93). This elegy for Samuel Coleridge-Taylor celebrates his work and life as a Pan-African artist and links his art to the poetry of Paul Laurence Dunbar. But it also mourns a potential lost future in which "there is no place for black children in this world" (585). The dead baby at the end of "The Comet" embodies this fear, as it hearkens back to Du Bois's elegy for his son in *Souls of Black Folk,* a figure who represents both despair and hope for change. If the image of the dead baby at the end of "The Comet" looks back toward *Souls,* it also looks forward to the end of Du

Bois's novel *Dark Princess*. In it a boy is born to a Southeast Asian woman and an African American man, who returns from Chicago to his roots in Virginia to rejoin his mother and his wife and constitute a new family. In a geography based on the cartography of *Darkwater,* Du Bois maps this birthplace at "the edge of a black world. The black belt of the Congo, the Nile, and the Ganges reaches by way of Guinea, Haiti and Jamaica, like a red arrow up into the heart of white America."[52] In *Dark Princess* the boy is born as a messenger to lead the colonized world, continuing the work of the black messenger of "The Comet."

Darkwater concludes with a final poem, "A Hymn to the Peoples," which prays for the "union of the World" to overcome the "Anarchy of Empire" (622). Why did Du Bois choose to end *Darkwater* by going back to a poem, based on Kipling's "Recessional," that he first wrote for the First Universal Races Congress of 1911?[53] Du Bois never lost his enthusiasm for this conference and wrote in several autobiographies that this gathering of men and women of all races around the world "would have marked an epoch in the cultural history of the world, if it had not been followed so quickly by the World War."[54] This statement has been ridiculed as an example of Du Bois's arrogance in inflating the importance of his own international endeavors.[55] Yet what meaning does this form of self-quotation take in 1920? *Darkwater* concludes with a gesture from the prewar past to project into the future an alternative untold story of what might have been and still might be. Du Bois devises an as yet uncharted map of the globe as a site of "world citizenship," for members of collectivities not bound solely by nation-states or colonies nor dislocated by the anarchy of empire.

Darkwater connects the problem of global reconstruction after the "awful cataclysm" of World War I to the unfulfilled legacy of Reconstruction in the aftermath of the Civil War. In the earlier period, wrote Du Bois, white opposition to the experiments of a new democratic rule

> based its objection on the color line, and Reconstruction became in history a great movement for the self-assertion of the white race against the impudent ambition of degraded blacks, instead of the rise of a mass of black and white laborers. The result was the disfranchisement of the blacks of the South and a world-wide attempt to restrict democratic development to white races and to distract them with race hatred

against the darker races. This program, however, although it undoubtedly helped raise the scale of white labor, in greater proportion put wealth and power in the hands of the great European Captains of Industry and made modern industrial imperialism possible. (552)

Here Du Bois begins to reconstruct a chapter of national history by placing it in a broader transnational context of the worldwide expansion of empire. In this revision, he imagines counter-histories to the rise of Jim Crow, histories that gesture toward alternative futures of what might have been and might yet be, an epoch of global interracial democracy as opposed to the African roots of war.

Du Bois would take up this challenge to rewrite history in *Black Reconstruction*, which ends with "The Propaganda of History," a scathing critique of historians for writing and teaching history as a means of "inflating our national ego."[56] Misrepresenting Reconstruction as a massive mistake, they based their historiography on the racist belief in black inferiority and refusal to credit black people as active agents in a revolutionary movement for freedom and social change. In Du Bois's view, this distortion of national history also had international repercussions, as his conclusion shifts abruptly from quoting a historian's approval of the triumph of white supremacy in reuniting the nation to the following vision: "Immediately in Africa, a black back runs red with the blood of the lash; in India, a brown girl is raped; in China, a coolie starves; in Alabama, seven darkies are more than lynched; while in London, the white limbs of a prostitute are hung with jewels and silk."[57] This depiction of simultaneity across geographic boundaries is the aesthetic analogue of the anarchy of empire, which cannot be represented in the linear narratives of national history. Du Bois claims here that these narratives perpetuate the intimate domination of empire inflicted on colonized bodies across the globe, and he calls for alternative histories and pedagogies that change the forms of representation as well as their content. His challenge remains with us today to develop the kinds of transnational historiographies and cartographies that can interlink what have traditionally appeared as disparate spaces and histories at the turn of the twentieth century: Black Reconstruction, the colonization of Africa and Asia, and U.S. imperialism in Latin America and the Pacific. Du Bois also challenges us to create new critical vocabularies that can represent current rearticulations of global power and the emergence of dispersed collectivities that go beyond the limits of the anarchy of empire.

I have been arguing that the anarchy of empire in its convulsive reach across the globe both erects and destabilizes the geopolitical boundaries of nation-states and colonies and the conceptual borders between the domestic and the foreign. Thus to analyze the culture of U.S. imperialism it is necessary to cross these same borders and challenge the interpretive framework of national paradigms, which use history for "inflating our national ego." Du Bois demonstrates ways of deflating that ego by turning to "unusual points of vantage" from which to map the anarchy of empire, just as Orson Welles turned the camera on Citizen Kane from below to make the viewer simultaneously feel the force of his power and perceive its undoing. In these chapters I have tried to convey this double perspective: to analyze the creative force of empire in the making of a national culture, and to trace the anarchic workings of empire in unraveling the coherence of this culture and opening it to the outside. We have seen how cultural representations of the anarchy of empire can shore up national borders against perceived external threats, or can decenter the nation with the recognition still vital today, "that the United States was living not to itself, but as part of the strain and stress of the world."

NOTES

ACKNOWLEDGMENTS

INDEX

Notes

Introduction

1. The name "Spanish-American War" is a contested political term that only presents a U.S.-centered perspective on the three-month war declared against Spain in 1898. It obscures the preceding Cuban War for Independence in which the United States intervened, as well as subsequent U.S. intervention in Cuba. Thus some call it the "Spanish-Cuban-American War." Furthermore, Spanish-American War does not refer to the three-year Philippine-American War that followed. In this book, my usage varies. I often refer to the traditional name when I am discussing the contemporary images of that war in popular culture and political discourse. In Chapters 2, 3, and 4, my analyses show how cultural representations contributed to legitimating that name by rendering the wider imperial wars in which the United States was engaged invisible to the contemporary public and later histories.

2. *Downes v. Bidwell,* 182 U.S. 244 (1901) at 341–42. I am indebted to Priscilla Wald for originally pointing out this case to me, and to her own work in *Constituting Americans: Cultural Anxiety and Narrative Form* (Durham: Duke University Press, 1995), p. 224.

3. Efrén Rivera Ramos, "The Legal Construction of American Colonialism: The Insular Cases, 1902–1922," *Revista Jurídica de la Universidad de Puerto Rico,* 65 (1996): 227–328. I am indebted to this article for my understanding of the legal and political contexts and ramifications of this case. For a collection of legal essays on the *Insular Cases* (which unfortunately came out after I completed this Introduction), see Christina Duffy Burnett and Burke Marshall, eds., *Foreign in a Domestic Sense:*

Puerto Rico, American Expansion and the Constitution (Durham: Duke University Press, 2001). For an important argument about how the project of mapping and imagining Puerto Rico in this period does not fit into a rigid binary between the colonizer and the colonized, and a gloss on the misspelling "Porto Rico" in this period, see Luis García Gervasio, "I Am the Other: Puerto Rico in the Eyes of North Americans, 1898," *Journal of American History*, 87 (June 2000): 39–64.

4. Rivera Ramos, "The Legal Construction," p. 264.

5. *Downes* 182 U.S. at 320.

6. Quoted in ibid. at 262 by Brown, and by Fuller at 357.

7. Ibid. at 262.

8. Ibid. at 263.

9. Ibid. at 373.

10. On the impact of U.S. colonial rule on Puerto Rico, see Kelvin Santiago-Valles, *"Subject People" and Colonial Discourses: Economic Transformation and Social Disorder in Puerto Rico, 1898–1947* (Albany: SUNY Press, 1994); and Eileen J. Findlay, *Imposing Decency: The Politics of Sexuality and Race in Puerto Rico, 1870–1920* (Durham: Duke University Press, 1999).

11. *Downes*, 182 U.S. at 287 and 315.

12. Ibid. at 308.

13. Ibid. at 288.

14. Ibid. at 381.

15. On the question of the Constitution following the flag in this case see Brook Thomas, "A Constitution Led by the Flag: The *Insular Cases* and the Metaphor of Incorporation," in Duffy and Marshall, eds., *Foreign in a Domestic Sense*, pp. 82–103.

16. *Downes*, 182 U.S. at 313.

17. Ibid. at 314.

18. Ibid.

19. Ibid. at 327.

20. Ibid. at 316.

21. On these interactions see Matthew Jacobson, *Barbarian Virtues: The United States Encounters Foreign Peoples at Home and Abroad, 1876–1917* (New York: Hill and Wang, 2000).

22. *Downes*, 182 U.S. at 306.

23. Ibid. at 340.

24. Vicente L. Rafael, "White Love: Surveillance and Nationalist Resistance in the U.S. Colonization of the Philippines," in Amy Kaplan and Donald Pease, eds., *Cultures of U.S. Imperialism* (Durham: Duke University Press, 1993), p. 185.

25. *Downes*, 182 U.S. at 315.

26. W. E. B. Du Bois, *Darkwater: Voices from Within the Veil* (1920), rpt. in Eric Sundquist, ed., *The Oxford W. E. B. Du Bois Reader* (New York: Oxford, 1996), p. 623.

27. Theodore Roosevelt, "The Strenuous Life," in *The Works of Theodore Roosevelt: The Strenuous Life* (New York: Scribner's, 1903), p. 11.

28. See Frederick Cooper and Ann Laura Stoler, eds., *Tensions of Empire: Colonial Cultures in a Bourgeois World* (Berkeley: University of California Press, 1997); Ann Laura Stoler, *Race and the Education of Desire: Foucault's History of Sexuality and the Colonial Order of Things* (Durham: Duke University Press, 1995); Mary Louise Pratt, *Imperial Eyes: Travel Writing and Transculturation* (London: Routledge, 1992); Jean Comaroff and John Comaroff, *Of Revelation and Revolution: Christianity, Colonialism, and Consciousness in South Africa* (Chicago: University of Chicago Press, 1991); Gayan Prakash, ed., *After Colonialism: Imperial Histories and Postcolonial Displacements* (Princeton: Princeton University Press, 1995); Gilbert M. Joseph, Catherine C. LeGrand, Ricardo D. Salvatore, eds., *Close Encounters of Empire: Writing the Cultural History of U.S.-Latin American Relations* (Durham: Duke University Press, 1998).

29. See, for example, Homi Bhabha, *The Location of Culture* (London: Routledge, 1994); Robert J. C. Young, *Colonial Desire: Hybridity in Theory, Culture and Race* (London: Routledge, 1995).

30. Edward W. Said, *Culture and Imperialism* (New York: Knopf, 1993). See also Gauri Viswanathan, *Masks of Conquest: Literary Study and British Rule in India* (New York: Columbia University Press, 1989).

31. Michael Hardt and Antonio Negri, *Empire* (Cambridge, Mass.: Harvard University Press, 2000), p. xii.

32. On the relation between exceptionalism and imperialism, see my introduction in Kaplan and Pease, eds., *Cultures of United States Imperialism.*

33. Similar arguments about American exceptionalism in two different historical periods are made by Anders Stephanson, *Manifest Destiny: American Expansion and the Empire of Right* (New York: Hill and Wang, 1995); and Nikhil Pal Singh, "Culture/Wars: Recoding Empire in an Age of Democracy," *American Quarterly*, 50 (1998): 471–522.

34. Lora Romero, *Home Fronts: Domesticity and Its Critics in the Antebellum United States* (Durham: Duke University Press, 1997).

35. On this historiography, see Edward P. Crapol, "Coming to Terms with Empire: The Historiography of Late-Nineteenth-Century American Foreign Relations," *Diplomatic History*, 16 (Fall 1992): 573–97; and the essays in "Special Section: Imperialism: A Useful Category of Analysis?" *Radical History Review*, 57 (Fall 1993): 4–84.

36. This approach can be seen in the following important works on the

study of U.S. culture: Richard Drinnon, *Facing West: The Metaphysics of Indian-Hating and Empire-Building* (New York: New American Library, 1980); Ronald Takaki, *Iron Cages: Race and Culture in Nineteenth-Century America* (New York: Knopf, 1979); Richard Slotkin, *The Fatal Environment: The Myth of the Frontier in the Age of Industrialization* (New York: Atheneum, 1985); *Gunfighter Nation: The Myth of the Frontier in Twentieth-Century America* (New York: Atheneum, 1992); Eric Cheyfitz, *The Poetics of Imperialism: Translation and Colonization from The Tempest to Tarzan* (New York: Oxford University Press, 1991).

37. Thomas Hietala, *Manifest Design: Anxious Aggrandizement in Late Jacksonian America* (Ithaca, N.Y.: Cornell University Press, 1985), p. 10.

38. W. E. B. Du Bois, *The Souls of Black Folk* (1903), rpt. in Sundquist, *The Oxford W. E. B. Du Bois Reader,* p. 107.

1. Manifest Domesticity

1. "Life on the Rio Grande," *Godey's Lady's Book,* 32 (April 1847): 177–78.

2. Influential studies of this paradigm by historians and literary critics include Barbara Welter, "The Cult of True Womanhood," *American Quarterly,* 18 (1966): 151–74; Kathryn Kish Sklar, *Catharine Beecher: A Study in American Domesticity* (New Haven: Yale University Press, 1973); Nancy Cott, *The Bonds of Womanhood: "Woman's Sphere" in New England, 1780–1835* (New Haven: Yale University Press, 1977); Ann Douglas, *The Feminization of American Culture* (New York: Knopf, 1977); Nina Baym, *Woman's Fiction: A Guide to Novels by and about Women in America, 1820–1870* (Ithaca, N.Y.: Cornell University Press, 1978); Mary Ryan, *Cradle of the Middle Class: The Family in Oneida County, New York, 1790–1865* (Cambridge: Cambridge University Press, 1981), and *Empire of the Mother: American Writing about Domesticity, 1830–1860,* special issue of *Women and History* (New York: Haworth, 1982); Mary Kelley, *Private Woman, Public Stage: Literary Domesticity in Nineteenth-Century America* (Oxford: Oxford University Press, 1984); Jane Tompkins, *Sensational Designs: The Cultural Work of American Fiction, 1790–1860* (Oxford: Oxford University Press, 1985). See also the useful review essay by Linda Kerber, "Separate Spheres, Female Worlds, Woman's Place: The Rhetoric of Women's History," *The Journal of American History* (June 1988): 9–39; Hazel Carby, *Reconstructing Womanhood: The Emergence of the Afro-American Woman Novelist* (New York: Oxford University Press, 1987); Sarah Deutsch, *No Separate Refuge: Culture, Class, and Gender on an Anglo-Hispanic Frontier in the American Southwest, 1880–1940* (New York: Oxford University Press, 1987); Peggy Pascoe, *Relations of Rescue: The Search for Female Moral Authority*

in the American West, 1874–1939 (New York: Oxford University Press, 1990); Gillian Brown, *Domestic Individualism: Imagining Self in Nineteenth-Century America* (Berkeley: University of California Press, 1990); the essays in *The Culture of Sentiment: Race, Gender, and Sentimentality in Nineteenth-Century America,* ed. Shirley Samuels (New York: Oxford University Press, 1992); Claudia Tate, *Domestic Allegories of Political Desire: The Black Heroine's Text at the Turn of the Century* (New York: Oxford University Press, 1992); Lora Romero, *Home Fronts: Domesticity and Its Critics in the Antebellum United States* (Durham: Duke University Press, 1997); Laura Wexler, *Tender Violence: Domestic Visions in an Age of U.S. Imperialism* (Chapel Hill: University of North Carolina Press, 2000).

3. On "domestic" in relation to colonialism, see Karen Hansen, ed., *African Encounters with Domesticity* (New Brunswick, N.J.: Rutgers University Press, 1992), pp. 2–23; Anne McClintock, *Imperial Leather: Race, Gender and Sexuality in the Colonial Contest* (New York: Routledge, 1995), pp. 31–36. On imperial contexts, see Jean and John L. Comaroff, "Homemade Hegemony: Modernity, Domesticity and Colonialism in South Africa" in Hansen, *African Encounters;* Anna Davin, "Imperialism and Motherhood" in Frederick Cooper and Anna Laura Stoler, eds., *Tensions of Empire: Colonial Cultures in a Bourgeois World* (Berkeley: University of California Press, 1997): 87–152; Inderpal Grewal, *Home and Harem: Nation, Gender, Empire, and the Cultures of Travel* (Durham: Duke University Press, 1996); Jane Hunter, *The Gospel of Gentility, American Women Missionaries in Turn of the Century China* (New Haven: Yale University Press, 1984); Vicente Rafael, "Colonial Domesticity: White Women and United States Rule in the Philippines," *American Literature,* 67 (December 1995): 639–66; Ann Stoler, *Race and the Education of Desire: Foucault's History of Sexuality and the Colonial Order of Things* (Durham: Duke University Press, 1995); Ian Tyrrell, *Woman's World/Woman's Empire: The Woman's Christian Temperance Movement in International Perspective, 1880–1930* (Chapel Hill: University of North Carolina Press, 1991).

4. Thomas R. Hietala, *Manifest Design: Anxious Aggrandizement in Late Jacksonian America* (Ithaca, N.Y.: Cornell University Press, 1985).

5. *Cherokee Nation v. the State of Georgia,* in Thomas G. Paterson, ed., *Major Problems in American Foreign Policy: Documents and Essays.,* 2 vols. (Lexington, Mass: Heath, 1989), vol. 1, p. 202. See Priscilla Wald's reading of this case in *Constituting Americans: Cultural Anxiety and Narrative Force* (Durham: Duke University Press, 1995), pp. 23–35.

6. Quoted in Walter LaFeber, *The American Age: United States Foreign Policy at Home and Abroad* (New York: Norton, 1989), p. 112.

7. *Democratic Review,* 20 (February 1847): 101.

8. Quoted in George B. Forgie, *Patricide in the House Divided: A Psychological Interpretation of Lincoln and His Age* (New York: Norton, 1979), pp. 107–108.

9. See Robert W. Johannsen, *To the Halls of the Montezumas: The Mexican War in the American Imagination* (New York: Oxford, 1984), pp. 175–204; Shelley Streeby, *American Sensations: Class, Empire, and the Production of Popular Culture* (Berkeley: University of California Press, 2002).

10. Hietala, *Manifest Design*, pp. 161–63.

11. Sarah Josepha Hale, "Editor's Table," *Godey's Lady's Book*, 44 (January 1852): 88.

12. Quoted in Ryan, *Empire of the Mother*, p. 112.

13. From "The Social Condition of Woman," *North American Review*, 42 (1836): 513, quoted in Annette Kolodny, *The Land Before Her: Fantasy and Experience of the American Frontiers, 1630–1860* (Chapel Hill: University of North Carolina Press, 1984), p. 166.

14. Catharine Beecher, *A Treatise on Domestic Economy* (Boston: Marsh, Capen, Lyon and Webb, 1841), p. 144. Subsequent page references are cited parenthetically in text.

15. Ryan, *Empire of the Mother*, pp. 97–114.

16. Sklar on *Catharine Beecher* is one of the few scholars to consider Beecher's domestic ideology in terms of nation-building. She analyzes *Treatise* as appealing to gender as a common national denominator, and as using domesticity as a means to national unity to counterbalance the mobility and conflicts based on class and region. She overlooks, however, that this vision of gender as a fulcrum for national unity is predicated upon a vision of that nation's imperial role. Jenine Abboushi Dallal analyzes the imperial dimensions of Beecher's domestic ideology in contrast to the domestic rhetoric of Melville's imperial adventure narratives in her "The Beauty of Imperialism: Emerson, Melville, Flaubert, and Al-Shidyac" (Ph.D. diss., Harvard University, 1996), ch. 2.

17. John L. O'Sullivan, "The Great Nation of Futurity," in Paterson, *Major Problems in American Foreign Policy*, vol. 1, p. 241.

18. Catharine Beecher and Harriet Beecher Stowe, *American Woman's Home* (Hartford, Conn.: J. B. Ford, 1869), pp. 458–59.

19. Karen Sánchez-Eppler, "Raising Empires like Children: Race, Nation and Religious Education," *American Literary History*, 8 (Fall 1996): 399–425; Stoler, *Race and the Education of Desire*, pp. 137–64.

20. Although the cleanliness and orderliness of the home promises to make American women healthier, Beecher also blames the lack of outdoor exercise for American women's frailty, as though the problematic space outside the home, the foreign, can both cause and cure those "difficulties peculiar to American women."

21. This generalized anxiety about contamination of the domestic sphere by children may stem from the circulation of stories by missionaries, who expressed fear of their children being raised by native servants or too closely identified with native culture. These stories would have circulated in popular mission tracts and in middle-class women's magazines, such as *Godey's* and *Mother's Magazine*. See, for example, Stoler, and Patricia Grimshaw, *Paths of Duty: American Missionary Wives in Nineteenth-Century Hawaii* (Honolulu: University of Hawaii Press, 1989), pp. 154–78. The licentiousness of men was also seen as a threat to women's health within the home. In general, domesticity is usually seen as an ideology that develops in middle-class urban centers (and, as Sklar shows, in contrast to European values) and then is exported outward to the frontier and empire, where it meets challenges and adaptations. It remains to be studied how domestic discourse might develop out of the confrontation with colonized cultures in what has been called the "contact zone" of frontier and empire.

22. Sklar, *Catharine Beecher*, p. 163; Douglas, *The Feminization of American Culture*, pp. 51–54.

23. Nina Baym, "Onward Christian Women: Sarah J. Hale's History of the World," *New England Quarterly*, 63 (1990): 249–70.

24. Sarah J. Hale, "Editor's Table," *Godey's Lady's Book*, 34 (January 1847): 53.

25. *Godey's*, 45 (November 1852): 303; *Godey's*, 34 (January 1847): 52.

26. Ruth E. Finley, *The Lady of Godey's, Sarah Josepha Hale* (Philadelphia: Lippincott, 1931), p. 199.

27. Sarah J. Hale, *Northwood, or, Life North and South* (New York: H. Long and Brother, 1852). See her 1852 preface, "A Word with the Reader," on revisions of the 1827 edition.

28. On the white ideological framework of African colonization, see George Fredrickson, *The Black Image in the White Mind: The Debate on Afro-American Character and Destiny, 1817–1914* (New York: Harper and Row, 1971), pp. 6–22, 110–17; Susan M. Ryan, "Errand into Africa: Colonization and Nation Building in Sarah J. Hale's *Liberia*," *New England Quarterly*, 68 (1995): 558–83; Bruce Dorsey, "A Gendered History of African Colonization in the Antebellum United States," *Journal of Social History* (Fall 2000): 77–103; Timothy B. Powell, "Harriet Beecher Stowe: *Uncle Tom's Cabin* and the Question of the American Colonization Society," in *Ruthless Democracy: A Multicultural Interpretation of the American Renaissance* (Princeton: Princeton University Press, 2000), pp. 103–30.

29. Sarah J. Hale, *Liberia; or Mr. Peyton's Experiments* (1853: reprint, Upper Saddle River, N.J.: Gregg Press, 1968).

30. On Liberia as a conservative rebuff to Stowe, see Thomas F. Gossett, *Un-*

cle Tom's Cabin and American Culture (Dallas: Southern Methodist University Press, 1985), pp. 235–36.

31. Ryan, "Errand into Africa," p. 572.

32. Reginald Horsman, *Race and Manifest Destiny: The Origins of American Racial Anglo-Saxonism* (Cambridge, Mass.: Harvard University Press, 1981), pp. 62–81.

33. Sarah J. Hale, *Woman's Record* (New York: Harper, 1853), p. 564.

34. Linda Kerber, *Women of the Republic: Intellect and Ideology in Revolutionary America* (Chapel Hill: University of North Carolina Press, 1980).

35. Sarah J. Hale, "An Appeal to the American Christians on Behalf of the Ladies' Medical Missionary Society," *Godey's Lady's Book*, 54 (March 1852): 185–88.

36. Nancy Armstrong, *Desire and Domestic Fiction: A Political History of the Novel* (New York: Oxford University Press, 1987); Brown, *Domestic Individualism;* Richard Brodhead, "Sparing the Rod: Discipline and Fiction in Antebellum America," in Philip Fisher, ed., *The New American Studies: Essays from Representations* (Berkeley: University of California Press, 1991).

37. Susan Warner, *The Wide Wide World* (1850; rpt., New York: Feminist Press, 1987); Maria Susanna Cummins, *The Lamplighter* (1854; rpt., New Brunswick, N.J.: Rutgers University Press, 1988); E.D.E.N. Southworth, *The Hidden Hand; or, Capitola The Madcap* (1859: rpt., New Brunswick, N.J.: Rutgers University Press, 1988); Harriet Beecher Stowe, *Uncle Tom's Cabin* (1852: rpt., New York: Viking Penguin, 1981).

38. Jane Tompkins, *Sentimental Designs: The Cultural Work of American Fiction, 1790–1860* (New York: Oxford University Press, 1985), pp. 160–65; Brodhead, "Sparing the Rod," pp. 153–57.

39. Forgie, *Patricide in the House Divided*, pp. 35–49.

40. On the connections between incest and race see Walter Benn Michaels, *Our America: Nativism, Modernism, and Pluralism* (Durham: Duke University Press, 1995), pp. 5–12; and Werner Sollors, *Neither Black nor White Yet Both: Thematic Explorations of Interracial Literature* (New York: Oxford University Press, 1997), ch. 10.

41. On the male characters' involvement in imperial enterprises in India in *The Lamplighter,* see Susan Castellanos, "Masculine Sentimentalism and the Project of Nation-Building" (paper presented at the conference on Nineteenth-Century Women Writers, Trinity College, June 1996).

42. On this split see Elizabeth Young, *Disarming the Nation: Women's Writing and the American Civil War* (Chicago: University of Chicago Press, 1999), pp. 30–47.

43. Toni Morrison, *Playing in the Dark: Whiteness and the Literary Imagination* (Cambridge, Mass.: Harvard University Press, 1992), p. 6.

2. The Imperial Routes of Mark Twain

1. Jonathan Arac, *Huckleberry Finn as Idol and Target: The Functions of Criticism in Our Time* (Madison: University of Wisconsin Press, 1997).

2. This paradigm of doubleness is as old as Twain criticism, since as early as Albert Bigelow Paine's *Mark Twain, a Biography*, 3 vols. (New York: Harper's, 1912) and Bernard De Voto, *Mark Twain's America* (Boston: Little, Brown, 1932). For more recent major examples see Justin Kaplan, *Mr. Clemens and Mark Twain* (New York: Simon and Schuster, 1966); Susan Gillman, *Dark Twins: Imposture and Identity in Mark Twain's America* (Chicago: University of Chicago Press, 1989); Shelley Fisher Fishkin, *Was Huck Black? Mark Twain and African American Voices* (New York: Oxford University Press, 1993).

3. For a collection of Twain's anti-imperialist writing see Jim Zwick, ed., *Mark Twain's Weapons of Satire: Anti-Imperialist Writings on the Philippine-American War* (Syracuse, N.Y.: Syracuse University Press, 1992).

4. Mark Twain, *Following the Equator; A Journey Around the World* (New York: Harpers, 1903) vol. 1, p. 47. Subsequent page references cited parenthetically in the text.

5. Mark Twain, *Roughing It* (1871; rpt. New York: Harper and Row, 1962), chs. 62–78.

6. Renato Rosaldo, "Imperialist Nostalgia," *Representations*, 26 (1989): 107–22.

7. My understanding of melancholia builds on Sigmund Freud's influential formulation in his essay "Mourning and Melancholia" (1917) in Philip Rieff, ed., *Freud: General Psychological Theory* (New York: Collier Books, 1963), pp. 164–79.

8. Ernest Renan, "What Is a Nation?" in Homi K. Bhabha, ed., *Nation and Narration* (London: Routledge, 1990), p. 11.

9. See Twain's "My Debut as a Literary Person," in *The Man that Corrupted Hadleyburg and Other Stories and Essays* (1900); and "The Turning Point of My Life," *Harper's Bazaar* (Feb. 1910).

10. For detailed accounts of Twain's lecture tours and extant texts of his lectures, see Walter Francis Frear, *Mark Twain and Hawaii* (Chicago: Lakeside Press, 1947), pp. 164–216, 421–59; Frederick William Lorch, *The Trouble Begins at Eight: Mark Twain's Lecture Tours* (Ames: Iowa State University Press, 1968), pp. 23–52, 271–84.

11. Frear, *Mark Twain and Hawaii*, p. 431.

12. Twain, *Roughing It*, p. 418.

13. Louis J. Budd, ed., *Mark Twain: The Contemporary Reviews* (New York: Cambridge University Press, 1999), p. 55.

14. *Mark Twain's Letters, 1853–1866*, vol. 1, eds. Edgar M. Branch, Michael

B. Frank, Kenneth M. Sanderson (Berkeley: University of California Press, 1988), p. 327.

15. Frear, *Mark Twain and Hawaii*, p. 437–41.
16. Ibid., p. 441.
17. Bret Harte quoted in Lorch, *The Trouble Begins*, p. 32.
18. Randall Knoper, *Acting Naturally: Mark Twain in the Culture of Performance* (Berkeley: University of California Press, 1995), p. 65.
19. Lorch, *The Trouble Begins*, p. 277. Subsequent page references cited parenthetically in text.
20. On Twain and Stanley see Kaplan, *Mr. Clemens*, pp. 31, 151–154; Martin Green, *Dreams of Adventure, Deeds of Empire* (New York: Basic Books, 1979), pp. 258–63.
21. In Hawaii, Twain also met the American minister to Japan and, what is of more significance, became close friends with Anson Burlingame, the American minister to China, who would two years later represent China in negotiating the Burlingame Treaty with the United States. While biographers credit Burlingame with encouraging Twain to climb the social ladder of gentility in the United States, they have not considered the way in which Burlingame also introduced Twain into an international circle of diplomats, travelers, and writers. He invited Twain to China, a trip Twain intended to make but never did. See Frear, *Mark Twain and Hawaii*, pp. 32, 112, 166, and Kaplan, *Mr. Clemens*, p. 81.
22. *Mark Twain's Letters*, p. 333.
23. Lorch, *The Trouble Begins*, p. 284.
24. *Mark Twain's Letters*, p. 349.
25. Frear, *Mark Twain and Hawaii*, pp. 449–50.
26. *Mark Twain's Notebooks and Journals, 1855–1873*, vol. 1, eds. Frederick Anderson, Michael B. Frank, Kenneth M. Sanderson (Berkeley: University of California Press, 1975), p. 189.
27. *Mark Twain's Letters from Hawaii*, ed. A. Grove Day (Honolulu: University of Hawaii Press), p. 42. Subsequent page references cited parenthetically in text.
28. See James Clifford, "Traveling Cultures," in Lawrence Grossberg, Cary Nelson, and Paula Treichler, eds., *Cultural Studies* (New York: Routledge, 1992), pp. 96–112.
29. This brief historical overview relies on the following sources: Gavan Daws, *Shoal of Time: A History of the Hawaiian Islands* (Honolulu: University of Hawaii Press, 1968), pp. 124–206; Ronald Takaki, *Pau Hana: Plantation Life and Labor in Hawaii, 1835–1920* (Honolulu: University of Hawaii Press, 1983); Lilikala Kame'eleihiwa, *Native Land and Foreign Desires* (Honolulu: Bishop Museum Press, 1992); Sally Engle Merry, *Col-*

onizing Hawaii: The Cultural Power of Law (Princeton: Princeton University Press, 2000).

30. Daws, *Shoal of Time*, p. 187.

31. Merry, *Colonizing Hawaii*, p. 238.

32. On the changing roles of Hawaiian women during the colonization of Hawaii, see Jocelyn Linnekin, *Sacred Queens and Women of Consequence: Rank, Gender, and Colonialism in the Hawaiian Islands* (Ann Arbor: University of Michigan Press, 1990).

33. Lorch, *The Trouble Begins*, p. 279.

34. On the politics of the hula as a spectacle for tourists in the past and present see Elizabeth Buck, *Paradise Remade: The Politics of Culture and History in Hawai'i* (Philadelphia: Temple University Press, 1993).

35. *Notebooks and Journals*, pp. 154ff.

36. Sidney Mintz, *Sweetness and Power: The Place of Sugar in Modern History* (New York: Viking Penguin, 1985) p. 47.

37. Daws, *Shoal of Time*, p. 178.

38. Eric Foner, *Nothing But Freedom: Emancipation and Its Legacy* (Baton Rouge: Louisiana State University Press, 1983).

39. Takaki, *Pau Hana*, pp. 127–52.

40. Foner, *Nothing But Freedom*, pp. 49–53; Eric Foner, *Reconstruction: America's Unfinished Revolution, 1863–1877* (New York: Harper and Row, 1988), pp. 199–201, 208–15.

41. Merry, *Colonizing Hawaii*, pp. 128–31.

42. Quoted in Takaki, *Pau Hana*, p. 22.

43. Foner, *Reconstruction*, illustration following p. 194.

44. *Mark Twain's Letters from Hawaii*, p. 31.

45. Quoted in Takaki, *Pau Hana*, p. 21.

46. Quoted in George Fredrickson, *The Black Image in the White Mind: The Debate on Afro-American Character and Destiny, 1817–1914* (New York: Harper and Row, 1971), p. 190.

47. *Notebooks and Journals*, pp. 149–50.

48. Ibid., p. 150.

49. *Mark Twain's Letters from Hawaii*, p. 112.

50. Daws, *Shoal of Time*, pp. 186–87.

51. For an excellent analysis of the remaining manuscript fragments see Stephen H. Sumida, *And the View from the Shore: Literary Traditions of Hawaii* (Seattle: University of Washington Press, 1991), pp. 38–56.

52. The reference appears on the last page of fragments of the manuscript, "Hawaiian Story," in the Bancroft Library of the University of California at Berkeley: The Mark Twain Papers, January 1884.

53. On Samuel Armstrong see Robert Francis Engs, *Educating the Disenfran-*

chised and Disinherited: Samuel Chapman Armstrong and Hampton Institute, 1839–1893 (Knoxville: University of Tennessee Press, 1999).

54. Samuel Armstrong, *Lessons from the Hawaiian Islands* (Hampton, Va.: Normal School Printing Office, 1884), quoted in Engs, *Educating,* p. 174.

3. Romancing the Empire

1. Mark Twain, "To the Person Sitting in Darkness" (1901), rpt. in Jim Zwick, ed., *Mark Twain's Weapons of Satire: Anti-Imperialist Writings on the Philippine-American War* (Syracuse, N.Y.: Syracuse University Press, 1992), pp. 33–34.

2. "Senator Albert J. Beveridge's Salute to Imperialism, 1900" in Thomas G. Paterson, ed., *Major Problems in American Foreign Policy: Documents and Essays* (Lexington, Mass.: Heath, 1989), vol. 1, pp. 389–91.

3. Quoted in Kristin Hoganson, *Fighting for American Manhood: How Gender Politics Provoked the Spanish-American and Philippine-American Wars* (New Haven: Yale University Press, 1998), p. 151.

4. Charles Major, *When Knighthood Was in Flower* (Indianapolis: Bowen and Merrill, 1898), p. 27.

5. William Dean Howells, "The New Historical Romances," *North American Review,* 171 (December, 1900): 936.

6. Henry Seidel Canby, *The Age of Confidence: Life in the Nineties* (New York: Farrar, 1934), pp. 191–92.

7. Many novelists identified as naturalists and realists also wrote historical romances; e.g., Edith Wharton, *The Valley of Decision;* Sarah Orne Jewett, *The Tory Lover;* Frank Norris, *Yvernelle;* Booth Tarkington, *Monsieur Beaucaire;* and of course Twain's parodic romance, *A Connecticut Yankee in King Arthur's Court,* and his more romantic *Joan of Arc.* Stephen Crane at his death was contemplating a conventional historical romance about the American Revolution. A literary history of these interpenetrating genres remains to be written.

8. This approach is almost too commonplace to document. For an influential formulation, see Richard Hofstadter, "Manifest Destiny and the Philippines," in Daniel Aaron, ed., *America in Crisis: Fourteen Crucial Episodes in American History* (New York: Knopf, 1952), pp. 173–200. John Higham includes imperialist adventure as one more form of antimodern muscularity in "The Reorientation of American Culture in the 1890's" in his *Writing American History: Essays on Modern Scholarship* (Bloomington: University of Indiana Press, 1973), pp. 73–100. This is a good example of an influential cultural history that relegates imperial-

ism to the margins, as does T. J. Jackson Lears in *No Place of Grace: Antimodernism and the Transformation of American Culture, 1880–1920* (New York: Pantheon, 1981), pp. 97–139. I argue against his view of the support for imperialism as an inadvertent consequence of the chivalric revival. For a rebuttal of the approach to American imperialism as antimodern nostalgia instead of modern rationalized force, see David Axeen, "'Heroes of the Engine Room': American 'Civilization' and the War with Spain," *American Quarterly,* 36 (1984): 125–38.

9. Edward Said, *"Kim:* The Pleasures of Imperialism," *Raritan,* 8 (1987): 27–64.

10. On masculinity and westward expansion see Michael Rogin, *Fathers and Children: Andrew Jackson and the Subjugation of the American Indian* (New York: Random House, 1975); Richard Slotkin, *Regeneration through Violence: The Mythology of the American Frontier, 1600–1860* (Middletown, Conn.: Wesleyan University Press, 1973) and *The Fatal Environment: The Myth of the American Frontier in the Age of Industrialization, 1800–1890* (New York: Atheneum, 1985); Richard Drinnon, *Facing West: The Metaphysics of Indian-Hating and Empire-Building* (New York: New American Library, 1980); and Ronald Takaki, *Iron Cages: Race and Culture in Nineteenth-Century America* (New York: Knopf, 1979). All four analyses work within a common framework based on a model of repression that joins its political and psychoanalytical meanings. In these accounts white masculinity is constituted by denying its threatening features and projecting its "primitive" desires onto the colonized "others" who are conquered and destroyed in the process of expansion. Drinnon and Takaki extend their analyses from westward to overseas expansion at the turn of the century and find the same dynamics at work in the later period.

11. The notion of an "informal empire" based on economic rather than territorial expansion has been propounded most thoroughly by William Appleman Williams, *The Contours of American History* (Chicago: Quadrangle, 1966), pp. 343–478, and Walter LaFeber, *The New Empire: An Interpretation of American Expansion, 1860–1898* (Ithaca: Cornell University Press, 1963).

12. Myra Jehlen, *American Incarnation: The Individual, the Nation, and the Continent* (Cambridge, Mass.: Harvard University Press, 1986), p. 5.

13. On the shift in the meaning of masculinity in this period see Gail Bederman, *Manliness and Civilization: A Cultural History of Gender and Race in the United States, 1880–1917* (Chicago: University of Chicago Press, 1995); E. Anthony Rotundo, *American Manhood: Transformations in Masculinity from the Revolution to the Modern Era* (New York: Basic Books, 1993); Joseph Kett, *Rites of Passage; Adolescence in America, 1790 to*

the Present (New York: Basic, 1977); Joe Dubbert, *A Man's Place: Masculinity in Transition* (Englewood Cliffs, N.J.: Prentice, 1979); and Elliot Gorn, *The Manly Art: Bare Knuckle Prize Fighting in America* (Ithaca: Cornell University Press, 1986). For an important interpretation of the Spanish American War in terms of these changing conceptions of masculinity, see Hoganson, *Fighting for American Manhood.*

14. Maurice Thompson, "Vigorous Men, a Vigorous Nation," *The Independent*, 50 (September 1898): 609–11.

15. Elaine Scarry, *The Body in Pain: The Making and Unmaking of the World* (New York: Oxford University Press, 1985), pp. 60–157.

16. *Downes v. Bidwell*, 182 U.S. at 301.

17. Franklin Henry Giddings, *Democracy and Empire* (New York: Macmillan, 1900), p. 3.

18. Quoted in Larzer Ziff, *The American 1890s: Life and Time of a Lost Generation* (Lincoln: University of Nebraska Press, 1966), p. 265.

19. On the meaning of this term, see Eric Hobsbawm and Terence Ranger, eds., *The Invention of Tradition* (Cambridge: Cambridge University Press, 1983), ch. 1, and on the late nineteenth-century context in which the historical romance takes its place, see ch. 7.

20. Renato Rosaldo, "Imperialist Nostalgia," *Representations*, 26 (1989): 107–22.

21. The popular romance draws on a long tradition of this form of nostalgia in British and American literature from Prospero recuperating his authority while marooned on an island, to Robinson Crusoe acquiring his island estate, to Twain's mechanic in *Connecticut Yankee* becoming "Boss" of King Arthur's England, to Kurtz regressing to an atavistic horror in *Heart of Darkness*. In Rosaldo's account of his own first encounter with the Ilongots, the subject of his anthropological fieldwork, he comments self-critically that he represented them in his journal as Hollywood Apaches in the Wild West.

22. On Roosevelt's theatricality see George Black, *The Good Neighbor; How the United States Wrote the History of Central America and the Caribbean* (New York: Pantheon, 1988), pp. 3–5. This relation between nostalgia and spectacle links other case studies of the period and merits study as a general cultural phenomenon: Roderick Nash's influential study of the Wilderness Cult centers on an example of an individual survival in the wilderness staged as a media event, *Wilderness and the American Mind* (New Haven: Yale University Press, 1982), pp. 141–60; Emily Rosenberg has shown that Buffalo Bill's international Wild West shows exported nostalgic values through technologically sophisticated productions in *Spreading the American Dream: American Economic and Cultural Expansion,*

1890–1945 (New York: Hill and Wang, 1982), pp. 35–37; and Donna Haraway has shown how the restoration of a vanishing Africa in the Museum of Natural History and of the great white hunter as a figure in that landscape was produced by the technologies of the gun and the camera, "Teddy Bear Patriarchy: Taxidermy in the Garden of Eden, New York City, 1908–1936," *Social Text*, 11 (1984–85): 20–64.

23. For different national formulations of this analogy see, for example, Stephen Kern, *The Culture of Time and Space: 1880–1918* (Cambridge, Mass.: Harvard University Press, 1983), pp. 224–40.

24. Maurice Thompson, "The Critics and the Romancers," *The Independent*, 52 (August, 1900): 1919–21.

25. Richard Harding Davis, *Soldiers of Fortune* (1897; rpt. New York: Scribner's, 1928).

26. George Barr McCutcheon, *Graustark* (New York: Grosset and Dunlap, 1901).

27. Mary Johnston, *To Have and To Hold* (Boston: Houghton, 1900).

28. In addition to these four novels, I draw on a number of novels chosen, for the most part, from the bestseller lists reconstructed by Alice Payne Packett, *Seventy Years of Best Sellers, 1895–1965* (New York: Bowker, 1967); and by Frank Luther Mott, *Golden Multitudes: The Story of Best Sellers in the United States* (New York: Macmillan, 1947). Additional sources can be found in James D. Hart, *The Popular Book: A History of America's Literary Taste* (New York: Oxford University Press, 1950), chs. 11 and 12; and Grant C. Knight, *The Strenuous Age in American Literature* (Chapel Hill: University of North Carolina Press, 1954), pp. 1–20, 61–65. This list is representative and by no means exhaustive, not only because it excludes non-American authors (the popular *Quo Vadis,* for example, by Polish author H. Sienkiewicz, typifies the genre) nor because of the great numbers of such romances, but because this genre overlaps with so many others: regionalism, the Southern plantation romance, the costume romance, the adventure tale. The fewest examples of the first category, the exotic contemporary romance, occur in this period, an absence that needs consideration: Davis's *The King's Jackal* (1899) and his story "The Reporter Who Would be King." By the 1910s, however, many popular adventure tales (and movies) were set in imperial arenas, like the Tarzan tales and Frank Merriwell novels. In the second category are Lew Wallace, *Ben-Hur* (1880), *The Prince of India* (1893); Francis Marion Crawford, *Via Crucis* (1898); S. Weir Mitchell, *The Adventures of Francis* (1898); Booth Tarkington, *Monsieur Beaucaire* (1899); Bertha Runkle, *The Helmet of Navarre* (1901). In the third are Davis, *Princess Aline* (1895); Harold McGrath, *Arms and the Woman* (1897) and *The*

Puppet Crown (1900); McCutcheon, *Beverly of Graustark* (1904); Gertrude Atherton, *Rulers of Kings* (1904). In the last category are Mitchell, *Hugh Wynne: Free Quaker* (1898); Paul Leicester Ford, *Janice Meredith* (1899); Winston Churchill, *Richard Carvel* (1898); Maurice Thompson, *Alice of Old Vincennes* (1900). Page references to these novels will be cited parenthetically in the text.

29. See also Hart, *The Popular Book;* Knight, *The Strenuous Age;* Mott, *Golden Multitudes.* The revival of Scott and of the martial ideal at large have been analyzed more acutely by Lears as part of the patrician rebellion against the routinization and weightlessness of bourgeois commercial life, a search for a primal authenticity by immersing the self in violence. Lears's antimodern argument, however, fits into a familiar paradigm of escape and nostalgia.

30. Frederick Jackson Turner, "The Problem of the West," *Atlantic Monthly,* 78 (September 1896): 296.

31. Frank Norris, "The Frontier Gone at Last" (1902), rpt. in *Frank Norris; Novels and Essays* (New York: Library of America, 1986), p. 1184.

32. Josiah Strong, *Our Country* (1886; rpt. Cambridge, Mass.: Harvard University Press, 1963), p. 213.

33. Johnston, *To Have and To Hold,* ch. 1.

34. Knight, *The Strenuous Age,* pp. 60–61.

35. Lears, *No Place of Grace,* pp. 119–24.

36. David H. Burton, *Theodore Roosevelt: Confident Imperialist* (Philadelphia: University of Pennsylvania Press, 1969), p. 190.

37. Frantz Fanon, *A Dying Colonialism* (New York: Grove, 1965), p. 39.

38. On the revival of Pocahontas as a national founding figure, see Martha Banta, *Imaging American Women: Idea and Ideals in Cultural History* (New York: Columbia University Press, 1987), pp. 492–494. Pocahontas is also the name of the American hero's canoe in Atherton's *Rulers of Kings;* the name represents his early sentimental attachment to a maternal native wilderness, which he leaves behind to become ruler of Europe.

39. Quoted in James Thompson, et al., *Sentimental Imperialists: The American Experience in East Asia* (New York: Harper, 1981), p. 117.

40. See Louis A. Pérez, *Cuba Between Empires, 1878–1902* (Pittsburgh: University of Pittsburgh Press, 1983), chs. 10 and 11, and Gerald Linderman, *The Mirror of War: American Society and the Spanish-American War* (Ann Arbor: University of Michigan Press, 1974), ch. 5.

41. Charles Brown, *The Correspondents' War: Journalists in the Spanish-American War* (New York: Scribner's, 1967), pp. 95–102. Hoganson, *Fighting for American Manhood,* pp. 58–61.

42. Quoted in Hoganson, *Fighting for American Manhood,* p. 61.

43. Ibid., p. 59.

44. Quoted in ibid., p. 61.

45. Quoted in Pérez, *Cuba Between Empires*, p. 204. For a brief view of this image of Latinos in general as feminized and light-skinned, see Michael Hunt, *Ideology and U.S. Foreign Policy* (New Haven: Yale University Press, 1987), pp. 58–62. Hoganson shows how Cubans were also portrayed as models of manly chivalry before the U.S. entered the war, pp. 434–67.

46. Quoted in Robert C. Hilderbrand, *Power and the People: Executive Management of Public Opinion in Foreign Affairs, 1897–1921* (Chapel Hill: University of North Carolina Press, 1981), pp. 44–45.

47. Theodore Roosevelt, "The Strenuous Life," in *The Strenuous Life: Essays and Addresses* (New York: Scribner's, 1906), p. 6.

48. I am suggesting that women readers (and writers) of the romance may have assumed roles analogous to those of female missionaries, reformers, anthropologists, and photographers at the time, who found new liberating social roles beyond the confines of domesticity by engaging in various imperial arenas and activities. See Jane Hunter, *The Gospel of Gentility: American Women Missionaries in Turn-of-the-Century China* (New Haven: Yale University Press, 1984); Louise Michelle Newman, *White Women's Rights: The Racial Origins of Feminism in the United States* (New York: Oxford University Press, 1999); and Laura Wexler, *Tender Violence: Domestic Visions in An Age of U.S. Imperialism* (Chapel Hill: University of North Carolina Press, 2000).

49. Francis Marion Crawford, *Via Crucis* (New York: American News Company, 1899), p. 363.

50. An important narrative inflection of this theatricality can be found in *Hugh Wynne*. Writing in the first person as a legacy for his heirs, the hero of the title quotes from his best friend's journal whenever he writes of his own duels or other belligerent acts, so that he can be seen by another in these poses. And this friend, uncommonly handsome, gentle, and unwarriorlike, is referred to throughout the novel as a "girl-boy." Here too masculine feats are given substance by the observation of a feminized figure, rather than narrated as an act of conflict.

51. Thorstein Veblen, *Theory of the Leisure Class* (1899; rpt. New York: Penguin, 1981), pp. 246–75.

52. G. Stanley Hall, *Youth: Its Education, Regimen, and Hygiene* (New York: Appleton, 1906), p. 103.

53. Lew Wallace, *Ben-Hur: A Tale of the Christ* (New York: Harper, 1880), p. 359.

54. J. A. Hobson, *Imperialism: A Study* (1902; rpt. Ann Arbor: University of Michigan Press, 1972), p. 215.

55. The role of the woman as spectator has not yet been studied, I believe, in recent accounts of the representation of women and modern warfare, from which they most often are rendered separate—as beneficiaries of more freedom at home, victims of aggressive fantasies, or emblems of patriotic nationalism. See Sandra Gilbert, "Soldier's Heart: Literary Men, Literary Women, and the Great War," in Margaret Randolph Higgonet et al., eds., *Behind the Lines: Gender and the Two World Wars* (New Haven: Yale University Press, 1987), pp. 197–226, and Banta, *Imaging American Women*, ch. 12. Susan Jeffords has powerfully analyzed the construction of the male body as spectacle in representations of Vietnam in *The Remasculinization of America: Gender and the Vietnam War* (Bloomington: Indiana University Press, 1989). Since she argues that these representations exclude women, blame them, or appropriate their powers, she does not consider their potential role as spectator or collaborator.

56. Strong, *Our Country*, p. 117.

57. Stephen Crane, *The Third Violet and Active Service*, ed. Fredson Bowers (Charlottesville: University Press of Virginia, 1969), pp. 171–72.

58. Ibid., p. 172.

59. Hobson, *Imperialism*, p. 215.

60. Walter Millis, *The Martial Spirit: A Study of Our War with Spain* (Boston: Houghton Mifflin, 1931), p. 357.

61. Quoted in Brown, *The Correspondents' War*, p. 427.

62. Albert Memmi, *The Colonizer and the Colonized* (Boston: Beacon, 1965), p. 66.

63. Homi Bhabha, "Of Mimicry and Man: The Ambivalence of Colonial Discourse," *October*, 28 (1984): 125–38.

64. For a wide-ranging article on spectacle and the post-World War II American empire, see Rogin "'Make My Day!', Spectacle as Amnesia in Imperial Politics," *Representations*, 29 (1990): 99–123.

65. Michael Kammen, *A Season of Youth: The American Revolution and the Historical Imagination* (New York: Knopf, 1978), p. 211 and chs. 5 and 6.

66. Quoted in Perez, *Cuba Between Empires*, pp. 197–199.

67. Beverly Seaton, "A Pedigree for a New Century: The Colonial Experience in Popular Historical Novels, 1890–1910," in Alan Axelrod, ed., *The Colonial Revival in America* (New York: Norton, 1985), pp. 278–93.

68. Owen Wister, "The Evolution of the Cow-Puncher," in Ben Merchant Vorpahl, ed., *My Dear Wister: The Frederick Remington-Owen Wister Letters* (Palo Alto: American West, 1973), pp. 77–96.

69. Owen Wister, *The Virginian* (1902; rpt. New York: New American Library, 1979).

70. Lee Clark Mitchell "'When you call me that . . .': Tall Talk and Male Hegemony in *The Virginian*," *Publications of the Modern Language Association*, 102 (1987): 66–77.

71. These are the arguments of Jane Tompkins, "West of Everything," *South Atlantic Quarterly*, 86 (1987): pp. 357–78; and Mitchell, "'When you call me that'."

4. Black and Blue on San Juan Hill

1. Nina Silber, *The Romance of Reunion: Northerners and the South, 1865–1900* (Chapel Hill: University of North Carolina Press, 1993).

2. Thomas Dixon, *The Leopard's Spots: A Romance of the White Man's Burden, 1865–1900* (New York: Grosset and Dunlap, 1902). Page references are cited parenthetically in the text.

3. Virginia Woolf, *A Room of One's Own, and Three Guineas* (London: Chatto & Windus, 1984), p. 75.

4. Seymour Dodd, *The Song of the Rappahannock* (New York: Dodd, Mead, 1898), preface.

5. Paul H. Buck, *The Road to Reunion, 1865–1900* (Boston: Little Brown, 1938).

6. Sutton E. Griggs, *Imperium in Imperio; A Study of the Negro Race Problem, a Novel* (1899; rpt. New York: Arno Press, 1969). Page references are cited parenthetically in the text.

7. Richard Harding Davis, *The Cuban and Porto Rican Campaigns* (New York: Scribner's, 1898), p. 217.

8. Theodore Roosevelt, *The Rough Riders: A History of the First United States Volunteer Cavalry* (New York: Scribner's, 1899), p. 133. Page references are cited parenthetically in the text.

9. This is the title humorist Finley Peter Dunne suggested that Roosevelt use for his book on the Spanish-American War. Quoted in Philip S. Foner, *The Spanish-Cuban-American War and the Birth of American Imperialism*, 2 vols. (New York: Monthly Review Press, 1972), vol. 2, p. 339.

10. Ada Ferrer, *Insurgent Cuba: Race, Nation and Revolution, 1868–1898* (Chapel Hill: University of North Carolina Press), chs. 6 and 7. On the Cuban War for Independence and U.S. intervention see also Foner, *The Spanish-Cuban-American War;* Louis A. Pérez, *The Spanish-Cuban-American War, 1878–1902* (Pittsburgh: University of Pittsburgh Press, 1983).

11. Each of these features can be found in accounts of the battle by Crane and Davis cited below; many more examples are brought together in Charles H. Brown, *The Correspondents' War: Journalists in the Spanish American War* (New York: Scribner's, 1967), ch. 15.

12. James Burton, "Photography Under Fire," *Harper's Weekly* (August 6, 1898): 774.

13. Elaine Scarry, *The Body in Pain: The Making and the Unmaking of the World* (New York: Oxford University Press, 1985), pp. 60–157.

14. For a pictorial example, see the illustration by H. L. V. Parkhurst, "The Charge at San Juan Hill," in Roosevelt, *The Rough Riders*, p. 132.

15. For an analysis of Roosevelt in juxtaposition with the Cuban perspective from the testimony of an ex-slave insurgent, see José David Saldívar, "Looking Awry at 1898: Roosevelt, Montejo, Paredes, and Mariscal," *American Literary History*, 12 (Fall 2000): 386–406.

16. On Crane's theatrical involvement in the war, see Brown, *The Correspondents' War*, p. 363; John Berryman, *Stephen Crane* (New York: Meridian Books, 1962), p. 78; Amy Kaplan, "The Spectacle of War in Crane's Revision of History," in Lee Clark Mitchell, ed., *New Essays on The Red Badge of Courage* (New York: Cambridge University Press, 1986), pp. 77–108; and Bill Brown, *The Material Unconscious: American Amusement, Stephen Crane and the Economics of Play* (Cambridge, Mass.: Harvard University Press, 1996), ch. 3.

17. Stephen Crane, "Stephen Crane's Vivid Story of the Battle of San Juan," *New York World,* July 14, 1898. Reprinted in Fredson Bowers and James B. Colvert, eds., *Stephen Crane: Reports of War* (Charlottesville: University of Virginia Press, 1971), pp. 154–65. Subsequent page references are cited parenthetically in the text.

18. Foner, *The Spanish-Cuban-American War,* vol. 2, pp. 358–61.

19. Crane, "The Red Badge of Courage Was His Wig-Wag Flag," in Bowers and Colvert, *Stephen Crane*, p. 135.

20. George Kennan, quoted in Perez, *The Spanish-Cuban-American War,* p. 204.

21. *New York Times* (August 9, 1898): 2.

22. *New York Times* (August 7, 1898): 2.

23. According to Ferrer, the U.S. racial arguments for disarming Cuban soldiers and excluding them from the formal surrender of Spain, and more generally denying them self-rule, echoed an age-old Spanish claim that Cuban independence would degenerate into a race war. She also shows how this fear informed some of the leaders of the insurrection as well, who were at pains to portray the Cubans through the lens of an implicitly white model of civilization, pp. 188–201. Ferrer's work challenges scholars of U.S. imperialism to explore how U.S. representations of race were not simply exported wholesale and imposed on Cuba, but interacted with and were also formed in response to the complex Cuban negotiations of racial identity.

24. Willard Gatewood, *Black Americans and the White Man's Burden, 1898–1903* (Chicago: University of Illinois Press, 1975), pp. 41–65.

25. Quoted in Gatewood, *Black Americans,* p. 59.

26. Willard Gatewood, ed., *'Smoked Yankees' and the Struggle for Empire: Letters from Negro Soldiers, 1898–1902* (Fayetteville: University of Arkansas Press, 1987), p. 79.

27. Gatewood, *Black Americans,* p. 59.

28. Gatewood, *'Smoked Yankees,'* p. 71.

29. Ibid., p. 96.

30. In his *A New Negro for a New Century* (1900; rpt. Miami: Mnemosyne Publishing, 1969), which depends heavily on the demonstration of black military heroism, Booker T. Washington not only reprints Holliday's rebuttal of Roosevelt (pp. 54–62), but also an earlier election speech Roosevelt gave at a political rally in Harlem, in which he praises the heroism of the Tenth and their harmony with the Rough Riders (pp. 50–52).

31. See the collection of editorials on this subject in George Marks, ed., *The Black Press Views American Imperialism, 1898–1900* (New York: Arno Press, 1971), ch. III.

32. Gatewood, *'Smoked Yankees,'* p. 73.

33. Quoted in Walter LaFeber, *The American Age: United States Foreign Policy at Home and Abroad Since 1750* (New York: Norton, 1989), p. 197.

34. Vicente Rafael, "White Love: Surveillance and Nationalist Resistance in the U.S. Colonization of the Philippines," in *Cultures of United States Imperialism,* ed. Amy Kaplan and Donald Pease (Durham: Duke University Press, 1993), pp. 185–218.

35. Christopher Lasch, "The Anti-Imperialists, the Philippines, and the Inequality of Man," *Journal of Southern History,* 25 (August 1958): 319–31. See also Walter Benn Michaels, "Anti-Imperial Americanism," in *Cultures of United States Imperialism,* pp. 365–91.

36. Gatewood, *'Smoked Yankees',* pp. 231–32, 270–71.

37. Ibid., p. 248. See Marks, *Black Press,* chs. v–vii.

38. Quoted in Foner, *Spanish-Cuban-American War,* vol. 2, p. 529.

39. *The Letters of Theodore Roosevelt,* ed. Elting Morison et al. (Cambridge, Mass.: Harvard University Press, 1951), vol. 1, p. 564.

40. Gatewood, *'Smoked Yankees',* pp. 95–96.

41. Washington, *A New Negro,* p. 56.

42. Gatewood, *Black Americans,* chs. 4–5; Gatewood, *'Smoked Yankees,'* chs. 2–3.

43. Quoted in G. Edward White, *The Eastern Establishment and the Western Experience: The West of Frederic Remington, Theodore Roosevelt, and Owen Wister* (New Haven: Yale University Press, 1968), p. 155.

44. Lieutenant John I. Pershing cited in Frank Freidel, *The Splendid Little War* (Boston: Little, Brown, 1958), p. 173.

45. Davis, *The Cuban and Porto Rican Campaigns,* pp. 210–11.

46. On the famous case of black desertion by David Fagen, see Gatewood, *Black Americans,* pp. 288–89; and Stephen Bonsal, "The Negro Soldier in War and Peace," *North American Review,* 186 (June 1907): 321–27. Bonsal laments the fact that black soldiers got along too well with their "little brown brothers" and learned their native languages. He notes that white soldiers deserted the army out of laziness, whereas black soldiers deserted out of principle, to join the insurgents in sympathy with their struggle against white racist colonial policies.

5. Birth of an Empire

1. Pauline Kael, *The Citizen Kane Book* (Boston: Little, Brown, 1971), pp. 181–86.

2. It is surprising how few Hollywood films have been made about the Spanish-American War, given how much media attention it commanded at the time. I am aware of one film about the war in Cuba, *The Rough Riders* (1927). More recently, Mario Van Peebles started *Posse* (1993) with a scene of black soldiers in Cuba during the war. *The Real Glory* (1939) is the only Hollywood film I know about U.S. colonial occupation of the Philippines. Several World War II films were made about battles in the Philippines, such as *The Bugle Sounds* (1942), *Bataan* (1943), *Back to Bataan* (1945), *American Guerilla in the Philippines* (1950). On these films see Charles Hawley, "'You're a Better Filipino Than I Am, John Wayne'; World War II, Hollywood, and U.S.-Philippines Relations," *Pacific Historical Review* (August 2002).

3. Michael Rogin, *Blackface, White Noise: Jewish Immigrants in the Hollywood Melting Pot* (Berkeley: University of California Press, 1996), p. 75.

4. This paragraph summarizes my viewing of the collection of Spanish-American War films in the Paper Print Collection of the Library of Congress. Some of these films can now be viewed on the Library of Congress American Memory website.

5. This overview relies on Charles Musser's magisterial research in *The Emergence of Cinema: The American Screen to 1907* (New York: Scribner's, 1990), pp. 225–62; *Before the Nickelodeon: Edwin S. Porter and the Edison Manufacturing Company* (Berkeley: University of California Press, 1991); and *High-Class Moving Pictures: Lyman H. Howe and the Forgotten Era of Traveling Exhibition, 1880–1920,* in collaboration with Carol Nelson (Princeton: Princeton University Press, 1991). See also the wealth of ex-

cellent material available on the website The Spanish-American War in U.S. Media Culture, by James Castonguay; see http://chnm.gmu.edu/aq/war/.

6. J. A. Hobson, *Imperialism: A Study* (1902; rpt. Ann Arbor: University of Michigan Press, 1972), p. 215.

7. Thomas Gunning, "The Cinema of Attractions: Early Cinema, Its Spectators and the Avante Garde," *Wide Angle*, 8 (Fall 1986): 63–70.

8. Early motion pictures did not emerge in a vacuum but often borrowed from other media, such as the magic lantern show, theater, political cartoons. The Spanish-American War films share many features with 3-D stereoscopic cards, a medium in which the war was a very popular subject. See William C. Darrah, *The World of Stereographs* (Nashville, Tenn.: Land Yacht Press, 1977), and Jim Zwick, Stereoscopic Visions of War and Empire, http://www.boondocks.com.

9. Charles Musser, *Edison Motion Pictures, 1890–1900: A Filmography* (Washington, D.C.: Smithsonian, 1998), p. 541.

10. Paul Virilio, *War and Cinema: The Logistics of Perception* (London: Verso, 1989), p. 5.

11. See Lynne Kirby, *Parallel Tracks: The Railroad and Silent Cinema* (Durham: Duke University Press, 1997); Anne Friedberg, *Window Shopping: Cinema and the Postmodern* (Berkeley: University of California Press, 1993).

12. Ella Shohat and Robert Stam, *Unthinking Eurocentrism: Multiculturalism and the Media* (London: Routledge, 1994), pp. 100–101.

13. Virilio, *War and Cinema*, pp. 6, 7.

14. See Charles Musser, "Nationalism and the Beginnings of Cinema: The Lumière Cinématographe in the U.S., 1896–1897," *Historical Journal of Film, Radio and Television*, 19 (June 1999): 149–76.

15. *War Correspondents*, Edison Company, 1898: Paper Print Collection, Library of Congress.

16. Musser, *Edison Motion Pictures, 1890–1900*, p. 414.

17. See *Cuban Refugees Waiting for Rations* and *Cuban Volunteers Marching for Rations*, Edison Company, 1898: Paper Print Collection, Library of Congress.

18. Edison Company, 1898: Paper Print Collection, Library of Congress.

19. Musser, *Edison Motion Pictures*, p. 418. See also the description of *Tenth U.S. Infantry, 2nd Battalion, Leaving Car*, where "real soldiers" marching with their equipment are contrasted with a "comical looking nigger dude" watching them (p. 423).

20. Musser, *Edison Motion Pictures*, p. 426.

21. Musser, *High-Class Moving Pictures*, pp. 86–90.

22. Basil Courtney, writing for *Motion Picture News* (1925), quoted in Anthony Slide, *The Big V: A History of the Vitagraph Company* (Metuchen, N.J.: Scarecrow Press, 1976), p. 10.

23. Quoted in Castonguay, the section on Film Studies. See n5 above.

24. Musser, *The Emergence of Cinema*, pp. 258–61; on the question of narrative in early film, see Thomas Elsaesser, ed., *Early Cinema: Space, Frame, Narrative* (London: British Film Institute, 1990).

25. On the relation between political and domestic spheres in early film, see Jonathan Auerbach, "McKinley at Home: How Early Cinema Made News," *American Quarterly*, 51 (Dec. 1999): 797–832.

26. *The American Soldier in Love and War*, #1, 2, 3, American Mutoscope and Biograph Co., 1903, Paper Print Collection, Library of Congress.

27. Kemp R. Niver, ed., *Biograph Bulletins, 1896–1908* (Los Angeles: Locare Research Group, 1971), p. 90, my italics. Three fictional films were made together under the title *The American Soldier in Love and War*, which I will refer to as scenes 1, 2, 3. The *Bulletin* recommended that the exhibitors intersperse them with two "actualities" made previously, one of real soldiers embarking for war and the other of a staged battle scene.

28. Miriam Hansen, *Babel and Babylon: Spectatorship in American Silent Film* (Cambridge, Mass.: Harvard University Press, 1991), p. 47.

29. *Love and War*, Edison Company, 1899, Paper Print Collection, Library of Congress. Similar to these films is a parallel six-card set of stereoscopic cards, which all take place in the same parlor from which the soldier departs, where his love faints, and to which he returns. The same cards were marketed as the Battle of Manila or of Santiago, with only a slight change of captions. See the cards and commentary on Zwick, http://www.boondocksnet.com/stereo/victorious3.

30. Musser, *Emergence of Cinema*, p. 342.

31. Theodore Roosevelt, "The Strenuous Life," in *The Strenuous Life: Essays and Addresses* (1899; rpt. New York: Scribner's, 1906). Kristin Hoganson shows how this project unraveled against the reality of the American conduct of brutal warfare against the Philippines in *Fighting for American Manhood: How Gender Politics Provoked the Spanish-American & Philippine-America Wars* (New Haven: Yale University Press, 1998), ch. 5.

32. Quoted in James Thompson, et al. *Sentimental Imperialists: The American Experience in East Asia* (New York: Harper, 1981), p. 117.

33. Oscar Campomanes, "Casualty Figures of the American Soldier and the Other: Post-1898 Allegories of American Imperial Nation-Building as 'Love and War'," in Angel Shaw and Luis Francia, eds., *Vestiges of War:*

The Philippine-American War and Its Aftermath (New York: New York University Press, forthcoming 2002).

34. Quoted in Castonguay, the section on The Female Spectator. See n5.
35. Ibid.
36. On early ethnographic uses of film see Fatimah Tobing Rony, *The Third Eye: Race, Cinema, and Ethnographic Spectacle* (Durham: Duke University Press, 1996), pp. 21–73.
37. "'Spaniards' Would not Fight: Vitascope Man Badly Treated by Men He Hired to Mimic the Battle of San Juan," *The Phonoscope* (April 1899): 15.
38. Quoted in Michael Rogin, "'The Sword Became a Flashing Vision': D. W. Griffith's *The Birth of a Nation*," in *The Birth of a Nation*, ed. Robert Lang (New Brunswick, N.J.: Rutgers University Press, 1994), p. 252. According to his biographers, Griffith viewed his first films in 1898; given their popularity, he most likely would have seen some of the war films.
39. Thomas Dixon, *The Leopard's Spots: A Romance of the White Man's Burden, 1865–1900* (New York: Grosset and Dunlap, 1902), p. 368. *The Birth of a Nation* is most often seen as a film version of Dixon's *The Clansman* (the film's name at first and the name of a play version as well), but the second half of the film, which focuses on Reconstruction, draws more from *The Leopard's Spots*.
40. Rogin, "'The Sword Became a Flashing Vision,'" p. 289.
41. G. W. Bitzer, *Billy Bitzer: His Story* (New York: Farrar, Straus and Giroux, 1973), p. 180; my italics.
42. Oscar Micheaux, *Within Our Gates* (1919; reissued in series, The Library of Congress Video Collection; v. 1, The African American Cinema, 1995).
43. Jane Gaines, "*The Birth of a Nation* and *Within Our Gates:* Two Tales of the American South," in Richard H. King and Helen Taylor, *Dixie Debates: Perspectives on Southern Cultures* (New York: New York University Press, 1996), pp. 177–92.
44. Micheaux's differentiation of African Americans from immigrants may also have been a way to claim a place in the world of film, a world identified with immigrants as both producers and consumers. Scholars have shown how the medium of film worked to Americanize immigrants, in part, as Michael Rogin has claimed, by teaching them antiblack racism and thus whitening them as well.
45. I thank Elizabeth Young for calling this scene to my attention and for first suggesting that I write about *Citizen Kane* in the context of empire.
46. James Naremore, *The Magic World of Orson Welles* (New York: Oxford University Press, 1978), p. 291.

47. Michael Denning, *The Cultural Front: The Laboring of American Culture in the Twentieth Century* (London: Verso, 1996), pp. 374–95; Laura Mulvey, *Citizen Kane* (London: British Film Institute, 1992).
48. Mulvey, *Citizen Kane*, p. 56.
49. Denning, *The Cultural Front*, p. 375.
50. Ibid., pp. 388–92.
51. Henry R. Luce, *The American Century* (New York: Farrar and Reinhart, 1941), p. 16. Subsequent references cited parenthetically in the text.
52. Quoted in Denning, *The Cultural Front*, p. 394.
53. On Bazin, see Mulvey, *Citizen Kane*, p. 20; Denning, *The Cultural Front*, p. 392.
54. André Bazin, *Orson Welles: A Critical View* (New York: Harper and Row, 1972), p. 75.

6. The Imperial Cartography of W. E. B. Du Bois

1. W. E. B. Du Bois, "The African Roots of War" (1915) in Herbert Aptheker, ed., *Writings by W. E. B. Du Bois in Periodicals Edited by Others* (Millwood, N.Y.: Kraus-Thomson Organization, 1982), vol. 2, p. 96.
2. Du Bois, "Hayti," *The Crisis*, 10 (September 1915): 291.
3. Du Bois, "The Clansman," *The Crisis*, 10 (May 1915): 33.
4. Du Bois, *Dusk of Dawn: An Essay Toward an Autobiography of a Race Concept* (1940: rpt. New Brunswick, N.J.: Transaction Publishers, 1994), p. 239.
5. Eric Sundquist, *To Wake the Nations: Race in the Making of American Literature* (Cambridge, Mass.: Harvard University Press, 1993), pp. 540–625. This is such a commonplace that it is hard to pinpoint. Sundquist, for example, often makes use of this assumption to structure his fine reading of *Darkwater* ("the rigid racial hierarchy supporting racism at home and colonialism abroad," p. 540; see also pp. 543, 547). This bifurcation also structures the views of Cornel West, *The American Evasion of Philosophy: A Genealogy of Pragmatism* (Madison: University of Wisconsin Press, 1989); and Adolph L. Reed, *W. E. B. Du Bois and American Political Thought: Fabianism and the Color Line* (New York: Oxford University Press, 1997). Although it is a cliché to say that Du Bois was interested in the national and international, scholars often emphasize one over the other. Ross Posnock, for example, discusses Du Bois's pragmatism without even mentioning the international content and context of the works he analyzes, such as *Dark Princess*, in *Color and Culture: Black Writers and the Making of the Modern Intellectual* (Cambridge, Mass.: Harvard University Press, 1998). For an especially useful analysis of the conjunction of Du Bois's national and international concerns see Wilson

Moses, *The Golden Age of Black Nationalism, 1850–1925* (Hamden, Conn.: Archon, 1978). See also Adam Lively, "Continuity and Radicalism in American Black Nationalist Thought, 1914–1929," *Journal of American Studies,* 18 (August 1984): 207–35. For a Marxist critique of Du Bois's internationalism see Cedric J. Robinson, *Black Marxism: The Making of the Black Radical Tradition* (London: Zed, 1983), and his essay "W. E. B. Du Bois and Black Sovereignty" in *Imagining Home: Culture, Class and Nationalism in the African Diaspora,* eds. Sidney Lemelle, Robin Kelley (London: Verso, 1994), pp. 145–57. For a collection that addresses Du Bois's international and national concerns, though in separate essays, see Bernard W. Bell, Emily Grosholz, James B. Stewart, eds., *W. E. B. Du Bois On Race and Culture: Philosophy, Politics, Poetics* (New York: Routledge, 1996).

6. In addition to those mentioned in the previous note see, for example, Manning Marable, *W. E. B. Du Bois: Black Radical Democrat* (Boston: Twayne, 1986); Paul Gilroy, *The Black Atlantic: Modernity and Double Consciousness* (Cambridge, Mass.: Harvard University Press, 1993); Richard Cullen Rath, "Echo and Narcissus: The Afrocentric Pragmatism of W. E. B. Du Bois," *Journal of American History,* 84 (September 1997): 461–95.

7. Gilroy, *Black Atlantic,* pp. 112–15.

8. Du Bois, *Dusk of Dawn,* p. 222.

9. Du Bois, "The Color Line Belts the World" (1906), in David Levering Lewis, ed., *W. E. B. Du Bois: A Reader* (New York: Holt, 1995), p. 42.

10. W. E. B. Du Bois, *The Suppression of the African Slave-Trade to the United States of America, 1638–1870* (1897), rpt. in *W. E. B. Du Bois, Writings,* ed. Nathan Huggins (New York: Library of America, 1986), p. 74.

11. Du Bois, *The Souls of Black Folk* (1903), rpt. in Sundquist, ed., *The Oxford W. E. B. Du Bois Reader* (New York: Oxford University Press, 1996), p. 107.

12. Du Bois, "To the Nations of the World," in Sundquist, ed., *The Oxford Reader,* p. 625.

13. Du Bois, "The Present Outlook for the Dark Races of Mankind" (1900), in Aptheker, ed., *Writings by W. E. B. Du Bois,* vol. 1, pp. 73–82.

14. On Du Bois's involvement in the Pan-African Congress of 1919 see David Levering Lewis, *W. E. B. Du Bois: Biography of a Race, 1868–1919* (New York: Holt, 1993), pp. 561–78; Marable, *W. E. B. Du Bois,* pp. 99–105; Du Bois, "The Pan-African Congress," *The Crisis,* 17 (April 1919), in Herbert Aptheker, ed., *Selections from the Crisis* (Millwood, N.Y.: Kraus-Thomson Organization, 1983), vol. I, pp. 182–85; Immanuel Geiss, *The Pan-African Movement: A History of Pan-Africanism in America, Europe, and Africa* (New York: Africana Publishing, 1974), ch. 12.

15. Du Bois, "My Mission" (1919), in Aptheker, ed., *Selections from the Crisis*, pp. 186–88.

16. On Du Bois and World War I see Lewis, *Du Bois: Biography*, pp. 525–34, 551–80; and Mark Ellis, "'Closing Ranks' and 'Seeking Honors': W. E. B. Du Bois in World War I," *Journal of American History* (June 1992): 96–124. For a good analysis of Du Bois's changing attitudes during the war, see Julia Liss, "Diasporic Identities: The Science and Politics of Race in the Work of Franz Boas and W. E. B. Du Bois, 1894–1919," *Cultural Anthropology*, 13 (1998): 146–53. I would only qualify her sense of Du Bois's progression from nationalism to internationalism as a result of disillusionment during the war. I see these positions of his as much more entangled and at play.

17. Du Bois, "Close Ranks" (1918), in Lewis, ed., *W. E. B. Du Bois: A Reader*, p. 697.

18. Du Bois, "World War and the Color Line," *The Crisis*, 9 (November 1914): 28–30.

19. Although Du Bois reports in *Dusk of Dawn* that he has "difficulty in thinking clearly" about his decision over twenty years earlier, he does explain: "I felt that for a moment during the war that I could be without reservation a patriotic American" (252–53). He then reprints parts of "Close Ranks" as well as an editorial responding to his critics only to conclude, "I am less sure now than then of the soundness of this war attitude" (255).

20. D. L. Lewis, *When Harlem Was in Vogue* (New York: Oxford, 1979), p. 13.

21. Du Bois did publish several essays containing part of this research in *The Crisis*. See his "An Essay Toward a History of the Black Man in the Great War" (1919) in Lewis, ed., *W. E. B. Du Bois: A Reader*, pp. 698–733, and the May 1919 issue of *The Crisis*.

22. Du Bois, "Returning Soldiers" (1919), in Sundquist, ed., *The Oxford W. E. B. Du Bois Reader*, pp. 380–81.

23. Lothrop Stoddard, *The Rising Tide of Color Against White World-Supremacy* (New York: Scribner's, 1922), p. 15.

24. Quoted in Marable, *W. E. B. Du Bois*, p. 116. See also William Ferris's scathing review of *Darkwater* for its elitism in *"Darkwater," African and Orient Review* (June 1920) in Theodore Vincent, ed., *Voices of a Black Nation; Political Journalism in the Harlem Renaissance* (San Francisco: Ramparts Press, 1973), pp. 342–48.

25. For reviews of *Darkwater* see Herbert Aptheker, *The Literary Legacy of W. E. B. Du Bois* (White Plains, N.Y.: Kraus International Publications, 1989), pp. 143–63.

26. The only full-length studies of *Darkwater* I have found are by Aptheker,

Sundquist, Arnold Rampersad, *The Art and Imagination of W. E. B. Du Bois* (Cambridge, Mass.: Harvard University Press, 1976), pp. 170–83, and John Carlos Rowe, *Literary Culture and U.S. Imperialism* (Oxford: Oxford University Press, 2000), pp. 197–215. My reading differs from both Rampersad and Sundquist, who emphasize the more spiritual and philosophical aspects of the figure of the Black Christ in Du Bois's Pan-Africanism; they both gloss over the centrality of World War I and his representation of empire that goes beyond the dichotomy between racism at home and colonialism abroad to explore the international dimensions of American race relations. My reading also differs from Rowe, who extracts from Du Bois's writing his changing political views of imperialism; I explore how the framework of empire shapes his textual as well as his political practices.

27. Sundquist suggests that the form and philosophy of *Darkwater* were influenced by J. E. Casely Hayford's *Ethiopia Unbound* (1911) in *To Wake*, pp. 610–12. Casely Hayford, a West African journalist and educator, attacked Du Bois's notion of double-consciousness as a limited and debilitating parochial American paradigm that ran contrary to a Pan-African vision. In drawing on the multigenre form of his book, Du Bois may have also been responding to this critique; J. E. Casely Hayford, *Ethiopia Unbound: Studies in Race Emancipation* (London: Frank Cass, 1969), pp. 179–82. On the national paradigm that informs *Souls*, see Hazel Carby, *Race Men* (Cambridge, Mass.: Harvard University Press, 1998), ch. 1.

28. Du Bois, *Dusk*, p. 96.

29. *Darkwater* does not fit the discussions of modernism in the African American literary tradition, in George Hutchinson, *The Harlem Renaissance in Black and White* (Cambridge, Mass.: Harvard University Press, 1995); Houston Baker, *Modernism and the Harlem Renaissance* (Chicago: University of Chicago Press, 1987); or Henry Louis Gates, "The Trope of the New Negro and the Reconstruction of the Image of the Black," in Philip Fisher, ed., *The New American Studies: Essay from Representations* (Berkeley: University of California Press, 1991), pp. 319–45.

30. Terry Eagleton, Fredric Jameson, Edward Said, *Modernism and Imperialism* (Minneapolis: University of Minnesota Press, 1990).

31. Du Bois, *Darkwater: Voices From Within the Veil* (1920) in Sundquist, ed., *The Oxford Reader*, p. 595. Subsequent references cited parenthetically in the text.

32. Du Bois, "The African Roots of War," p. 101.

33. Much of this debate has responded to Anthony Appiah, "The Uncompleted Argument: Du Bois and the Illusion of Race," in Henry Louis

Gates, Jr., ed., *"Race," Writing, and Difference* (Chicago: University of Chicago Press, 1986), pp. 21–38.

34. Du Bois, "Worlds of Color" (1924) in Aptheker, ed., *Writings by W. E. B. Du Bois in Periodicals Edited by Others,* vol. 2, p. 241.

35. David Roediger, *The Wages of Whiteness: Race and the Making of the American Working Class* (London: Verso, 1991). I am not arguing that Du Bois originated his idea of the wages of whiteness in *Darkwater* rather than in *Black Reconstruction,* which itself took root in an essay of his in 1910; rather, I believe that there are important international dimensions to this concept used by Roediger and others to analyze the relations between class and race within the United States.

36. Du Bois, "African Roots," p. 98.

37. Ibid., p. 99.

38. Toni Morrison, *Beloved* (New York: Knopf, 1987), p. 190.

39. See, for example, Geiss, *The Pan-African Movement,* and Robinson, *Black Marxism.*

40. Sundquist, *To Wake the Nations,* pp. 555–81.

41. See Moses, *The Golden Age,* and Robinson, who focuses on Du Bois's complicity with American policy in Liberia in "Du Bois and Black Sovereignty."

42. "President Woodrow Wilson's 'Peace without Victory' Speech, 1917," in Thomas Paterson and Dennis Merrill, eds., *Major Problems in American Foreign Relations,* 2 vols. (Lexington, Mass.: Heath, 1995), vol. 1, p. 534.

43. Lewis, *W. E. B. Du Bois: Biography,* pp. 566–67.

44. Du Bois found it difficult to attribute political agency to Africans throughout his work of the 1920s. The novel *Dark Princess* (1928), for example, which is based on the geography of *Darkwater,* imagines an international anticolonial organization composed of representatives from Asia, Egypt, India, and the Caribbean. Yet there are no black Africans in it, and the council enlists the black American hero for leading the African struggle. In examining Du Bois's relation to Liberia from 1923 through the 1930s, Robinson has excoriated his blindness to the Liberian imperial posture, supported by the United States, toward its own people. I suggest that this issue be reconsidered not only in relation to Du Bois's class status and elitism, but also to the components of his internationalism that were consonant with American internationalism and imperialism.

45. Du Bois, "Awake America," *The Crisis,* 14 (Sept. 1917): 216–17.

46. Du Bois, "A Letter to the President," *The Crisis,* 13 (April 1917): 284.

47. Du Bois, "The League of Nations," *The Crisis,* 18 (May 1919): 10–11.

48. There is more evidence of Du Bois's ambivalence toward the political

agency of black women in "The Damnation of Women": while he pays homage to women of the past whom he names, such as Phillis Wheatley, Mary Still, Harriet Tubman, Mary Shad, and Sojourner Truth, when he quotes at length a contemporary leader, Anna Julia Cooper, he does not name her. It is not clear to me whether he assumed that her statement "when and where I enter" was so well known as to require no name, or whether he subsumed as his own both her words and her claim to represent the race as a woman, "then and there the whole Negro race enters with me" (569–70). Du Bois's complex representation of black women and his treatment of gender unfortunately goes beyond the scope of this chapter. See Cheryl Townsend Gilkes, "The Margin as the Center of a Theory of History: African-American Women, Social Change, and the Sociology of W. E. B. Du Bois," in Bell et al., eds., *W. E. B. Du Bois on Race,* pp. 111–39; Joy James, "The Profeminist Politics of W. E. B. Du Bois, with Respect to Anna Julia Cooper and Ida B. Wells-Barnett," in ibid., pp. 141–60.

49. Du Bois, "Rape" (1919), in Aptheker, ed., *Selections from the Crisis,* pp. 186–188; "An Essay Toward a History of the Black Man in the Great War" (1919), Lewis, ed., *W. E. B. Du Bois: A Reader,* p. 731.

50. Du Bois, "Viva La France," *The Crisis,* 17 (March 19): 215–16.

51. When the woman first realizes that she is alone with a black man, she too expresses a terror of rape that is followed by her realization of Jim's humanity and their common plight. It is interesting that she experiences this fear when she looks at the mouthpiece of a telephone that gets no response from the outside world: "it was wide, black, pimpled with usage, inert, dead, almost sarcastic in its unfeeling curves" (616). This phallic rendering suggests the importance of technologies of communication in producing racial stereotypes that have the power to shape social relations.

52. Du Bois, *Dark Princess: A Romance* (1928; rpt. Millwood, N.Y.: Kraus-Thomson Organization, 1974), p. 286.

53. Lewis, *Biography,* p. 440.

54. Du Bois, *Dusk,* p. 230.

55. Lewis, *Biography,* p. 441.

56. W. E. B. Du Bois, *Black Reconstruction in America, 1860–1880* (1935; rpt. New York: Atheneum, 1992), p. 714.

57. Ibid., p. 728.

Acknowledgments

Completing a book this long in the making has helped me realize concretely what I have always known in the abstract, that the production of knowledge is truly a social practice. More colleagues and students have contributed to this project than I could possibly acknowledge, through their questions at lectures, their participation in seminars, and their own scholarship. I am grateful to the people who have read or heard parts of the manuscript in different stages and offered their valuable advice: Jonathan Arac, Jonathan Auerbach, Nancy Bentley, Brenda Bright, Richard Burt, Rob Corber, Cathy Davidson, David Eng, Jenny Goodman, Robert Gregg, Gordon Hutner, Leslie Moore, George Lipsitz, Lisa Lowe, Dana Nelson, Donald Pease, Vince Rafael, José David Saldívar, Michelle Stephens, Shelley Streeby, Brook Thomas, Donald Weber, Laura Wexler, Elizabeth Young. Chris Wilson and Matt Jacobson were ideal readers of the entire manuscript and helped the book cohere at the final stages. I am indebted to Edward Said, whose worldly scholarship has always been a model, and to Lindsay Waters, my editor at Harvard University Press, for their patient yet persistent commitment to this project. I would like to honor the vibrant memory of Mike Rogin, his intellectual generosity and enthusiasm, and the inspiration of his work.

I wish to thank the following presses for permission to reprint revised versions of earlier essays: Duke University Press for an earlier form of Chapter 1 in *American Literature* (1998) and of Chapter 4 in Amy Kaplan and Donald Pease, eds., *Cultures of U.S. Imperialism* (1993); Oxford University Press for a version of Chapter 3 in *American Literary History* (1990); and the Modern Language Association for a part of Chapter 5 in *PMLA* (1999). Thanks to Charles Musser for giving me a copy of his still print of *The American Soldier in Love and War* and permission to reprint it. An NEH fellowship helped launch this project, and leave time and research funds from Mount Holyoke College helped to keep it going. I had the opportunity to teach some of the material discussed in the book at Dartmouth College, University of California, San Diego, University of Massachusetts at Amherst, and Yale University, where students and faculty provided me with challenging new perspectives.

I am fortunate to have dear friends, near and far, who have seen me through this project from beginning to end. They have taught me as much from their own work as from their careful reading and spirited conversation about mine. Mary Renda has shared the journey of writing her book on imperialism and culture, which has deeply informed my thinking. Priscilla Wald has been indefatigable in her willingness at a moment's notice to discuss, read, and edit. Their insights helped give shape to incipient ideas and expressions throughout the process of writing and revising. Susan Gillman has brought her unflagging enthusiasm and knowledge to our parallel tracks through the turn of two centuries. Carla Kaplan has walked me through countless versions of the argument on long walks at the Cape, where she generously opened her home to me. Day by day, with wit and grace, Judith Frank has taught me about the life of the writer, and much more. I thank Becca Leopold for her gentle sarcasm and bedrock support, Nina Gerassi Navarro for her high-spirited team teaching, Kavita Kory for Scrabble and sushi breaks, Liz Garland for traveling and coming home, and Ken Talan for his wisdom and compassion. This extended family has sustained me in mind, body, and soul.

I would like to thank my parents, Sol and Eunice Kaplan, for trying not to ask me, "are you almost done yet?" and for always believing that I would be. This book is dedicated with love and gratitude to my daughter, Rose Kaplan Weiss, who at a young age once came to hear her mother lecture and bravely raised her hand to ask the question: "what does utopia mean?"

Index

Adams, Brooks, 96

The Adventures of Francis, 229n28

The Adventures of Huckleberry Finn, 51, 55, 78, 86, 87, 88

Africa: European colonization of, 1, 171–172, 173, 195–196; and World War I, 171–173, 176, 181, 183, 186–187, 196, 197; Pan-African Congress of 1900, 176, 178; Pan-African Congress of 1919, 178–180, 197; attitudes of Du Bois toward Africans, 199, 206, 244n44

African Americans: and *Plessy v. Ferguson,* 9; white attitudes toward, 9, 17, 18, 20, 21, 26, 35, 36–40, 41, 48, 50, 75, 79–80, 85–86, 89–90, 121–128, 133–136, 137, 138–142, 143, 144, 145, 160–161, 172–175, 176–178, 179–180, 181–183, 185, 188–189, 191–193, 195–197, 200, 201–206, 207–209, 210–212, 235n30, 239n44, 240n5, 243n26, 245n51; Jim Crow legislation regarding, 9, 17, 18, 21, 123, 125, 137, 138, 140–141, 145, 173, 207–208; during Reconstruction, 9, 79–80, 82, 83–84, 86, 89–90, 121–123, 172, 209; in Spanish-American War, 18, 20–21, 124–125, 126–128, 133–145, 152, 161, 163, 181, 209, 235n30, 236n2; colonization of Africa by, 35, 36–40, 41, 48, 162; imperial citizenship sought by, 134–136,

141–142, 163–164, 181, 187, 189–190, 198–199, 208; in Philippine-American war, 145, 236n46; in World War I, 181–182, 189–190, 207, 208, 209; migration from the South, 201–202; African American women, 203–206, 245n48

"The African Roots of War," 171–173, 176, 181, 183, 186–187, 196, 197

Aguinaldo, Emilio, 115, 117

Ajax, 58, 63, 75

Alaska, 4

Alexander, Prince Liholiho, 84

Alice of Old Vincennes, 110, 230n28

"The American Century," 16, 21, 167–169, 170, 198

American exceptionalism, 14–16, 17, 174, 175, 177–178, 198–199, 244n44

American Guerilla in the Philippines, 236n2

American Revolution, 101, 117, 118–119, 226n7

The American Soldier in Love and War, 154–156, 158–159, 161, 238n27

The American Women's Home, 31–43

anarchy, relationship to American imperialism, 12–15, 26, 27–28, 28, 50, 125, 170, 172–173, 185, 198–199, 211–212

Aptheker, Herbert, 242n26

Arac, Jonathan, 51

Arizona, 4

Armstrong, Nancy, 43

Other books in the *Convergences* series:

CPSIA information can be obtained
at www.ICGtesting.com
Printed in the USA
BVHW070731020719

552428BV00014B/64/P